EIGHT LONDON HOUSEHOLDS

EIGHT LONDON HOUSEHOLDS

Sandra Wallman

Tavistock Publications
London & New York

First published in 1984 by
Tavistock Publications Ltd
11 New Fetter Lane, London EC4P 4EE

Published in the USA by
Tavistock Publications
in association with Methuen, Inc.
733 Third Avenue, New York, NY 10017

© 1984 Sandra Wallman

Printed in Great Britain at the University Press, Cambridge

British Library Cataloguing in Publication Data

Wallman, Sandra
Eight London households.
1. Households—England—London   2. Battersea
(London, England)—Social conditions
3. London (England)—Social conditions
I. Title
942.1'660858   HN398.L7

ISBN 0-422-78390-0
ISBN 0-422-78400-1 Pbk

Library of Congress Cataloging in Publication Data

Wallman, Sandra.
Eight London households.

"Published in the USA ... in association with Methuen, Inc."—
T.p. verso.
Bibliography: p.
Includes indexes.
1. Family–England—London—Case studies.   2. Cost and
standard of living—England—London—Case studies.
3. Battersea (London, England)—Social conditions.
I. Title.
HQ616.W34   1984   307.7'62'094212   84-2568
ISBN 0-422-78390-0
ISBN 0-422-78400-1 (pbk.)

aug.85

Contents

Preface and Acknowledgements

There are two points to be made at the start. First, these households do not constitute a full range of London types or a representative sample of inner city households. But to say that these eight do not represent a wider population is only to say that they should not be made the basis for statistical statements of any kind. It does not mean that they are atypical or out of the ordinary. As case studies in the anthropological tradition, they are used to illustrate aspects of social process and to demonstrate certain general theoretical principles. It is important that the inferences drawn from this study are qualitative, not quantitative (although neither illogical nor untrue for that), and that the very ordinariness of these eight households is part of the point.

Second, the members of these households are perceived as active subjects who have choices to make within the constraints of the environment they share. The effect of this perspective is to take the emphasis of the book off the institutional framework which all these households have in common, and to put it on the scope for variation within that framework. For this reason the reader may find that the book goes against conventional views of the role that class and/or ethnic origin play in the organization of livelihood in the inner city. This study does not argue that they have no significance, only that their significance depends on other things happening within each household system.

The interviews which have become Chapters 4–7 are products of the sympathetic skills of David Clark, Yvonne Dhooge, Stephanie D'Orey, Hazel Flett, Mai Wann, and Bawa viii *Preface and Acknowledgements*

Yamba, and of the patience and generosity of the eight households that are the focus of this book. The fact that I have not used the real names of any member of these households does not diminish my debt to them as individuals.

I owe a general acknowledgement to colleagues in the SSRC Research Unit in Ethnic Relations at the University of Bristol, and in the Resource Options Unit at the London School of Economics and Political Science (LSE). Among them, I am specifically indebted to David Clark for the design of the layered time budget chart reproduced in Chapter 3; to Andra Goldman for adapting the psychotherapeutic network map to our ethnographic purpose (also in Chapter 3), and for explaining the difference between problem families and families with problems; and to Ian Buchanan and Yvonne Dhooge for their critical efforts to extend my understanding of the anthropology of the city with perspectives from their own disciplines. I would like also to thank members of the Department of Social Anthropology at the University of Stockholm who, at crucial points in the gestation of this book, told me about other people's households and gave me hospitality in various of theirs. Finally, I am happy to acknowledge in print that the most essential insights into households as resource systems have come from twenty years' participation in my own.

This book reports one phase of an enquiry funded by a programme grant from the Social Science Research Council (SSRC). Parts of it are adapted from previous publications: Chapter 1 draws from *Living in South London* (published by Gower for the London School of Economics); and from *Man* 13 (2) (1978) (published by the Royal Anthropological Institute), and parts of Chapter 3 appeared in *Ethnos* 45 (1–2) (1980) (published by the Ethnographic Museum, Stockholm) and/or in *Energy and Effort* (edited by G. A. Harrison and published by Taylor and Francis as *Proceedings of the Society of Human Biology*).

S.W.
London
May, 1984

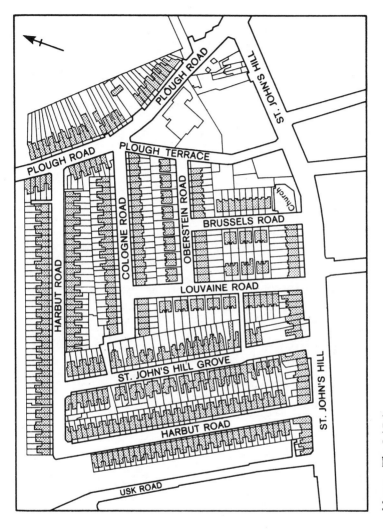

Map 1 The LARA area

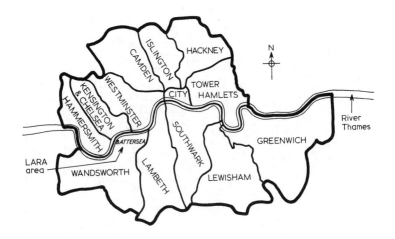

Map 2   Inner London

1 Inner-city setting

PROBLEMS AND ISSUES

This book is about eight inner-London households and it therefore addresses current policy issues – not because these eight are 'problem households', but because the inner-city label inevitably implies social problems of one kind or another. In a literal sense of course, it is no more than a spatial or geographic referent. Once an urban centre has been defined, then the urban districts that make up the city can be mapped or visualized in ever-widening circles around it. In relation to the centre, any part of the city is then more or less close in or far out, and the 'inner city' is simply that part of town which falls within the circle designated to mark a significant change of population density, housing stock, business activities, traffic patterns, and the like.

The reason for a sudden focus of popular interest and academic enquiry on these areas in the recent past is not so bland. It reflects the fact that they have come to be associated with particular kinds of political and economic failure and with a concentration of urban problems. In ordinary use therefore, the inner city is defined less by where it is than by the excesses of disadvantage and distress so often found in it. In this perspective any 'inner city' is widely assumed to be the kind of area where no one with any option would choose to live. The assumption implies not only that inner-city areas are uniformly non-viable, but also that inner-city residents must always be worse off than suburbanites in the same town: if they were not, surely they too would have organized themselves to move 'out' into the suburbs by now.

The picture is complicated by factors of colour and ethnicity. It is observed in Britain and the USA, indeed in polyglot cities everywhere, that ethnic minorities (although not always the same ethnic minorities) tend to be over-represented in inner-city areas. Relative to their proportion in any urban population, there are said to be too few minority group members in the 'nice' suburbs and too many in the 'blighted' centre. On this basis, and with a little help from the media, three elements – disadvantage, the inner city, and minority ethnic status – have come to be associated together. Hence the popular idea that ethnic minorities (who happen to live in the inner city) are disadvantaged; and that inner-city areas (which happen to have sizeable minority group populations) are unpleasant places to live. Although there is no doubt that both these statements are or have been true in some contexts of place and history, the point to be made is that they cannot properly be applied to all members of ethnic minorities in all inner-city areas at this time.

If the implications of minority status and urban decline had no bearing on practical concerns, it would not matter very much how they were defined. But on the contrary, a good part of current political and social argument rests on assumptions about the differences between people and the uniformity of inner-city areas, which combine to obscure the realities of urban livelihood. As the ways in which we classify people and places both reflect and confirm these assumptions, the terms we use and the way we use them do not simply affect our understanding of events, they may also influence those events, even to the extent of moving them in directions that no one intended.

It is important therefore to stress that our findings on these eight London households go against current expectations in two respects. First, although this book is about four black and four white households in a mixed inner-city area, it does not find race or ethnic relations a central or even a consistently important issue. It takes national/regional/racial origin into account throughout, but only as one of a number of character-istics that may, or indeed, may not, effect the way households organize a livelihood or relate to the area and people around them.

Second, although the subjects of this book are typical inner-city residents, their collective story is not a bleak tale of deprivation and disadvantage. It is not that they want for nothing: all of them work hard to make ends meet and can remember times when even everyday life was too much to cope with. But most of the time they get by well enough, and as they see it, the inner-city setting offers as full a range of possibilities for a decent life as any other.

This 'best view' perspective is entirely practical. It matches the strategy of Lancelot 'Capability' Brown, the famous eighteenth-century gardener, who tackled each new landscaping problem by asking himself: 'What are the capabilities of this environment?' Here the 'capabilities' of one inner-city environment are approached through a number of common-sense questions. What kinds of people live in the inner city? How do they manage? Who do they know? Who do they depend on? Where do they work? Where do they shop? What do they buy? If some households manage 'better' than others, what 'better' resources do they have? Does everyone use or even try to use the local environment in the same way? How does this inner-city setting differ from any other? If markedly different reactions to outsiders or markedly different household strategies occur in a single neighbourhood, are there particular household characteristics that account for them? In what circumstances does the bond of local loyalty or local identity override the divisions of ethnic, cultural, or racial origin?

Questions of this kind might usefully be asked of any polyethnic urban area, but the answers expressed or implied in this volume apply specifically to eight households in one neighbourhood in the south London area of Battersea.

CHANGE AND CONTINUITY

The boundaries of Battersea have changed many times since the name first appeared on any map, and the implications of living in Battersea have always varied according to who is defining it and for what purposes. Changes of both kinds are inevitable: new administrative fashions and responsibilities regularly alter official notions of how big a local government unit should be; and even if boundaries on the ground are fixed, their significance to the way people define themselves and others is not. Change is not, of course, the whole story. Some aspects of the life and identity of Battersea have certainly been characteristic of it for more than a century and probably for much longer. Perspectives on the livelihood of several generations of Battersea people show both the change and the continuity of it quite clearly.

These perspectives are set out at length in *Living in South London* (Wallman *et al.* 1982), which was the first product of our Battersea studies. Details from it are repeated here to sketch the environment of the eight households described later in this book, and to emphasize the features of Battersea that distinguish it from other inner-city settings.

Change here as anywhere is not all of one kind: *historical*, *personal*, and *situational* perspectives reveal different processes. Although the events that make them up are related, they belong to different time scales and can be distinguished from each other.

In the *historical* frame, Battersea has experienced many social and economic changes over the last century. Some of them were explicitly imposed on it from outside, although it is likely that no one intended all their consequences. Certainly Battersea did not choose to dissolve its own metropolitan status in 1965 (following the Government of London Act, 1963), to lose 'grass roots' access to its elected politicians (Kosmin 1982), or to decrease the number of jobs available in local industry (Buchanan 1982). Other changes came as implicit reactions to national or international events: wars of one kind or another, population movements in and out, industrial growth and recession, fluctuations of interest in the Commonwealth, the spread of state services and welfare bureaucracies, renegotiations of the social division of labour between men and women, rich and poor, white and black, etc. No sub-set of people can have been immune to trends like these. Some show in the census figures for Battersea over the period from 1911–71 (*Table 1*). In sixty years its population dropped by a half, but nearly five times as many of its people were born outside Britain. The proportion of residents born outside the British Isles rose from less than 2 per cent to 15 per cent, the influx from the New Commonwealth coming late in the period and more than a decade after the beginning of the postwar decline.

Table 1 *Birthplaces of the population of Battersea Metropolitan Borough*

	1911	*1921*	*1931*	*1951*	*1961*	*1971*
Old Commonwealth	259	303	252	—	366	385
New Commonwealth	659	604	651	—	5,030	7,914
total Commonwealth	918	907	903	831	5,396	8,299
Foreign countries and at sea	1,573	1,291	1,208	2,743	2,364	3,993
total outside British Isles	2,491	2,198	2,111	3,574	7,760	12,292
British Isles	163,843	164,635	157,435	113,566	97,517	71,558
birthplace not stated	1,409	906	6	—	593	—
total population	167,743	167,739	159,552	117,140	105,870	83,850

Source: Censuses of England and Wales (OPCS 1911, 1921, 1931, 1951, 1961, 1971).
Notes: Some categories are only approximately comparable. A dash means that the figure is not available.

Other changes have happened and continue to happen on quite another level. They are the effects of ordinary social process – changes within the local system that do not alter it overall, and that, in a bird's-eye view, would happen even if the world outside went away. The most obvious of them follow on the passing of life time – *personal* as opposed to historical time – and are repeated in every generation: families progress through their separate domestic cycles; daughters grow into mothers and babies into grandfathers; households get bigger and again smaller; houses, flats, and corner shops change hands, and so on.

Changes in the position and content of the boundaries that divide 'insiders' from 'outsiders' are less obvious but no less normal. Social boundaries reflect the ordinary permutations of social context; because they are processes in *situational* time, they move in rhythms apart from historical trends or individual cycles. Yet they are not independent of them. There is no one measure that defines 'us' – the people entitled to share the resources we call 'ours' – but the continual shifting of the boundary of us is not random. Social process at any level is not free; it is constrained by other things happening in and around the local environment, and by the scope of the resources it offers. People who live in or move into an area can only take up the options that are there. Similarly public policy and generalized social change have different effects even in different parts of the same inner city because each local area has a characteristic style of response.

THE BATTERSEA STYLE

In the case of Battersea there is a continuity of style throughout the local system. All the expressions of it put some kind of emphasis on local over ethnic identity, and on heterogeneous over homogeneous forms. On the former account there is minimal interest shown in status ascribed by ethnic origin, and there is maximum scope for newcomers to achieve local status. On the second there is both an unusually wide variety of resource stock and relatively open access to it: housing, jobs, and people are mixed and there are so many separate 'gates' into local resources that no single group, institution, or ideology can claim a controlling share. Evidence for Battersea's particular style is cumulated in *Living in South London* (Wallman *et al.* 1982). Two summary items will serve to spell it out here: the first refers to Battersea's consistent boundary patterns; the second to the creation of the identity defining the Louvaine Area Residents' Association (LARA) neighbourhood in which the eight households of this book are situated.

Item 1 The population of Battersea is mixed in a way that leaves plenty of scope for ethnic solidarity or discrimination, but ethnic origin did not mark significant boundaries in historic Battersea and has little bearing on its livelihood even now. In the matter of politics, Battersea has 'always' considered outsider status to be more a matter of newness than of colour or foreign origin, and it has 'always' made the local area a prime focus of identity and loyalty. Thus in 1913 the metropolitan borough elected the pan-Africanist John Archer as mayor – the first popular election of a black man to this office in the English-speaking world; and in 1922 it sent Saklatvala, an Indian (and a Communist) to represent it in Parliament. Battersea's traditional style did not change when the electorate expanded to include poor men (in 1918), women (in 1918 and 1928), or immigrants (in the 1950s), and there are echoes of it in contemporary political life (Kosmin 1979, 1982). In the matter of labour market economics the pattern is no less consistent. No incoming population category has been exclusively associated with one industry or one industrial role, and there is no evidence of ethnic niches or ethnic-specific patterns of employment. Recent figures for unemployment sustain the pattern. A follow-up count three years after our 1978 LARA neighbourhood survey shows the same appalling increase in the number of men without jobs in LARA as elsewhere. But amongst LARA residents, men born outside south London are almost twice as likely to be unemployed as those born in it; men who have lived in south London for one to five years are three times as likely to be unemployed as those resident for more than five years and less than ten; and these probabilities are largely independent of birthplace or colour (Wallman *et al.* 1982: 183). By this measure also, Battersea's style is at once localist and a-ethnic.

Item 2 The south Battersea neighbourhood now called LARA was declared a Housing Action Area (HAA) in 1975. One implication of this special status is that extra resources are vested in the area by the Government bureaucracy. Since membership confers rights to those resources, the question of who belongs becomes an explicit public issue.

At the start of housing action the LARA area existed only as half a dozen streets within a rectangle clearly demarcated on the map, distinct only because it was bounded on two sides by main traffic arteries and on two more by fenced, now derelict ground designated for a new council housing estate. Although the Housing Act (1974) provides that grants for rehabilitation can be made available only to established communities (in 'technically appropriate' areas), residents tend to date the beginning of community from the beginning of housing action. On this basis 'the neighbourhood' is less than ten years old.

Of the 500 households in the area, more than one third are put into the official category 'New Commonwealth origin', which is to say that their members, or most of their members, are non-white. But neither colour nor language nor the presence of 'blacks' or 'foreigners' are central or persistent issues. Those issues most often cited are: faceless bureaucrats, ambitious politicians, people who ignore the council's skips and leave their large rubbish by the dustbins, council employees who will not take this large rubbish away, people who have noisy and frequent parties, and worse, who are thought to charge a gate fee and therefore admit strangers to those parties, and also, in a looser category, those newly arrived, perhaps eccentric, without connections 'in this part of London'. Thus a Newcastle man, three years' resident, with a wife from the other side of London, is called a 'foreigner' by a Jamaican woman resident of ten years' standing who clearly is not.

As the regulations for housing action entail, the houses and flats are being refurbished for established residents of the area. Households may move or be moved within the area, either temporarily while their own quarters are rehabilitated, or permanently, into accommodation better matched to household size. They may on no account be ousted from the area, although some few do profit from their special bureaucratic status to acquire council accommodation elsewhere in the borough. But even without mass exodus, better use of the housing stock has created a surplus over the residents' requirements. This must, again according to the rules, go into the council's hopper to be allocated to 'anybody' on the housing lists.

This possibility is a focus of anxiety: '"Anybody" will not

be known to us . . . will only use the place to get a house . . . will not really want to live here . . . will not have family here . . . will not care about the place . . . will run it down . . . will move on.' Residents therefore encourage each other to find amongst their acquaintance 'somebody' who wants to live in the area; who would move in and stay; who would become 'us'.

The challenge to local identity assumptions is explicit. Who belongs in the LARA area anyway? In 1981 most of the residents on the original housing list had been accommodated, and the council had begun to implement Conservative Party policy by selling its properties to the private sector – to present tenants if they were both willing and able to purchase, and to buyers on the open market if they were not. At the same time the letting of council and housing association property was controlled by the borough, not the neighbourhood office, and all new claimants had to join the borough queue. Even residents with long-standing connections or kin in the area now have no guarantee of accommodation in it and inevitably wait longer to be rehoused than their neighbours did.

Both procedures have brought new people into the area and have focused attention on the LARA boundary. There is no real evidence that newcomers are being housed at the expense of established residents, but some say that 'outsiders' are moving into housing units that should have been allocated to 'locals'. It is characteristic of Battersea that even in this competitive context ethnic ratios and affiliations are beside the point. 'We' are, in the most general sense, those who belong here; specifically 'we' are defined as those who were in the area when it was earmarked for housing action and so designated a 'community'. (That this occurred a short time ago does not prevent its having the force of tradition.) At that time the area was distinguished only by being marked off on an official map. But the cartographer's boundary marked a categorical differ-ence between those entitled to particular resources and those not eligible for them. It became a *social* boundary only when residents identified themselves by it. This happened when it began to be used to define 'us', the people entitled to share the resources we call 'ours'.

BOROUGH, NEIGHBOURHOOD, AND HOUSEHOLD

This book is, as we have indicated, the second part of an extensive local study of Battersea. Like the first (Wallman *et al.* 1982), it refers at various points to the local system, local resources, local status, local attitudes, local involvement, and local livelihood. But these locally based items and ideas do not belong to a fixed local unit. They may pertain to a context as large as London or as small as one individual's network. The units referred to most importantly are, from largest to smallest, the borough, the neighbourhood, and the household – specifically, Battersea, a neighbourhood within Battersea, and households that make up that neighbourhood. In each book the larger unit provides a context for the smaller and the smaller illustrates aspects of the larger, but the two volumes take different perspectives.

The earlier volume provides a historical description of the whole of Battersea over the last century, and a contemporary sketch of one Battersea neighbourhood. It covers the growth of new political and ethnic identities in the area, changes in the population and in the economic opportunities open to it; and the development of local labour markets, both formal and informal. The historical chapters deal specifically with Battersea, even though the official identity of the old metropolitan borough was erased with the reorganization of London's local government in 1965. Battersea (with a population of about 75,000) was then absorbed by the new and much larger London Borough of Wandsworth (with a population of about 250,000) and it no longer appears by name in official census enumerations. Its constituent small areas are not, however, affected and it was therefore possible to reconstruct the old Battersea boundaries from small area statistics of the 1971 census, and to complete a time series of census data on the Battersea area which stretches back to 1901 and forward into the present.

The contemporary chapters refer to the small LARA neighbourhood in south Battersea. One documents the progress of its housing action, the rest are based on material collected by ethnographic survey in 1978. The neighbourhood then contained approximately 1,300 people in just over 500 households. Our material refers to 1,167 people in 446 households; the shortfall is made up of those who could not be contacted or who did not want to answer the survey questionnaire. Their number is unusually small for inner-city studies, and probably reflects the fact that we employed neighbourhood residents to do the neighbourhood interviewing (Wallman *et al.* 1980).

The neighbourhood referred to as 'LARA' or 'the LARA area', covers the Louvaine Area Residents' Association Housing Action Area as defined by the local government London Borough of Wandsworth. The boundaries of this area do not however match the boundaries of central government census enumeration districts. Seeking the maximum amount of census information about the area over the longest possible period, we identified the four 1971 census districts that are wholly contained within the LARA area and account for about two thirds of the total LARA population. This smaller area is referred to as the *core* area of LARA (*Tables 2* and *3*). Data on it has been drawn from the 1961, 1966, and 1971 Census small area statistics, the 1974 local authority housing action survey, and our 1978 neighbourhood survey. *Table 2* in effect shows the rapid decline of population numbers in the neighbourhood since 1961.

Households appear in different guises throughout the first book. As the social context shifts, so do the boundaries of the household unit: like all social boundaries they depend on who is defining them, what they are defined for, and whether they are defined from inside or outside. It is these shifts in the boundaries of household that are explored in the present book: it concentrates on describing and analysing the resources of eight households living in the area of the neighbourhood survey. Whereas the purpose of *Living in South London* is the mapping of the history and ethnography of the area as a whole, without differentiating the livelihood and experience of individual households within it, this volume deals with the details of particular cases and focuses on the options and expectations of each household. A demographic profile of the neighbourhood in 1978 links the two volumes: it indicates both the characteristics of the neighbourhood and the typicality of these eight households.

THE NEIGHBOURHOOD IN 1978

The 1978 neighbourhood survey took place at the end of a period of great change. Most inner-London areas suffered a loss of people during the 1960s and 1970s; LARA also experienced the upheaval of housing action. Between 1961 and 1978 the core area population fell by about half (*Table 2*). Despite these losses however, the area is not at all homogeneous: perhaps the variety of its housing maintains the original mixture of people and household types.

Table 2   *Population of the core area of LARA, 1961–78*

	1961	1971	1974	1978
men	785	654	494	361
women	807	651	506	392
total population	1,592	1,305	1,000	753

Table 3   *Age and sex of the LARA area population, 1978*

age in years	men	women	all	(%)	core area only	(%)
0–14	137	128	265	(23)	182	(24)
15–59	357	375	732	(63)	461	(61)
60 and over	66	102	168	(14)	108	(15)
no information	—	—	2		2	
totals	560	605	N = 1,167		N = 753	

Sources: 1961, 1971 Census (OPCS 1961, 1971)
1974 Housing action survey (Wallman *et al.* 1982)
1978 Neighbourhood survey (Wallman *et al.* 1982)

Table 4   *Household sizes in the whole LARA area, 1978*

household size	no. of households	no. of persons
1	123	123
2	136	272
3	78	234
4	53	212
5	30	150
6	15	90
7	4	28
8	5	40
9	2	18
totals	446	1,167

Average household size: 2.6 persons.

The age structure of the area has not been affected and remains unremarkable (*Table 3*). The lack of change in this respect runs contrary to expectation: in most inner-city areas the number of old people increases proportionately as the population declines. The stability of the age ratio in this case may be a product of housing action, which can influence the population structure through the bureaucratic allocation of housing; certainly housing action has had an indirect effect by making the area relatively more attractive to families.

Although many of the 446 households in the LARA area contain only one or two people, almost two thirds of the population live in households containing three or more, and the average household size is 2.6 people (*Table 4*). Couples and nuclear families make up over half of all households. The nuclear family is the commonest household type, followed closely by single person households; a small proportion of households are collectives, either of unrelated individuals or collateral kin (such as brothers, sisters, or cousins in the same generation), and there is a handful of extended families. The only other numerically significant type is the single-parent family which accounted for 14 per cent of households. In some of these the resident children are themselves adults; only one household in ten is a single-parent family with dependent children under the age of sixteen (*Table 5*). Nor has there been any major change in the birthplaces of the population of the LARA area during the 1970s. The New Commonwealth-born population has accounted for about a quarter of the total throughout the decade. By 1978 most of the Caribbean-born had been settled for a generation; over half had lived in the UK for twenty years or more.

Table 5   *Family structure of households in whole LARA area, 1978*

structure of households	number	% of all households
single person	123	28
couples	97	22
nuclear families	130	29
single parents alone with children under 16	39	9
single parents alone with all children over 16	16	4
extended families including single parents with children	4	1
other extended families	11	2
collectives with family links	7	2
collectives without family links	19	4
total (N)	446	

Although the birthplace data tells us that in-migration from the New Commonwealth was not numerically important in the 1970s, the proportion of non-white residents increased by natural means. In 1978, in addition to the 26 per cent of the LARA area population born in the New Commonwealth, a further 15 per cent were people born in Britain with one or both parents born in the New Commonwealth.

The label New Commonwealth ethnic origin (NCEO) appears to take both cultural factors and birthplace into account. In effect it classifies people by skin colour, allowing

only the superficial observation that 41 per cent of the LARA
population was black or brown and 59 per cent was white in
1978. But colour has no direct effect on ethnicity or on
livelihood, and the option of an ethnic identity applies equally
to everyone in the population. Thus people of Caribbean and
African origin have been distinguished, even the British-born
are classified by birthplace, and among these a south London
ethnic origin (SLEO) category is defined to indicate those who
have special ties through long association with the area. It is
limited to people born in south London of south London
parents (*Table 6*).

Table 6   *Birthplace of whole LARA area population, 1978*

birthplace	number (%)	number (%)
UK born		769 (66)
SLEO[1]	161 (14)	
NCEO[2]	179 (15)	
NC born		303 (26)
Africa	101 (9)	
Asia	44 (4)	
Caribbean	158 (14)	
Eire		51 (4)
other European		28 (2)
other foreign		6 (—)
no information		10
total (N)		1,167

Notes: [1] SLEO: South London Ethnic Origin = south London born of south
London parents.
[2] NCEO: New Commonwealth Ethnic Origin = UK born of New Commonwealth parent(s).

Like the household, the ethnic group is a unit in process; but
the implications of ignoring the difference between inside and
outside views of it are politically more relevant. People of the
same ethnic origin do form an ethnic *category* once an ethnic
category has been designated from the outside – that is if
people are sorted on the basis of their origins without reference

to how they behave or feel. The same people do not form a *group* unless they identify together from the inside, whether for purposes of action or affect. Both category and group, ethnic category and ethnic group, can be respectable units of study or ways of defining aggregates of people, but they imply very different things about what is happening on the ground. Throughout this study we have been careful to make that difference plain.

Economic change in this small part of south London has created new local boundaries and identities. This process in turn altered the meaning and management of 'local' resources. Similar change can be expected similarly to affect boundaries and resource management wherever it occurs. But it need not affect them in the same way: its outcome depends in each case on the kinds of people included and excluded in the new local system, and on the style and scope of local livelihood. Even where comparable areas have equal access to the same resources, they may not have the same organizational options.

What is true for large 'local' units applies equally at the level of household. The next chapter adapts this perspective to account for variations between households that have structurally similar options but very different styles of organization; Chapter 3 describes the research strategies used to unravel them; Chapters 4–7 are narratives of the everyday life of the eight households at issue in this book; and Chapter 8 returns to the general questions of 'what are the capabilities of this environment?' and 'In how many ways do ordinary households manage livelihood in one inner-city area?'.

2 Households as resource systems

HOUSEHOLD AS IDEAL

According to the Office of Population and Census Statistics (OPCS), the British household is a co-residential and commensal unit: its members live under one roof and eat together – or if they do not eat together, at least they 'share catering facilities'. Furthermore, standard census forms are designed to fit complete nuclear families with an explicit bias towards patriarchy: each 'head of household' is 'the male breadwinner' whose employment both provides for the household and determines the status of the wife and children who share it with him.

These definitions are set up for statistical convenience and are not supposed to represent normative ideals. But official statistical categories inevitably reflect the values of the culture from which they are drawn. Knowing this, anthropologists trying to understand domestic economy or family patterns in other cultures reject this mum-dad-and-the-kids model as ethnocentric and inappropriate. They continue to seek concepts of household which will do justice to each special ethnographic case, and yet will allow the comparative discussion of a wide range of cases.

In these discussions the British household and industrial society households in general are left out of account, partly no doubt because one's own society has not been a traditional subject for anthropological study, but also because, as householders in this society ourselves, we feel we already know how it is. Certainly we know that *our* households vary from one to another and alter from one year to the next, and that few of them come anywhere near matching the census ideal. For some amongst us the variety is amusing, and the inevitable gap between the ideal and the normal – between the way we ought to be and the way we are – is not a problem. For others it is. The statistical ideal becomes normative when public servants must decide who is or is not entitled to official resources. So while all of us fail to fit the system in some way, the failure is a problem precisely for those most dependent on it. Households disadvantaged by any measure that puts them in need of the welfare state are also households that are, by the same measure, outside 'the moral community' of people entitled to a share in its benefits. Morally speaking, the unemployed, the homeless, the helpless, and any households whose organization or structure is too different from the ideal are outcast (Goffman 1968; Flett 1979: 143–45).

HOUSEHOLD AS TYPE

The point of this discussion of households is neither to castigate the official system for categorizing its clients in a particular way, nor to propose a typology that would classify them better. Any typology is tidier than real life: its function is to fix boundaries between like items for some purpose or other, and no one way of classifying anything – butterflies, citrus fruits, people, or indeed, households – is appropriate to every purpose. This quite normal limitation accounts for some of the difficulties in the way of comparing households across cultures or at different periods in the same setting. How and whether the social groupings we choose to call households are like or unlike is less a matter of fact than of the measures used to define them; inevitably and quite properly, those measures depend on what it is we want to know.

Within anthropology, the focus of interest in households has changed with the development of new perspectives in the discipline as a whole. During the long period in which typology itself was a central issue, households, like lineages or political systems or societies, were classified by characteristics that could be used to mark them off as discrete units at a fixed point in time (see for example Schapera 1950). For this purpose, physical markers like 'under one roof' and 'around a common pot' are very appealing. They allow a conceptual snapshot of any society's suppertime that shows its members grouped in clusters, each person belonging only to one, and each cluster like every other, or at least matching some proportion of the others in the matter of size, shape, or composition. The British census achieves exactly that. Its purpose is to count the nation's households on one particular night every ten years. For that purpose the criteria serve: they fix the boundaries of each household and the place of every citizen while the picture is taken.

Typology can of course be more intricate. In the business of cross-cultural comparison, it is useful to know how the members of these snapshot units are related to each other and to households round about. For that purpose a kinship dimension can be built into the basic analytic structure and the typology of households changed to accommodate it. The relation between family and residence patterns is now a standard element in ethnographic description. Building on the kinship base it becomes possible to ask what kinds of people do which household tasks (Who produced and who cooked that food in the common pot? Who called the children to eat it?), and to consider the rights and obligations that come with belonging to the household group (What does each member do for the others? What are the social effects of membership?).

But the extra dimension creates new problems. Family and household are not the same kind of unit. One is based on kinship (How are people related?), the other on propinquity (Who lives with whom?), and the two units need not overlap at all. People can live together without being kin, and will remain kin when they live apart (Yanagisako 1979). So while the household is based under one roof and may house a family of some kind, it is not realistically defined even by place and kinship together. To understand the livelihood of any one household we need to know what it *does*; and for the purpose

of comparing one household with another we need a typology
that will take domestic functions and activities as well as
structure into account (Bender 1967). Once typology is that
complex, however, its usefulness begins to break down. Some
household activities involve non-members, and many do not
require that people live together or function as an economic
corporation of any kind. The sensible reaction to this complex-
ity is a sub-set typology. Rather than seeking to compare
households in this complicated way, it may be better to
compare, say, shelter groups, eating groups, hearth groups,
and production groups in which the household's tasks are
performed (Aijmer 1975).

HOUSEHOLD AS PROCESS

But no matter how many or complicated the variables used to
type households, typology remains tidier than life. Lately there
is less interest in mapping social forms for the sake of a natural
science of society: the definition of species and sub-species, the
creation of types and sub-types. More attention must be paid
to the fluidity of social units of every sort. The new problem of
household, which is the problem taken up here, is not a matter
of discovering how units of production, consumption, and
residence interrelate and change over time (Goody 1958)
because it cannot be posed in terms of bounded units at all. It
concerns itself instead with processual themes: How do
households *manage*? How and when do their boundaries shift?
How is household process affected by change in the society at
large? What makes for viability in particular economic or
social settings? (see Arnould and Netting 1982; de Tray 1977;
Gershuny 1979; Laslett and Wall 1972).

Three kinds of factors affect the form and the content of
household process. The first is *developmental*: in the course of
the ordinary domestic cycle, households grow or blend or split
(Goody 1958). The second is *ecological*: the scope and
strictures of the environment set a society-wide household
pattern (Sahlins 1974), and special events or catastrophes
(famine, economic recession, labour migration, etc.) foster or

inhibit changes in it (Gonzales 1970; Murray 1979). And the third is *strategic*: each household assesses the options available to it and deploys them according to its own needs and priorities in any given period or set of circumstances (Bohman 1981; Pahl 1980), and the cumulation of these separate decisions generates new options and new patterns of livelihood (Barth 1966; Paine 1974).

These processes are distinct only as levels of analysis, and do not represent different types of household. In reality everything happens in combination. A model of households as resource systems comes nearer to it by incorporating all three processes in one analytic frame. It conceives households as being differently bounded in respect of different resources; and as differing from each other in respect of the resources available to them, the resources they choose to deploy, and the kinds of value they vest or invest in them for particular purposes in local or cultural contexts of various kinds.

RESOURCE-KEEPERS

Where household survey, whether carried out by social anthropologists or by the OPCS, defines the household as an economic unit and identifies a single head-of-household figure, the real division of household labour is obscured or distorted. One effect is that the distribution of power and control within the household can only be described in the formal or legal domain which has no necessary bearing on non-formal authority patterns. Another is that the viability of a particular household system in a crisis can neither be predicted nor understood, and the contribution made by the young, the old, and any others designated unemployed or economically non-active, is left out of account. Where the household is viewed instead as a system of resources of various kinds, we may notice that the formal/legal head of household is not necessarily the manager of all its resources or the decisive focus of its livelihood. On the contrary, particular members of the household system tend to be allocated or to take over the management of particular household resources such as money, information, grandparents, social workers, and so forth. For this reason it is useful to set the head-of-household ideal aside, and to expand the notion of *kin-keeper* (Firth, Forge, and Hubert 1969) so that each resource-keeper, whether the keeper of a designated resource or, less commonly, of household resources as a general stock, can be recognized.

The parallel notion of a kin-mobilizer makes the analogy still more useful. While the kin-keeper keeps track of family members and tells each the others' news, the kin-mobilizer actually brings them together for ceremonial occasions, or to focus their collective effort on the emergency need of one of their number, whether for money or for support of a less material kind. Kin-keeping and kin-mobilizing tasks may be carried out by different people. The possibilities are similar in respect of other kinds of resources: the person who knows about and has access to, say, information, need not be the one who puts it to work for the household. The allocation of responsibility for these tasks is partly a matter of household structure, partly a matter of personality or individual preference. In the specific domain of kinship, at least among the middle-class English, both seem most often to be done by middle-aged adults on the fringe of the kinship group (Firth, Forge, and Hubert: 140). The keepers or mobilizers of other household resources are more variously qualified and some are outside the kinship system altogether. (It is in their relation to its resources that social workers, neighbours, etc. constitute part of the household system.) Either way the rights and obligations of household resource management are now less rigid than they were (see for example Gershuny 1982). What has been called the renegotiation of the social division of labour in industrial society is substantially a matter of renegotiating responsibility for the resources of livelihood at every level.

HOUSEHOLD LIVELIHOOD

Livelihood is never just a matter of finding or making shelter, transacting money, and preparing food to put on the table or exchange in the market place. It is equally a matter of the ownership and circulation of information, the management of relationships, the affirmation of personal significance and group identity, and the interrelation of each of those tasks to the other. All these productive tasks together constitute the work of livelihood. A similarly expanded concept of work is implicit in studies of unenumerated economic organization or the informal sector (McGee 1974; Pahl 1980; Santos 1979). It also underlies recent efforts of various disciplines to monitor changes in the form and concept of work in contemporary industrial societies (Gershuny 1979; Wallman 1979b). Two trends are clear: one is that the availability, experience, organization, and function of employment in the formal economy is changing; the other is that the value of work outside the formal economy is increasingly widely recognized. Although the attention of political or public policy analysis tends still to concentrate on the *economic* values and implications of such work, other perspectives emphasize *other than economic* issues, so that work is seen to entail the performance of necessary tasks and the production of moral as well as economic values. By this logic the livelihood of a London household involves all kinds of work. It depends on the achievement of a sense of identity and belonging (Cohen 1982; Jahoda 1982; Jahoda, Lazarsfeld, and Zeisel 1972; Wadel 1973, 1979); on its ability to differentiate *us* and *them* in apparently transient and impersonal urban settings (Hannerz 1980); and on its capacity to manage social relationships and information (Paine 1970, 1974; Wadel 1979: Wallman 1979b: 1–24), as much as it depends on informal economic organization inside and outside the home (Pahl and Gershuny 1979), and on some member of the household having a job in the formal economy.

This approach to livelihood is built on two tenets of economic anthropology. First, that the resources used in the pursuit of goals and the maximization of benefit are not only and not always material objects. Time, knowledge, symbolic systems, skill, organization, and the goals, values, and valuations of the actor are equally to the point (Belshaw 1967). Second, that the social system can be visualized in terms of spheres, domains, or sub-systems – whether of activity, exchange, or meaning – to which particular resources or kinds of resources pertain, and between which those resources can be transposed when the right conditions of structure and context apply. The systems idea is not peculiar to social anthropology, nor, of course, is the idea of resource conversion. But the perspective of anthropology enhances it to the extent that it notices and tries to account for the fact that not everyone classifies or evaluates the same resources in the same way, and that any one person may not do so consistently (Sahlins 1974: 1–39; Wallman 1979b: 7–10).

SYSTEMS OF RESOURCES

Systems logic has two implications here. First, the boundaries of a household are doubly fluid: they change empirically throughout the domestic cycle, and analytically according to which resource is in focus. Second, the value of any of the household's resources is not fixed. We need to ask: what *kind* of value, for what purpose, and from whose point of view? And where a resource is exchanged or negotiated in more than one domain of the household system, we can see that the effect, if not the purpose, of converting it from one to another is to alter its value in some way.

The classic definition of the entrepreneur as a person able and willing to convert social reserves of skill, contacts, and information into economic capital for business purposes makes the point very plain (Barth 1963). But it is not only 'social facts' that are so volatile: physical energy itself has different value in different domains of livelihood. We may assume, for example, that the calorific energy cost of digging so many square metres of garden is constant, at least for one individual (Harrison 1982). But its economic value changes if I dig to grow potatoes instead of ornamental shrubs; and its moral value is drastically different if, having no horticultural purpose at all, I am digging to bury stolen goods or a dead alley cat. Similar shifts occur on the level of relationships. The moral, social, economic, and existential value of the effort I put into relating to my own spouse changes when I apply the same effort to relating to someone else's. And any of us who has a family of any kind knows that the same kinsman can be an economic liability and an affective resource, a locus of support and the cause of stress in different contexts at the same time, or in similar contexts on different occasions (Saifullah Khan 1979; Wallman 1974).

Ethnic origin is like a kinship tie in this respect. Sometimes it has resource value; sometimes it is a liability. Sometimes, indeed, it has no relevance to the economy or the identity of the household system at all. But from the outside, and most importantly in the official observer's framework, the ethnic origin of minority group members is given a once-for-all quality that obscures quite ordinary changes in the definition and value of anything called an ethnic resource. (Members of the ethnic majority are not classified in the official ethnic schema and therefore are not credited with ethnic resources of any kind.) Just as the census view of households is built on a typology that ignores household process, much of the current discussion of ethnically mixed inner-city areas assumes that people of the same ethnic origin use the ethnic tie in the same way all the time, and that the livelihood of ethnic minority households will be dominated by ethnicity whatever other interests, characteristics, or resources they have to deploy. At least where such households in Battersea are concerned, these assumptions are quite wrong. Age and family stage can be better predictors of a household's organization and work patterns (Buchanan 1982; Dhooge 1982), and employment or locality more important loci of its identity (Wallman 1983a). In this case the structure and style of the local context – that is the Battersea area – apparently diminishes or neutralizes the resource value of ethnic origin. A different kind of local system would have a different effect (Wallman 1983b).

OPTION AND CHOICE

There is a proposition formulated by physical scientists which can be applied here to good sociological purpose: the viability of any resource system is limited by the availability of the least available resource. By this logic, all the elements of the household resource system are interconnected and its viability depends on the appropriate functioning of all its parts. And by the same logic, the crude quantity of any one resource bears no necessary relation to its effective value because usefulness of any sort depends on other things happening at the time. Its value is governed by other options, other constraints, and other obligations in the household system. For example, there may be plenty of labour or labour incentive, but if there is a lack of information about job opportunities or of the time it takes to go out and look for them, then the economic value of labour power or willingness to work cannot be realized. The same is true of the whole range of resources. It explains the failure of apparently well-off households to cope with unexpected change or to take up options and opportunities which they themselves regard as desirable. In the particular matter of some new immigrant residents' failure to find the house or the job they want in the Battersea survey area, there is evidence that such failure is better explained by their lack of access to, or their non-acceptance of, some complementary local resource or resources than by local attitudes to their ethnic origin (Buchanan 1982; Wann 1982).

Differences in the livelihood of immigrant and native households in the same city neighbourhood are rarely a simple function of ethnic status. The limiting factor can occur or not occur at any level in the system. A household may fail to take up a particular option in, say, the matter of child care because it has other possibilities ('Grandma lives around the corner'); because the option is not acceptable ('That's not the way *we* look after children'); or because no one in the household knows that such child care services exist. Whether the household does not know because it has not been around long enough to find out, because it cannot understand the pamphlet advertising the service, or because someone deliberately sets out to ensure that it is excluded or misled makes no difference to the outcome in patterns of child care. But it is the systematic logic of households' success or failure to use the state services that will decide the success of any policy designed to improve them, or of any private strategy to make them more accessible.

Most fundamentally, the household cannot take up options that are not there. It can neither use resources it does not have, nor deploy resources that are not marketable/exchangeable/convertible in the local system that contains it. Some adjustments can, of course, be made internally. Different allocations of time and tasks between members of the household, and even renegotiations of the division of labour happen in the privacy of the home. These are either idiosyncratic changes of strategy (Clark 1982; Pahl 1980), or a reflection of global economic and ideological developments. Either way they vary little from one industrial setting to another (Gershuny 1979, 1982). Other aspects of household livelihood seem to be geared much more closely to the scope and constraints of local context.

Two kinds of local area are identified in this book: the neighbourhood in which the eight households of the title are situated, and the Metropolitan Borough of Battersea to which that neighbourhood belongs (see Chapter 1). In the framework of this study they are assumed also to represent significant levels of local *context*. Some such assumption is inevitable. The context of any analysis must be a matter of arbitrary judgement because the boundaries of social worlds and social systems are never obvious (see Gellner 1973). The special features of defining context in a dense and polyglot urban setting are taken up at the beginning of Chapter 3. Here it is important only that all the households at issue live in the same part of London and within the same small set of streets, so they are sub-sets of the same local system. Any variation between them therefore comes from somewhere within the separate household systems.

WHICH RESOURCES?

If urban households are to be defined or even discussed as resource systems, a number of limiting questions needs to be asked about the resource concept itself. The first is: how far does it extend? One version of the answer includes all those items that might have, or by some formal definition do have, economic value in the city. The other version is more restrictive, covering only those items that are now actually used in some 'resourceful' way.

In operation the distinction between the two usages is hard to justify. Each varies according to whose valuation of the item is at issue. We need therefore to ask for whom and in what way an item has economic potential and whether its owners recognize that potential. Do they have other than economic priorities for it? And in any case, how direct must this economic potential be? Do we include in the resource category items whose value cannot be converted into money? The real difficulty is that as soon as the resource notion moves out of narrowly economic bounds it is hard to know where to stop it (Townsend 1979: 55, 116).

This difficulty leads into the second question: what *kind* of items are to be included in the resource concept? Since it is fundamentally an economic concept, a resource tends to be visualized as a material item. But this usage is based on a misunderstanding of economic notions and, more important, conceals too many of the realities of livelihood. Even those who limit the resource concept to material items will recognize that resource *management* involves organization and some number of layers of social and cultural embroidery. To include perceptions, skills, symbolic structures, organizational strategies, and any sense of commitment to those structures or strategies within the scope of the resource concept is not therefore outside the bounds of common sense. Doing so, however, creates a third problem: which of all these resources is *necessary* to livelihood?

The conventional model of economic resources talks of *land, labour,* and *capital,* and of the relations between them. At the level of households organizing livelihood in the inner city, land becomes *housing,* labour becomes *services,* and capital becomes *goods and money.* These three resources are in some form necessary to livelihood everywhere, but none is sufficient to it even when they are abundantly available.

Using the resource concept for the specific purpose of sorting out the processes of household livelihood in this highly industrialized urban setting, we have added only three extra resources to the classic land–labour–capital trio. They are referred to simply as *time*, *information*, and *identity*, but each covers a whole range of cognate items. There is no doubt that they are necessary to livelihood: each is, in the matter of London household resources, no less essential than bread.

In some respects these 'extra' resources are like the others. Given the question: 'When and how does ethnic origin count?' we can ask when and how is it relevant to the way time is spent, information is obtained, and the world is experienced by someone living in a mixed inner-city area just as readily as we can consider its significance to the getting and keeping of land, labour, and capital resources. And when ethnic origin is itself useful in, for example, the business of borrowing money or getting information about a flat – that is when ethnic resources are converted into money or information or a flat – we may notice that it is not always the same *kind* of resource. When someone lends me money because I belong to the same church or come from the same village, the face value of my ethnic origin is economic. But he/she lent me the money because he/she identified with me, and I had the confidence to ask for it because I identified the bond between us. In this context ethnic origin for both of us is also an identity resource. Similar shifts in resource value apply even in the case of material resources. Most people recognize, for example, that a fast motor car is worth *money*, conveys a relatively affluent *identity*, and, traffic permitting, saves the driver and passengers some amount of *time*.

So the six necessary resources – land, labour, capital, time, information, and identity – are analogous to the extent that they can be valued in the same variety of ways. They are also, in the right conditions, interchangeable. In other respects the two sets of three remain distinct. Land, labour, and capital resources are not only material, they are structural. Their form and scarcity provide the framework for action by deciding which options are available in a given setting at a given time. Together they make up the objective *structure* of livelihood. By contrast, time, information, and identity have more to do with *organization*. It is these resources that decide what is done with or within the objective structure and that limit 'the conditions of possibility' (Bourdieu 1977). In so doing they account for who does better within the constraints of a single environment: who finds the opportunities, who solves the problems, and who takes best advantage of the options available.

Although this approach requires only that these non-material/organizing resources be given as much weight as the material/structural kind, there are indications that their prior importance is a characteristic of industrial society. Apter (1964) and Gellner (1982) have argued the case for *identity* and *information*, Gershuny (1979) for *time*. It could be that they are in their separate ways observing the limitation of the least available resource in operation: housing, services, and money resources are not scarce in industrial welfare states in the way that land or labour or capital are scarce in non-industrial settings. In the latter case, society as a whole is concerned with overall shortages. In the former there is no overall shortage; the supplies of individuals or individual households are limited more importantly by impediments to distribution and access than by any poverty of the industrial system itself. In these matters very plainly it is information, time, and identity resources that make the real difference. The following short discussion of each of them begins to sketch their part in the livelihood of the households which are the focus of this book.

INFORMATION

None of the resources necessary to livelihood is sufficient to it but, in the local context, the resource value of information is particularly striking. It governs the use and usefulness of all the material/structural resources. Members of a household have no access to formal or informal employment unless someone has told them where it is available, how to get it, and how to do the work. No household can make use of welfare statutory services or public housing unless it knows its rights, what benefits are offered, how to apply for them, and how to deal with the officials in charge. The control of information therefore, controls livelihood as effectively as formal job reservation controls access to employment. But the scope of information resources and the mechanisms of their control are seldom explicit for two reasons. First, because the most valuable information is broadcast exclusively on non-formal, private and firmly bounded networks whose relevance to the formal resources of livelihood is often ignored or misunderstood. Second, because the usefulness of information to household X does not depend simply on its being absolutely or relatively unavailable to household Y. It sometimes depends more importantly on the Ys being quite unaware that the Xs have information which they lack or, on the contrary, on their being convinced that the Xs are keeping from them information which they need. Nothing is more controlling than a secret, real or imagined.

This means that what people say about their access or lack of access to local information resources may reflect their sense of belonging in the local system without revealing how much they do belong. They cannot report not having information they do not know about. The usefulness of asking direct questions about information is therefore limited to specifics: 'Where did you hear about *that*?' Thus the replies to the neighbourhood survey question asking where employed members of each household found out about the jobs they now have indicate that the majority used local information sources, even though a majority of jobs are outside the local area. But these responses say nothing about the form and content of local or household information systems.

Where the survey questions failed, the survey procedure succeeded. The neighbourhood survey was designed to be administered by local residents employed as interviewers. We knew this strategy would have implications for the quality of the data collected, and for access to a 'difficult' inner-city area (Wallman *et al.* 1980). Data on access to local information resources were, the first time around, an unplanned bonus. They are an indirect result of allowing each interviewer to choose the households he/she will visit, and of recording the households chosen and the sequence in which they are chosen in the normal course of survey administration. This routine produces maps that show an important segment of the local networks of a score of individual residents, namely the households each feels he/she knows well enough to approach, to talk to, and to co-operate with. These are likely to be households to whom local information is passed, at least by that interviewer. And in so far as information systems are exchange systems whose purpose is either to transact for personal benefit, or to incorporate oneself and others within a common boundary (see Paine 1970, 1974, 1976) a collation of interviewers' local networks suggests the mode of social relationships in the neighbourhood system and so the position of households within it. The interviewing pattern of Mrs C is typical of the Battersea mode.

Mrs C is sixty-five and a widow. She is of south London origin and has lived in Battersea since birth. She has two sons, both living outside London, a sister-in-law in Battersea, and a brother in the next district with whom she is 'very close'. Her close friends all live in Battersea and other parts of south London. These relatives and friends form the inner core of her social network. Mrs C also has a relatively large number of local contacts. The map shows that in her case the street is an important boundary marker for knowing and interacting with local people. Except for five (out of thirty-one), all the households with whom she had the kind of relationship she felt made an interview possible are clustered in *her* part of the road. These relationships are not all of the same type or degree of intimacy. The sequence in which Mrs C chose the households reflects this. The first batch includes friends and neighbours she is on good terms with. Next she interviewed people she is less close to but meets regularly in the local community centre, and households with whom she has exchanged services – one of them uses her telephone in emergencies, a member of another assists her with the distribution of the Residents' Association newsletter, and so forth. The interviews she conducted last involve households whose members she recognizes by sight because she sees them occasionally in the street or at the community centre. From the questionnaires she completed we know the characteristics of households in Mrs C's local network. They include a full range of people in terms of age, occupation, and ethnic origin. At the same time, most of them have lived many years in Battersea.

Because there is a relation between the order in which the households were visited and their perceived closeness to the person visiting them, a cumulation of residents' interviewing patterns produces a local map showing which households are more or less 'in' the local system, with those interviewed last being further 'out' than those interviewed first. And because every household's questionnaire records its main characteristics, the same map can be used as an indicator of the relative significance each has to processes of inclusion and exclusion in the area. The households contacted last have a number of other characteristics in common. Many actually see themselves as 'passing through', 'not really resident'. More important, they are largely households whose members are not involved in the neighbourhood because of study programmes, family or job commitments, and who tend to spend much of their free time in other parts of London or outside it altogether. Consistent with the boundary style of Battersea, households of New Commonwealth or foreign origin are not significantly 'outside' by this measure. It is attitudes and activity patterns that define those least involved in the local system.

TIME AS LENGTH OF RESIDENCE

On the whole, information that governs access to other resources and resource options is exchanged through informal and personal networks. The time it takes to become part of those networks entails the exclusion of newcomers by virtue of their newness (Cohen 1982; Paine 1970, 1974) and may be more significant to the integration of minority group households than their ethnic status as such (see Sowell 1975).

Whether and how integration is taking place at all shows in the extent to which newcomers have started to resemble locals of long standing, that is those born in south London of south London parents (SLEO) (see Chapter 1). Data on *finding a job* and on *kin and friends in the residential area* provide some evidence of the integration of black immigrants and their children in the survey neighbourhood. Employed residents of New Commonwealth origin (NCW) use friends, neighbours, family members, and other informal channels to find employment nearly as much as do residents of south London origin (NCW 58 per cent; SLEO 61 per cent). They are also beginning to resemble the original locals in terms of having kin and friends in the survey neighbourhood itself. The importance both of local ties and of the time it takes to create them shows most dramatically in the unemployment figures given as evidence of Battersea's localist style in Chapter 1 (page 7).

TIME AND WORK

The crisis of unemployment strikes different households in different ways. The differences are not only a matter of relative abilities to get money on the side (Pahl 1980), to manipulate the social service bureaucracies appropriately or at least effectively (Wadel 1979), or to deploy any marketable or exchangeable items, such as skills, empty rooms, or friendly relatives, which may be lying latent in the household resource system. Clearly a job in the formal economy has value beyond its wages. On one hand the proper management of non-monetary resources is a necessary part of getting and performing a job. On the other, the loss of a job is commonly experienced as the loss of identity, status, and the structure of time (Jahoda 1982; Jahoda, Lazarsfeld, and Zeisel 1972; Wadel 1973). And in every case the meaning or crisis of unemployment is mediated by or suffered by families or households as systems, not by individuals in isolation (Fagin 1979; New Universities Quarterly 1979).

Emphasis on the household system allows more realistic assessment of the value and the management of time as a productive resource. Although this emphasis is not new to anthropology (see for example, Belshaw 1954; Bourdieu 1977; Minge-Klevana 1980; Young and Willmott 1973), it does represent a departure from the traditional economic theory of consumer behaviour. Family or household production–consumption decisions at any point in time and over time depend not only on the price of market goods and services, but on the value attributed to time by the people spending it. This value is not as much a matter of absolute scarcity as it is of resource options (What else could I be doing? Who else could be doing this task?). It is also a matter of what else is happening. Thus, while the neighbourhood survey told us who does the shopping, who cooks the family dinner, and how long these tasks normally take in each of 446 households (Wallman *et al.* 1982: 142–44, 151), the household survey time budgets asked this small sub-set of these households who else was at home and what *they* were doing at the same time (*Figure 2*, p. 54). It makes a difference to the value of time spent, say, washing dishes, if there is someone drying them. There is more difference still if he/she is working on a social relationship with the person washing up at the same time.

Time management affects the local system too. There is good evidence that divergent categories of people are spending less time at places of employment than they did, say, twenty years ago (Gershuny 1979). What are they doing instead? Improving their property and/or their minds? Looking for or travelling to formal employment? Dealing with the complexities of state bureaucracies? Looking for ways to fiddle the formal system? Watching television? Relating to their children? (Ingelstam 1980; Wadel 1979). How far do changes in the proportions of time allocated to working on different resources reflect changes of cultural, personal, or local resource options? (Liljeström 1979). This study does not pretend to answer such important general questions, but the two-stage research strategy begins at least to indicate what resources are available to each household and how these resources are evaluated, managed, and allocated in two different time dimensions: throughout the working life cycle, via work histories, and throughout the week, via time budgets. Both strategies are described at length in Chapter 3.

TIME AS PERSPECTIVE

Since the value I put on any kind of work is in some part a function of what else I could be doing, what I see others doing, what I expected to be doing at this time, what I hope to do next year, whether my position has changed and whether that change is for the better, whether I am prepared to sweat for the sake of my own or my children's future benefit or must have my returns *now* – we need not be surprised to find that different categories of people have different kinds of perspectives on past, present, and future time resources. Migrants in any system are said to work harder and to put up with conditions that no indigenous worker would tolerate, exactly because they tend to be future oriented and to see conditions 'away', however inhospitable, as somehow better than conditions at home.

But the migrant/non-migrant distinction is not the only one affecting time perspectives. At different ages time passes at different speeds. A year to a child is 'long', to its busy parent 'short', to its grandparent 'flying'. Biology itself may make a difference. When the human organism is changing fast, as it does in early childhood, time outside it is bound to feel slow. And where certain life stages combine with culture-specific preoccupations or anxieties, chronology alone is a crisis. In industrial societies everybody is said to be at least disconcerted by the future (Toffler 1970), but the more introspective members of adolescent and mid-life age grades commonly deny their own relation to it. For those among the young who expect either nuclear war or a lifetime of unemployment, the twin horsemen of the new apocalypse are reason enough to be present-oriented; and the middle-aged who become more than normally anxious about the waning of economic and cosmetic success may even try to 'turn time around' so they can start the whole business again (de Beauvoir 1971; Lessing 1973).

The fact that these time perspectives are fanned by consumerism and the commercial media may contribute to their special association with industrialized settings (Goffman 1978; Wallman 1978b). Certainly it is possible that, by making ready explanations of the current life crisis of any household member available to the rest, the media exaggerate its effect on the identities and anxieties of the rest. But the effect of normal cycles of social or domestic responsibility pertains in some way everywhere. Different aspects of livelihood become matters of central concern at different stages. Notable among these is the change wrought on the time perspectives of adults by the arrival and development of their children.

There is strong evidence too of a relation between ecology and time perspectives of this sort. Hunter-gatherers are 'oriented forever in the present'. They are described as optimistic or at least unconcerned about the future on the grounds that they regularly 'eat right through all the food in the camp, even during objectively difficult times'. The propensity to do so makes sense where storage is either impossible or economically and socially undesirable, and where more than minimal possessions of any sort get in the way of movement to the next hunting ground. In this setting the 'utility' of all material resources 'falls quickly at the margin of portability' (Sahlins 1974: 30–3). So apparently does the utility of long-range planning. All the work of livelihood is directed towards immediate returns for effort and even investment in children falls away (Woodburn 1982). Similar reasoning has been used in analyses of the culture of class in Britain: people categorized as 'working class' were said to want immediate returns for any effort they made, and some part of the relative success of 'the middle class' was attributed to its members' willingness to defer gratification of all sorts (Zweig 1949). In the British case neither nomadism nor physical environment have been held to account, although a parallel American version of the same model builds a time culture on something like the ecology of poverty itself: the poor are poor because they are unwilling and/or unable to concern themselves with the future (Lewis 1967; see also the critique in Valentine 1968).

These approaches talk of the time perspective of whole societies or cultural groups as if the relative weights of past/ present/future were as unchanging as the shape of time itself (Bloch 1977; Leach 1961; Wallman 1977: 2–10). An approach at the level of household resource systems shows the extent to which time perspectives vary within a single cultural frame. At that level it may be *only* the time perspective that differentiates one style of livelihood from another.

Exactly this possibility is raised by comparing the Bates and Mason households whose narratives are combined in Chapter 7. Both centre on young English working-class couples with two children under five. Each couple claims the same formal educational level, and each household's system includes a large locally-based network of kin. The two women worked at apparently identical jobs before they married, the two men are equally healthy and resourceful, and both couples are council tenants in the Battersea survey neighbourhood.

There is so little to differentiate the material/structural resources of the two households that they can be said to have the same economic options. But because one is resolutely present-oriented, and the other just as consistently looks towards the future, they organize those options in quite different ways. Because other things are so equal between them, the effect of time on the business of livelihood is drawn out by the contrast.

IDENTITY

Identity is the most pervasive of the three organizing resources. It is also the most slippery. Identity issues arise whenever the question 'Who am I?' is asked or answered. The question is seldom raised explicitly and there is no single answer to it because individuals do not consistently identify themselves by the way they look, or the way they behave, or the people they associate with. For this reason the significance put upon signs of similarity by non-members outside a group may differ from their meaning for members inside it. The identification of people by signs the observer can see has no necessary bearing on their internal identity processes (Wallman 1978a). While there is no logical limit to the number of identity options available to ordinary individuals, discourse on identity in industrial society at this time is dominated by references to three loci: ethnic origin, work (in the narrow sense of occupation and employment), and local community. It is possible that the identity strength of each depends on the identity strength of the others. Certainly there is evidence that ethnic sentiment is enhanced by unemployment and that it is not a useful organizing principle in areas with localist traditions of the Battersea sort (Wallman 1983a/b).

Whether or not the three stand in some kind of complementary relation, it is important to analyse localism and work identity in ways analogous to the study of ethnicity. We need to ask in what context each is used by or useful to whom, and for what purposes. We need moreover to allow the possibility that either can be more valuable/negotiable/convertible than ethnic or kinship ties, even in the livelihood of people who manifestly enjoy 'shared understandings' with (some?) fellow members of an ethnic group when they get together (Epstein 1978: 97–9).

One special caution concerning localism needs to be noted. The term is most often used to refer to a geographic locus of kinship, to ethnic or other associative ties, or to length of residence in a demarcated area, or to combinations of these (Gans 1962a/b, 1967: Hannerz 1969, 1980; Liebow 1967; Suttles 1968; Whyte 1943; Young and Willmott 1957). These measures may be useful predictive indicators of involvement or investment in a local area, but they do not amount to local identity in the sense intended here. Localism as an identity option is not the same as being there, just as ethnicity is not the same as phenotype or culture, and people do not invariably define themselves by their formal occupational status. Localism is not always important, nor is it always important in the same way. Although in Battersea it tends overall to count for more than ethnicity, it does not play the same part in every Battersea household system. Its significance varies according to which of the household's resources are vested in the local area and which are vested outside it, or in other than geographic domains.

The variation could be demonstrated by ordinary social process in any household. It is implicit in all the eight accounts of livelihood that make up Chapters 4–7. But the point is emphasized by reference to differences among households that are identified alike *from the outside*. Thus, although the Abraham, Irving, Charles, and Ellison households all belong in the official 'New Commonwealth Ethnic Origin' category and all have the same objective local identity options, each one's narrative (Chapters 4 and 5) suggests a different balance of local/ethnic involvement.

Occupation and employment status account for some of the variation, but inevitably all kinds of other factors get in the way of predictable correlations: ethnicity is unusually important in the Irving household because all its ethnic and occupational identities are concentrated in the same set of people and activities. Matthew Irving is the Minister in a Pentecostal Church, and all the members of his household identify with the West Indians who make up his congregation. The strength of their household's involvement in Matthew's vocation seems to preclude any of them from identifying with the people, the tasks, or the status associated with jobs they have or have had in the formal economy. By contrast, the Charles household has no occupational identity options (apart from the stigma of living on state welfare) because its only adult member is unskilled and unemployed. Somewhat surprisingly in this circumstance, the household does not even try to take up ethnic identity options as such. Its only sense of belonging is vested in the local area. The Abrahams is also a one-parent household, but its identity is altogether less fragile. Its members energetically involve themselves in ethnic *and* occupational *and* local networks and they identify equally comfortably with each of them as context demands. The Ellison household does not distinguish its options in the same explicit way. As ethnicity and work identities are compounded in the case of the Irvings, here it is ethnic and local domains that overlap. The adult Ellisons have each lived in the area since early childhood and both now identify as Battersea people. Their ethnic origins are represented by their parents and a small circle of kin among the people they grew up with and know well as individuals. It is because all these people live in and around Battersea that the Ellisons' ethnic and local identities are not separated. In this respect they match the Bateses (p. 37–8 and Chapter 7), more nearly than the Irvings. Like many among the Black English in Battersea, their identity resources are more like those of 'south London ethnics' than of the 'New Commonwealth immigrants' with whom they are officially identified.

VARIATION AND VIABILITY

Even households with similar objective characteristics living in the same urban neighbourhood may have markedly different styles of livelihood. This happens because the values of the separate resources that constitute and define the household system are not fixed, and because each of them is combined with or converted into others in different ways throughout the ordinary processes of livelihood. The variation is not random: the effectiveness of each household system depends on the context in which its resources are being used or assessed, on the particular purposes of its members on particular occasions, and on which options are both available to the household and recognized by its resource-keepers.

As much as the details of livelihood vary from one household to another however, the necessities of life are remarkably similar. People everywhere need food, shelter, companionship, and self-esteem; livelihood anywhere is a matter of balancing a household economy and getting on with the neighbours. The point is only that there is not just one way of defining or achieving one set of ends. On the contrary, the admission of the three 'organizing resources' admits also that priorities need not always be ranked in the same way and that different households, whether with the same or different objectives, invest their various resources in a variety of ways with equal satisfaction. Most people cope well enough, in their own terms, to get by. Some look as though they manage a great deal better than that. In the area of this study certainly, there are far more households with problems they can solve than there are problem households burdening the state. In any case there is more than one kind of successful performance:

> 'only a virtuoso with a perfect command of his "art of living" can play on all the resources inherent in the ambiguities and uncertainties of behaviour and situation in order to produce the actions appropriate to each case, to do that of which people will say "There was nothing else to be done" and do it the right way. . . . It is the art of necessary improvisations which defines excellence.'
>
> (Bourdieu 1977: 8)

3 Unravelling household processes

ANTHROPOLOGY IN THE CITY

Until quite recently the settings of ethnographic enquiry were always rural. This is not only because social anthropology was from its beginning defined by a specialist interest in small-scale and 'whole societies' whose members expected no change in their relationships with each other or with the natural environment. It is also because the discipline built its reputation on an appreciation of the context in which events occur and are evaluated, and it knows that context is dauntingly hard to perceive, let alone to control, in town. We have therefore a number of durable professional excuses for not venturing into cities at all – particularly our own cities – and all kinds of professional anxieties to face when we get there. Significant on both counts is the fact that other social scientists seem to have pre-empted the study of 'us' in general and of the urban setting in particular. Even now we are curiously willing to connive in the rumour that we are working in our own (urban) countries because we cannot get the money or the research permission to go back to (rural) Africa, and to accept the small exotic corners of the urban scene, the residuum of the other disciplines, as our only and proper due. Indeed, what conceptual room is there left? What is there in our professional repertoire that is worth transposing and can be transposed out of the setting in and for which it was developed – out of the periphery and into the centre of the social research map?

The popular answer tends not to go beyond participant observation. In the popular image, social anthropology is a technique of enquiry, nothing more. By this metonymic logic, its means are equated with its ends, its method with its methodology; if it is not possible to 'do' participant observation – which, in the traditional paradigm, requires year-round isolation from one's own ordinary life and round the clock immersion in the ordinary lives of others – then it is not possible to 'do' social anthropology. In these terms it is difficult to work as a social anthropologist in any town and impossible in your own.

But these are not the right terms. The proper criterion of the craft is in the perspectives we bring to the analyses we attempt, not in the deceptively simple act of 'hanging in'. Participant observation is a means to understanding social life in the round, to the appreciation of context and meaning, and to the relational perspective, all of which are distinguishing marks of social anthropology. 'The typically anthropological assumption (is) that a social field does not consist of units of population, but of persons in relation to one another' (Leach 1967: 80).

The crucial problem has been to devise research strategies that are feasible in a dense urban setting (as participant observation is not) and yet do not distort the realities of ordinary life by dealing with people as 'units of population', classified only by characteristics that can readily be seen and counted by outsiders in the way that conventional social survey tends to do. We may agree that 'the typically anthropological assumption' is worth transposing out of the typically anthropological setting, but do we know what to do with it when we get it home? Is it possible to map context without sitting in the middle of it?

The strategies described in this chapter aim to do so. They were used in the second stage of a programme of research into aspects of livelihood in inner London. They are designed to unravel processes which make up the households that are the focus of this book. The strategies of the first stage of the study are reported elsewhere (Wallman *et al.* 1980; Wallman *et al.* 1982). At one level they brought historical and demographic perspectives to bear on the whole of Battersea as a part of inner London; at another they were concerned with the ethnographic survey of LARA – the neighbourhood in south Battersea that is the most immediate local context of the households at issue.

The project has not been a purely anthropological venture. Researchers from several different disciplines have been so closely associated in its procedures that there is a sense in which this is the report of an exercise in interdisciplinary ethnography. We have been explicitly aware of the methodological charters of sociography (Jahoda, Lazarsfeld, and Zeisel 1972) and mass observation (Harrisson 1976) in the design and execution of the first stage neighbourhood survey; of techniques of psychotherapeutic intervention (Speck and Attneave 1974) in the mapping of household resource systems; and of traditional ethnography throughout.

It may be that some form of interdisciplinary collaboration is a necessary condition of effective urban anthropology (Foster and Kemper 1974). This study makes no such general claim. We do not here define what urban anthropology is or might be and should not be thought to be offering an all-purpose blueprint of procedures for doing it. These strategies are adaptations of others, each invented to deal with its own combination of theoretical and practical constraints. No doubt they will be used again – other researchers have taken them up – but not without modification *ad hoc*. Their usefulness to us is in strict relation to the problem we were set to study, to the characteristics of the setting in which we had to study it, and to the generous but still limiting conditions of the research grant.

NEIGHBOURHOOD AND HOUSEHOLD SURVEYS

The first-stage neighbourhood survey mapped the resource dimensions of the local area by cumulating household responses to the survey questionnaire. This second-stage household survey aims to chart the resource systems of a small number of households in the survey neighbourhood. Superficially it is asking the same questions of units of a different size. The similarity between the two stages is limited in one essential respect: the survey questionnaire was designed to exclude matters of personal interpretation or meaning – whether of the researchers, the interviewers, or the respondents – while these strategies deliberately broach those questions. The first stage of the study seeks to find out what the resources of the setting are; the second to account for variations in the way they are used.

The first-stage neighbourhood survey questionnaire takes about 35 minutes to complete and yields information on more than 800 variables. It is cast in eight sections, each dealing with a separate facet of livelihood. When all the responses are combined, the survey produces a generalized ethnographic profile of the whole neighbourhood – who lives there, what kind of households they keep, etc. Machine reading of the data allows combinations of specified variables to be made, and the typicality of the patterns of particular households or ethnic groups to be tested. One of the survey's effects is to show whether the various population categories use the area in the same way. We know from it something about how far they travel to shop and to work; how they found the jobs they have; how they organize certain household tasks; how much time they spend on them; what household machinery they have; whether they have significant kin or close friends around; whether they use (or at least whether they admit to using) support services, etc. (see Appendix). Overall the survey material is rich in inference for the comparison of the life patterns of people who come from different places but now live as neighbours. For example, the section that records the geographical distribution of close friends and kin shows which households have support or potential support in the neighbourhood or the wider south London area. These data can be aggregated to suggest how far the kinship and friendship contacts of the various ethnic categories are localized. Since having 'close' local contacts implies some degree of local involvement, the same data reflect the extent to which each ethnic category is integrated into the local system and is more or less 'localist' in its orientations (pp. 38–40).

But the value and validity of the first stage neighbourhood survey is limited to statements about the area or categories of household in it. The case material for the second-stage household survey, by contrast, describes the resource systems of particular households that constitute sub-systems of the 'whole' neighbourhood. As this stage of the enquiry set out to compare styles of resource management, all the households studied had to be similar in respect of need for and formal access to resources. For these reasons, all the second-stage households have five characteristics in common. Each of them (i) has lived in the neighbourhood for at least five years; (ii) has kin living in south London but at a different address; (iii) has children under sixteen living at home; (iv) falls into the same socio-economic status category; and (v) has experienced a normal crisis (a birth, a death, a move, a marriage, a redundancy, or the like) in the preceding twelve months.

Criteria (i) and (ii) ensure that all the households studied have the same possibility of involvement in the local area and the option of calling on locally based kin for assistance or support; (iii) puts them at a similar stage in the domestic life cycle; (iv) confines them to a range of skilled and semi-skilled, manual and non-manual occupations (in OPCS categories 3 and 4) which are both non-executive and weekly paid. Each of these criteria controls, to some extent, the resources available to each household and the tasks of livelihood over which they must be deployed; and (v) provides a focus for discussion ('What did you do when . . .?') of a situation requiring extra attention to resource options and resource management.

Sorting both by computer and by hand, we searched among the 446 households covered in the first stage survey and found thirty-five which met all five criteria. Given our own resource constraints, we calculated that we could manage four visits to each of a maximum of twelve households. We then sent letters to small batches among the thirty-five, referring to the first stage of the enquiry and inviting them to participate in the second. The letters underlined the overall theme (How does your household manage?) and at the same time stressed the four-visit limit to the commitment that was asked of them. Apart from making sure that each batch was ethnically mixed so that the case studies would reflect the cosmopolitan character of the neighbourhood, there was no reason to stratify the eligible households any further; given the criteria already imposed, willingness to co-operate was sufficient ground for selection. In the event, four white and four black households, some London born and some immigrant, make up the eight that are the subject of this book.

Initially it was our plan to focus each of the agreed four sessions on one aspect of household resource management:

– How did you manage through that recent crisis?
– How do you and have you in the past organized your working life?
– How do you manage time?
– Who and where are the important people in your network? How, when, why are they important?

At the same time we agreed to aim for 'objective' interviewing devices so that the material collected from different households and by different interviewers would be comparable. After more discussion and some pilot inquiry however, it became clear that any device we might invent could do no more than round out the household picture. In effect, comparison would be less tidy but more realistic and more interesting if the devices and the topic order could be adapted to each household as an individual case. The reasons for this change of strategy and its implications for the research procedure were set down in the following memorandum, circulated among us at the time (the references in brackets have been added).

Research memo (1)

(Since we are an interdisciplinary team) no collective effort that we make within the programme can or should exactly fit the conceptual frame of any one of us. Each has his own slant on the resources notion, would give priority to a different aspect of it, and would want his favourite device or topic administered best and so last, when the relationship with the respondent had warmed up and/or when the interviewer could risk *the* definitive question – 'Do you pay tax on that?' 'Do you *really* feel comfortable with your husband's kin?' – and beat a definitive retreat when the conversation suddenly sours.

The second reason hinges on our discovery that we do not, after all, want to know the same things about each of the households in our stage two set. The questionnaire and the interviewers' comments on it give us a profile of each household and the beginnings of a description of how its members 'manage' in the city. When we read off a household from its questionnaire there are many things we know about it. The same process indicates things we do not know but feel we should know about that household. They show up as gaps or as question marks. These consolidated form the basis of an *aide mémoire* (Firth, Forge, and Hubert 1969), a what-we-need-to-know-about-household-X list, which the interviewer will be familiar with before setting foot in the household at all.

The version of 'case' analysis that we are now evolving looks like being a combination of the case conference technique that psychotherapy groups sometimes use, and the extended case study/situational analysis strategy that social anthropologists have used in various ways elsewhere (van Velsen 1967; Mitchell 1983). The success of our effort probably depends on our spending some amount of time discussing and mapping every case *together*, both before and after interviewing. It will therefore entail more time than we had originally supposed, and may actually reduce the number of families we can deal with in the second stage. But it will be interesting to do and will make another innovation for our record – if we can pull it off. Its peculiar charm is in the combination of a brief that indicates to the interviewer which topics need to be discussed, with a degree of autonomy that leaves him the scope to decide the order of those topics or – better – to respond to the inclination of his informants.

One further point has begun to emerge: in trying to answer the question 'Who, in each household, should be the main informant?' we looked for a similar combination of consistency and flexibility. For consistency our only demographic option is the mother of the children who, by our selection, is present in all the households we are studying. But such a person is not always available, not always articulate, not always knowledgeable. Besides, how can we assume that the mother plays the same role in each family? We realized, in effect, that it was a particular *role* we wanted at the centre of discourse: the role of *resource-keeper* (Firth, Forge, and Hubert 1969 and see pp. 21–2). Being intrigued by this notion, but not entirely sure what it entails, I suggest we hang on to it for a while, but give it room to take shape.

Notwithstanding these reservations, a framework for the comparison of households as resource systems is provided by the devices used. These are: two day-round time budgets showing who was doing what, with whom, and where on one work day and one weekend or holiday day; detailed and dated job histories of each adult member of the household; and two network maps, filled in by or with the informants, and designed to record the geographic and affective distance of kin and non-kin in the resource universe of the household. Building on the basic description of the structure and history of every household made available by the neighbourhood survey (see Appendix), these strategies provide qualitative dimensions which the neighbourhood survey lacks.

But the information contained in time, employment, and network maps of the sort shown here is equally only a partial picture of livelihood. To make full sense it has to be integrated with other dimensions of the household system which are not described in this chapter. Most explicit among them are the *structural resources* revealed by the neighbourhood survey itself: demographic, sociographic, and geographic facts; shops, consumer durables, patterns of transportation, housing, etc. Other strands of the analysis are less specific but, since they relate to equally essential *organizing resources*, are no less significant to it (pp. 29–40). Least measurable of all are the expectations and orientations implicit in the narrative material (Chapters 4–7) which amount to something like a *philosophy of life* and so come closest to revealing the overall style of each household's livelihood. Most generally, of course, every household's processes are affected by options and events in the world around it, and in this respect the features of the neighbourhood, the characteristic style of Battersea, and the problems and opportunities of the inner-London environment are also integral parts of every household system. (Both the survey results and demographic, sociographic, and political profiles of Battersea are set out at length in Wallman *et al.* 1982, and in summary here in Chapter 1.)

The point of defining households as resource *systems* is to recognize that the value, the use, or the operation of each resource element is affected by the value, etc. of each of the others, and that the whole system is more dynamic than any catalogue of its constituent parts. This is only to say that context counts: when seeking to evaluate a household 'item' of any kind or to interpret the processes that make up the household system, it is important to ask, 'What else is happening? What else could be happening? How much of other things happening counts and in what way?'. The answers will vary according to the way context is defined; and since there is nothing in real life to indicate which 'other things happening' make up that context, its boundaries can only be arbitrarily drawn (p. 27), and so they are here. The three strategies described in this chapter are designed to take account only of options and events which bear *directly* on the household or its members, but also to record a range of 'things' in the household system which are 'happening' at the same time. We do not know whether any one 'thing' causes any other: co-variance is not, after all, the same as a causal sequence. But the format of these research devices serves both to separate the dimensions of household process and to suggest why the value of each is so variable.

Their scope is made plainer by contrast to single-stranded models. The conventional forms of time and people resource maps (*Figures 1* and *4*) record only a single dimension of the resource at issue. The maps developed for this study (*Figures 2* and *5*) are similar in that they too record how much time is spent on particular tasks and how many people are 'available' to the household, but differ in that they take account of things happening that affect the way amounts of time and numbers of people are evaluated by the actors who 'use' them, and they imply the relation of events happening in different domains of livelihood. The format of the job histories (*Figure 3*) is most explicit in this last respect: besides recording past and present jobs of each adult member of the household and the sequence in which they were held (much as an academic *curriculum vitae* or job centre questionnaire would do), it encourages the respondent to remember what each job was like, how he/she heard about it, why he/she left it, and what else was happening around the time of leaving.

TIME CHARTS

Time has been used as a measure of relative value in the analysis of economies without a money currency and to evaluate anything that, like 'the quality of life', cannot be measured or bought by industrial wealth in our own (Brenner 1979). Cross-national time 'budgets' demonstrate consistencies and developments in time expenditure and activity patterns. Nation states have used them as a basis for everything from government plans to broadcasting policy throughout the industrial world (Gershuny and Thomas 1982), and social analysts use them to monitor trends in domestic technology and the sexual division of labour in specific settings (Gershuny 1982; Young and Willmott 1973).

In the business of assessing how people value what they do, time is probably the best proxy for money that we have. But time and money are very different: quantities of time cannot be tallied like cash; two hours is not always twice as valuable as one, nor can it be exchanged for twice as much of anything. A specific amount of money can be converted into predictable quantities of goods and its value is fixed by the conventions of the economy it represents: exchange rates and inflation notwithstanding, we know what we mean when we say six eggs 'cost' the same as a pound of apples. Time does not play the same intermediary role and its value is a good deal more slippery: it 'takes' as long to listen to a symphony as it 'takes' to clean the kitchen, but the two activities are neither interchangeable nor alternative to one another. It is possible to do two things at the same time, but impossible to buy eggs and apples with the same piece of money. More important perhaps, the value of a piece of time 'spent' on a given activity changes according to whose time it is and where and when it is spent. Time values are dependent on all sorts of other things that are happening or could be happening in the same period (pp. 35–8, see also Wallman 1979b: 10–12).

The perspective taken here dissolves none of these constraints. On the contrary, its chief function so far has been to complicate the time budget procedure. But if it provokes a better set of questions for evaluating time resources, it will suit our general purpose very well.

Research memo (2)

The whole of our second stage survey is about the work of livelihood (pp. 22–4). All four of the focal questions are asking people about the work they do, whether to earn or pay out money, to meet the obligations of their various social roles, to affirm personal significance and group identity, or to clean the house and cook the family dinner.

Every sort of work involves time and energy 'costs' of some sort. In instrumental terms these may be raised or lowered by machines or tools or labour-saving devices. But objects are not only used as instruments. In other-than-instrumental domains they can become resources of very different kinds: people exchange things for affection, define themselves as owners of particular motor cars or colour television sets, and identify with (some) items as strongly as with (some) people. Conversely, people are not just the other half of relationships, not only affect. They can be used instrumentally. Either way people and objects are part of the same scene. So, in the matter of the division of labour–time, we want to know how much time people spend using/relating to people *and* things. We know from the first stage survey which appliances, tools, labour-saving devices, and residents each house contains. Here we have some chance of discovering how they are combined. When we ask people to fill in two separate 24-hour time charts we want to get from them some idea of the relative and cumulative value of all these kinds of work – even of the non-events which they may think of as empty time, free time, 'standing about'. The real difficulty, of course, is to know what it all *means* in relation to the household system.

The best we can do is first to ask who in the household spends time how, and who does which necessary household tasks and how long each takes, and then to try to find out what else they recognize to be happening at the same time. Who chats to whom? What kind of time does each parent spend (or think it spends?) with its partner, with each child, etc? While X was standing at the stove cooking, was the TV on? We have asked on the first stage survey questionnaire who prepares the main meal. Here we can also ask who else was in the house (and what were *they* doing?), and was anyone else in the kitchen not helping with the cooking but relating to the cook? In the long run it may even be possible to see whether less time spent at one kind of work means more to spend at another. Does the unemployed man at home *in fact* spend more time (at the work of) relating to his wife and children than he did when he had a job which kept him out of the house all day? How elastic is the time curve anyway? If my partner is away for days or weeks I have many more household tasks to perform. Logically I must spend his share of task time as well as my own. But if he is absent I have time 'spare' from the 'work' of relating to him. The balance of the day's work is altered – more household tasks, less social exchange – but the number of 'working' hours in the day is not significantly different. At what point is the lack of emotional recharge reflected in overt energy levels? Can we consider this kind of equation in our resource survey of large versus small households? Single-parent versus conventional nuclear families?

Figure 1 Simple time schedule, to show portions of time spent on each kind of task or activity.

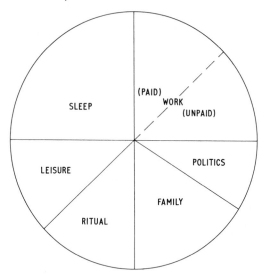

Figure 2 Contextual time schedule, to show other things happening during each task period

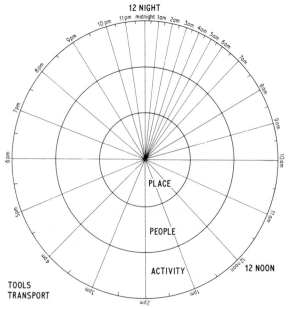

Figure 1 represents a conventional time/work schedule. It shows energy expenditure in terms of crude proportions of time spent on categories of activity or in particular domains of livelihood. Changes in the designation of any category will not lift the one-dimensional constraint. By contrast, the time chart filled in by these eight households (*Figure 2*) shows time and energy expenditure in a number of dimensions. It records time spent in designated activities along with 'other things happening' which affect both the energy spent on each activity and the actor's feeling about the time it takes to do it. Because those 'other things' are also work, they too must be consuming calorific energy; and because the meaning of any task is altered by its context, so the worker's affective energy investment in it will change with the logic of the situation in which it is performed. Whether these two kinds of energy are analogous is not to the point here (but see Harrisson 1982). Either way they combine to govern the value of the time in which they are spent.

JOB HISTORIES

The job history chart (*Figure 3*) deals with similar issues, but on different scales: the notion of work is narrowed to focus only on employment, and the time perspective is widened to take in the chunks of months or years that add up to an individual's job life – that is, to the periods of his or her 'economic activity' according to official census definitions. Also in contrast to the time charts, the job history is linear: *Figures 1* and *2* reflect the circularity of 24-hour periods, 'the daily round', and *Figure 3* the sequential experience of a career. Some informants' entries extended over several column pages; for others – whether because they were younger, less frequently employed, or more steadfast in the job or jobs they held – one page was more than enough. But whatever the content of each job life, the linear 'shape' of job time is common to all of them.

The baseline of the job history is a record of which jobs were held by each adult member of the household, and for how long (columns (i) and (v)). The extra columns on it, like the inner

Figure 3   Job history chart

JOB HISTORY OF . . . .   Given by: self ☐   partner ☐   other . . . .

(i) Name of job?	(ii) Short description: what was it like?	(iii) How did you get the job? WHO HELPED?	(iv) Where was it? How far away?	(v) How long, and what dates were you there?	(vi) Why did you leave it?	(vii) What else was happening around the time you left?

rings of the time chart, are designed to set each job in the context of the household resource system and to relate it to other domains of household livelihood. Answers given in columns (iii) and (iv) for example, show how far job information resources and jobs themselves are localized, and any entry in column (vii) shows that the real reason for changing jobs may have been 'other things happening' and nothing to do with the work or the workplace at all. In columns (ii) and (vi) the reasons given for liking or disliking and keeping or leaving jobs often fall into patterns which say as much about the workers as about the work. Some rank every job as more or less interesting and leave it (where they have themselves chosen to change) because they 'got bored'; others concentrate on the pay and move to anything that pays better; still others are interested in each job for a while, but invariably want to move to better wages as their interest wanes. Put together, any one person's answers will show up consistencies of strategy not revealed by simplistic where-did-you-work-when questions. In this form the job history reveals contrasts between households whose members apparently have the same job options and similar objective experiences of employment. The fact that one stays in one place and moves up a single job hierarchy, and the other does the same job for three employers in succession; that a man has had six jobs before he married and the same one for six years since; or that some women work out of the house only until they have children and others begin to do so only when their children are older – all these job history items are both cause and effect of each household's style of livelihood.

The procedure for recording each person's job history begins with a discussion of the present job or, in the case of anyone retired or unemployed, with a discussion of their last employment. The object of the exercise is a general picture of experience and attitudes in each case, *not* the specifics of actual earnings, taxes, or benefits. There is no interview schedule, but a checklist of questions can be used to make sure that the same points are raised every time (see also Firth, Forge, and Hubert

1969). Some of the answers given fill in the specifics of the present job on the job history form, others serve to nudge the informant's memory, and make it easier to talk about jobs he/she has held in the past.

It is striking that informants in all the eight households readily extended their 'work histories' beyond the description of jobs and job sequence to include work outside the formal economy, that is the work of livelihood as a whole, while in relation to the time charts they had to be encouraged to report or even to remember 'work' which was not employment. Such opposite tendencies confirm the elasticity of people's definitions of work, but left us with very diffuse material. Some of it reappears in the household narratives that follow (Chapters 4–7), but for the sake of trying to understand the experience of each job, we focused the discussion on a handful of specific dimensions:

Research memo (3)

Around all jobs in the formal economy the same questions can be asked, but do not expect too much detail about past jobs. Work backwards in time from now. It is said to be easier for informants to remember that way, but might be worth trying in both directions. Consider, first for the current job, then for the others:

Degree of *autonomy*. Who makes decisions, e.g. when to work, when to take a tea break, go to the washroom, etc? Is it a person or a machine process? *Supervision* How close? How precise? How punitive is it? Can you decide who you work with, eat with, etc? *Authority* Who allocates perks, overtime? Who controls the resources and actions of the work group?

What *incentives* are there to work harder? Bonus payments? Prospects? Expectations? Time orientations? Plans for the family?

How much *concentration* does the job need? Heavy drudgery? Mindless button pressing? Boredom *and* concentration seems a bad combination: you cannot let the mind wander, but the work is not interesting enough to hold the attention. If the job does not need concentration, the worker can think about something else. These latter kinds of work may be quite relaxed. The drudgery does not have to be all-embracing.

How *sociable* is it? Jobs that do not need concentration allow the workers to chat. (The best part of some work situations?) Are the people worked with pleasant, your kind, etc? 'Trouble with work is usually people.' How is time structured? Flexitime? Teabreaks? Time clocks (punching in)? Work by the hour? Does the lunch period come out of work time or is it in effect unpaid? Unpaid breaks imply work by the hour or by the item i.e. piece work. Who or what controls the pace?

These thoughts apply to clerical work as much as to manual or factory work. The general notions are: what do people like about it, dislike about it? What are they indifferent about? (Maybe everything except the pay.) What did they expect? In relation to their job/life what would they like to see happen to them next? Do they or did they identify with the job, the place of work, the people at work – none or all of these? What would – or did – unemployment take away?

NETWORK MAPS

It is not a coincidence that the society-as-network metaphor joined the currency of our analytic notions only when anthropologists ventured into the cities. It is a model which allows the ethnographer to consider who knows whom, who goes where, and what kinds of cross-linkages there are in a given social field even when it is not possible to sit in the middle of that field and watch it all happening. Where that is possible, as it is said to be in small, closely-bounded rural communities in which all relationships are played out in a single arena, network as a conceptual tool is neither necessary nor particularly useful. It is not that the quality of relationships differs from one place to another, only that different kinds of research strategy suit different research environments and different research questions.

The network notion has been articulated in a number of

ways in urban anthropology (see Hannerz 1980: Chapter 5). The two most common are normally contrasted: one involves drawing an arbitrary line around a total social field and mapping all the linkages and cross-linkages happening inside it; the other conceptualizes an ego-centred social field and involves following one person through the universe of his or her contacts. The first, it is said, is like describing the activity in a fish tank; the second, is like tagging one fish and watching to see where it swims and who it swims with. But to say that X and Y live in the same 'fishtank' is only to say that there is a chance of one encountering/meeting/colliding with the other; and the fact that X 'knows' Y (because Y is 'on X's network') says nothing about what they do together, what each thinks of the other, or what kind of relationship they share. Neither model *as such* reveals the meaning of the links in the social net.

The strategy used here combines both versions in a way designed to raise exactly those questions of meaning with the informant. Two different maps of each household's network are drawn. One (*Figure 4*) situates its contacts in relation to the local context; the other (*Figure 5*) classifies these contacts in terms of their practical or emotional resource value. Combined, they imply the household's relation to the neighbourhood: the extent to which its 'valuable' contacts are also geographically close gives some indication of the household's investment or involvement in the local area (pp. 38–9).

The map structure is the same for both purposes. It consists of concentric rings around the household unit, left and right segments to distinguish kin from non-kin, and a pie slice section at the bottom to encourage informants to express difficult, hostile, or ambiguous relationships. The rings on both maps are named to show degrees of 'closeness' to the household: they differ only in the kind of closeness that is recorded.

Figure 4 represents the conventional form of people/distance schedule. It allows the informant to record significant others (that is, actual or potential people resources) in terms of geographic distance: How close are you to each of them in fact? *Figure 5* places the same others in terms of their relative affective distance from household members: How close are

Figure 4 Map to record geographic distance of people in the household
network

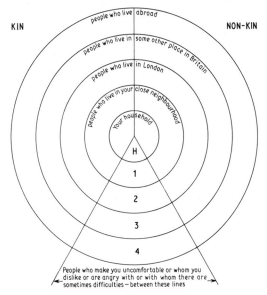

KIN

NON-KIN

people who live abroad

people who live in some other place in Britain

people who live in London

people who live in your close neighbourhood

Your household

H

1

2

3

4

People who make you uncomfortable or whom you
dislike or are angry with or with whom there are
sometimes difficulties – between these lines

Figure 5 Map to record affective distance of people in the household
network

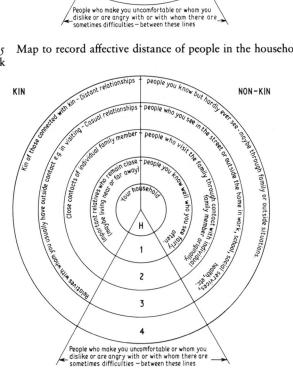

KIN

NON-KIN

Kin of those connected with kin – Distant relationships

people you know but hardly ever see – maybe through family or outside situations.

Close contacts of individual family member - Casual relationships

people who you see in the street or outside the home in work, school, social services, health, etc.

Important relatives who remain close
(maybe living near or far away)

people who visit the family through contact with individual family member

Your household

people you know well who you see fairly regularly.

Relatives with whom you usually have outside contact e.g. in visiting

H

1

2

3

4

People who make you uncomfortable or whom you
dislike or are angry with or with whom there are
sometimes difficulties – between these lines

you to each of them in feeling? Most informants find the second classification no more difficult than the first; some, on the contrary, tackle it with more enthusiasm. (The triangular section marked off in both versions for antipathetic or ambiguous relationships does sometimes give them pause, but no one has denied that such relationships are 'extra' in some way.) Despite their similarities, the affective network map (*Figure 5*) is the more controversial of the two and needs particularly careful handling (Wallman *et al.* 1980; see also key to *Figures* 6 and 7). The rest of this section deals with its main features.

The affective network device is adapted from a family therapy model built on the assumption that the very activity of mapping resources and relationships would provide the family in therapy with information about its social universe, and would at the same time indicate points of intervention to the therapist wanting to change patterns within the family. In effect, the network map could help to make the family situation plain so that its problems could begin to be dealt with constructively (Speck and Attneave 1974). The same logic is adapted here to the non-interventionist study of household resource systems. In this case the households are not 'problem families' or families with an expressed need for psychotherapy, but ordinary households who have ordinary problems from time to time (Bott 1957).

The adapted strategy was first used in a pilot study of thirty households in another part of inner London. Both there, and in the study of these eight Battersea households, the maps provoked so wide a variety of responses that we found it necessary to vary the filling-in procedure rather freely. On the whole, each one was completed at one interview and no time limit was imposed. Given the household-as-process frame-work, it might have been better to complete one diagram as quickly as possible on one occasion and to do another at some other time which would show additions or changes of the overall picture. It is important anyway to remember that the alteration of information or the interpretation of it is not a matter of error, but of the fact that the constructs of respondents vary from day to day; shifts in bias or resource valuation are normal and inevitable (pp. 24–9; see also Gellner 1973). Inconsistency, moreover, is a key to discussion in the interview situation, and an illustration of the boundary processes that are an important focus of this study.

Research memo (4)

The affective network is delicate because it is all about identity (Who am I?) and identification (Who/what are they?) (pp. 6–9, 38). The processes are intertwined: we identify ourselves by what we are not, and we use some kind of 'them' to do it. Any line of difference will serve to define 'them' but ethnic difference makes the point most readily: ethnic identification categories defined by outsiders – the OPCS or the first stage neighbourhood survey – are not the criteria used or felt by households to distinguish in-groups and out-groups, the close from the not-so-close on the network map. Ethnic categories are marked off by objective difference, identity by subjective investment in that difference (Wallman 1978). Thus, people with the same birthplace, 'race', mother tongue, etc. can logically be lumped into ethnic categories, but criteria of this kind do not of themselves constitute ethnic groups. No single identity locus counts for the person identifying all the time, or always in the same way; sometimes it does not count at all. Likewise ethnicity.

We should not therefore assume that individuals or households 'feel close to' the people we think they resemble; or that, if fellow ethnics do appear in the 'close' circles of the network they are there by virtue of ethnicity alone. By the same token, not 'choosing' an 'available' fellow ethnic, for some social purpose does not amount to rejection. Questions concerning when, how, and to what purposes the ethnic origins of people on a household's network do count must be left as open as we can manage and we should look at ethnicity as only one dimension of the total picture of household livelihood. Using the network map it should be possible to know which other identities and identifications are in play.

This is where the notion of a system of resources is useful. We have been asking people how they manage in the city. They manage by organizing their resources in particular ways. Obviously they can only use the resources that are available to them, and that they know are available to them, but however limited, they always have a range of options. Consider 'help resources' in the household network: Mrs X, for example, lives on her own with young children; she must go to hospital for a fortnight. What does she do with her children? She casts about among her options and makes a 'choice', but how is it to be interpreted? If Mrs X gives her children to a co-ethnic who is also a neighbour, are we seeing an ethnic or a locality tie 'heated up'? Two levels of questions together tell us something: Who (else) is, objectively speaking, available to look after her children? and, How does *she* perceive the relationship? Both of these questions can be posed directly: How are the people in her social universe identified or ranked on the network diagram? Which of them did she call on for support during that recent normal crisis?

Figures 6 and 7 show the affective networks drawn by two different households from another area. The contrast between them is marked in terms of the absolute number of people recognized as important in each case, and in the quality or closeness of the people resources they designate. The real meaning of these differences does not emerge from the maps alone, but a number of observations are suggestive. *Figure 6*, for example, shows a total absence of entries in ring 2 which represent individuals who have been brought into the household by one of its members and, while remaining important to that member, are now close to the whole household. The same map indicates that, of a reasonable number of kin recognized and named (ring 4), only two are important for particular purposes (ring 3) and rather few are held in specially close esteem (ring 1). Similarly on the non-kin side, only three people are consistently or specially close (ring 1), but quite large numbers are important for some purposes (ring 3) or recognized and named but not often used as resources (ring 4). *Figure 7* shows quite a different balance, with relatively more people in the inner rings on both sides – but the outermost ring is unusually loaded in the tension triangle. Clearly these two households are organizing their affective social lives differently.

But even so marked a contrast in numbers of entries does not signify that one household is inevitably more viable than the other. Three cautionary points need to be made. First, the large numbers 'claimed' in *Figure 7* may be inversely related to their quality as support resources: the household may need to know a lot of people because none is powerful enough to meet its needs for practical or emotional support. Since the status of entries counts as much as the number, the few claimed in *Figure 6* may actually reach higher and further than the many in *Figure 7*. Second, the balance between quality and quantity could reflect household style or ethnic culture as much as resource options. Some people invest in (or only report investing in) a handful of relationships as a matter of deliberate choice: for them few is better; for others more is best. And third, in every case the overall situation of the household makes a difference to the value of the people it knows. Individuals who are resources for some purposes can be liabilities for other purposes, and a change of circumstance – the loss of a job, for example – can turn a supportive network of friends and relations into a financial drain or a social embarrassment overnight.

The amount and depth of information that can be read off these network maps is of course enhanced by using them in combination with the other household research strategies, against the background of the neighbourhood survey data; and we have since realized that a full household genealogy would make more sense of the kin entries because it would allow us to know whether few entries means few kin, or few useful kin (Wallman 1974). But a number of ethnographic items can be read off the diagrams alone. At the simplest level, it is possible to count the number of resource people

Figure 6   Affective network map of a household recording relatively
few 'close' contacts

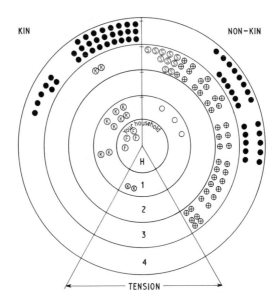

⑤	Family, members of the household
ⓒ	Lodger, non-family. (This category is rare in the inner-London setting.)
⑱ (ring 1)	Important relatives. These may not live nearby, but their involvement with the household makes a difference to its livelihood or quality of life. Often they have figured in the lives of members of the household from birth; sometimes they occupy positions of power in the dynamics of the family though they may be far away. Dead relatives have been mentioned in this category.
⑱ (ring 2)	Kin who are in close contact of some kind but may have a particular relationship with one member of the household.
⑱ (ring 3)	Kin who are seldom well known directly and have therefore limited resource value except as sources of information. They are often but not necessarily of the same ethnic group as the respondent. (For our purposes it made sense to indicate ethnic origin when the informant made a point of it, but not to note it as a characteristic of people on the map if we had learnt it from the informant in passing or knew of it from elsewhere. In these cases it would be recorded in the interviewer's notes only.)
⑤ᐟ (all rings)	Statutory worker, someone employed in the state social, medical, or educational services who is perceived as having professional contact with the household – although this perception may change. This category often embodies a lot of information about the network: the informant is likely to remember how, for what reason, and through whom the contact was made in the first place, and to be specifically aware of the resources made available through it.

Figure 7   Affective network map of a household recording a large
number of 'close' contacts

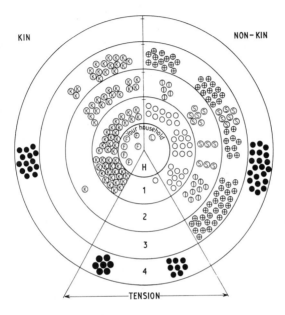

○ (ring 1)	Non-kin who are well known to all the household and likely to provide resources not available through kin or statutory workers by virtue of consistent involvement and commitment to the household and all its members.
⊕ (ring 2)	Non-kin who are accepted into the household and who become known to all members of it, although intimacy and closer contact continues with the introducing member. Friends of children, workmates of one adult would be likely to appear here.
⊕ (ring 3)	Non-kin known in the more public sphere and occupying more public roles, although they may know a lot about the household. Much of the success of the neighbourhood survey was a function of this category of relationships.
● (ring 4)	These may be kin or non-kin but are not considered integral to the household's livelihood in any way. They would be recognized and acknowledged on encounter, but often contact no longer exists. When it occurs it is likely to be through other links in the network, activated by a kin-keeper (as in the matter of weddings and funerals), or in relation to a specific public or institutional event (a political meeting or a local or occupational issue). Hannerz's (1980) traffic and provisioning relationships might be perceived here. In our study there is evidence that locals once placed in ring 4 'moved in' to ring 3 in the course of the neighbourhood survey when simple recognition was activated and residents 'got to know each other better'. Processes of this kind may be graphically recorded by inward or outward arrows.

designated by the informant(s). Comparing one diagram with another on this basis we get something like a measure of social or affective energy: some people recognize/define/feel something about few others, some about many others. Similarly the diagram shows the number of people placed in particular relationship categories and at each degree of intimacy, and makes immediately visible the balance of kinds of relationship perceived by the informant.

The essential usefulness of the diagram is not, however, in its mathematical or quantitative accuracy, but in the levels of meaning it makes available. It allows the mapping of the *affective* network – which, for the sake of clarity, must be distinguished from the *effective* network (as defined in Epstein 1969; the question of affect is raised in Epstein 1978) – and indicates that links of kinship or propinquity alone cannot be used as indicators of intimacy or resource value. It also shows that neither categorical distinctions of colour or ethnic origin, nor structural distinctions between personal and official resources are consistently significant to the informant. They are not therefore reliable predictors of his/her actions and identities. If public sector employees, brought into the family circle by virtue of professional role performance, can be placed in ring 2 and named kin or fellow ethnics relegated to rings 3 or 4 (as shown in the figures), then we have evidence that the classification of relationships in terms of any one set of characteristics of the individuals involved misses the basic anthropological point: relationships are not units, they are processes whose meaning and value changes in response to other things going on at the time. By the same token it can be demonstrated that even if kinship solidarities are displaced or replaced by bureaucratic support systems in the city as many models of urbanism and urbanization propose (see Hannerz 1980: Chapter 3), the new resources are not necessarily any less 'personal' than the old.

Equally there are aspects of structure and process that the diagram does not and cannot show. Because every entry appears in some direct relation with the centre, whatever its affective distance from it, all the entries represent first order relationships. Relationships one link (or more) away from the informant(s), and relationships between the people that the informant knows do not appear: the diagram cannot cope with range and 'reach', or with density and connectedness. Indeed, it is not required to. What it is required to do it begins to do very well. It gives us a way into understanding how a variety of individual households conceptualize the people they know, how they experience the inner city, and how they manage the business of livelihood in an inner-city setting.

The chapters that follow incorporate the detail of these research devices into narrative descriptions of the eight households that are the focus of this book. The charts and maps that each filled in during the interview series are not reproduced here because they would identify the households too precisely: but the dimensions of household process that they signal are annotated throughout, and the final chapter compares them accordingly.

Each of these eight households is a separate case which was interviewed and analysed apart from the rest. They appear here in pairs only so that the resource theme can be brought into sharper focus by comparison. Four pairs could have been defined in any number of ways: all eight households have things in common, and each is at the same time different from every other. These pair headings have been chosen deliberately to reflect official classifications of households and their problems. As such they focus on only one or two dimensions of the household system and on dimensions that are 'objective' and consistent: for formal/official purposes, household types have to be defined by characteristics that can be seen (and counted!) by an outside observer, and that are independent of the shifts of identity and strategy that make up the inside stuff of household process (see Chapter 2). Here the emphasis is on exactly those processes so the labels have a different purpose. Pairing households by static and structural qualities emphasizes differences of process and organization within each pair. In effect, the crucial importance of at least one of the organizing resources – *identity*, *information*, and *time* – is underlined by each comparison.

4 Two single-parent households

In material/structural terms, the Abraham and Charles households are remarkably alike. Not only are they both headed by
single parents, and living on similar money in equivalent
housing in the same neighbourhood, but both single parents
are black women in middle age with relatively young children.
More striking still, the circumstances of their becoming single
parents are very similar, and their stories begin with a litany of
personal tragedy and disappointment.

Both women are now caring and careful mothers whose
livelihood centres on the well-being of their children. In their
concern to feed them properly, they each prepare food as it was
prepared by their mothers at home when they were children
themselves. The English call it 'ethnic food', but neither
woman calculates that eating it will make her children identify
with the culture of their grandparents: it is good for children
simply because it is 'proper' food; English food is only filler.
The extent of each one's identity investment in 'ethnic' food
shows in the special pleasure each takes in preparing it for
guests at weekend meals. Here the difference between the two
households begins to show: the Abraham flat is full of people
every Saturday and Cynthia Abraham's life is full of people the
rest of the week; if the Charleses have one or two guests for
Sunday lunch, these may be the only social contacts Olive
Charles has, apart from people she meets shopping in the
winter, or walking her toddler outside in good summer
weather.

As resource systems in fact, the two households are starkly
different. The Abrahams enjoy the support of three effectively

separate networks – one established through Cynthia Abraham's job, one focusing on contacts with the home country, and one based on neighbourhood ties – and each domain expands the household's information resources and identity options. Each network also, inevitably, demands work of one kind or another – travelling, organizing, talking, listening, receiving, shopping, cooking – yet there is no sense of shortage of time or energy in the household system. It is as though the costs of social involvement are invisible and only the benefits count. Olive Charles in contrast, spends most of her time cleaning her house and waiting for and being with her children at home. She lacks the energy to organize even resources that are readily available. For example, she obtained vital information about her welfare entitlements from her neighbours because they brought it to her, pushed it at her, not because she asked it of them: her household's access to local networks is a function of Battersea's localist style (Chapter 1), not of the Charleses' active involvement. Although mother and children have friendly contacts in the area, the household is neither confident of its local identity, nor sustained by accessible ethnic resources.

Olive Charles's unemployment status has a lot to do with all these shortages, and with the general depression of the household. Comparison with the Abraham case highlights its effect. Cynthia Abraham has a steady job and Olive Charles depends on state welfare; roughly the same money comes into each household every week, but one makes autonomous decisions about spending it, and the other is stigmatized by its source. Olive's fear of losing the single mother's allowance prevents her setting up house with her child's father, constrains her ability to plan for the future, and seals her isolation by keeping her at home and off the job market. She is by all these measures a classic welfare victim. Whether unemployment is cause or effect of it, the Charles household system is trapped by its own limited scope.

The Abrahams

Cynthia Abraham came to Britain from West Africa in 1964. She came over in the company of her husband as a newly married woman. She had not known him long when they married, but he came from the same region and had good prospects. He claimed to have completed the first part of his bar examinations[1] in London, and had come home to find a wife to live with him in Britain while he completed his legal training. So even though she was leaving behind the good job she had held for six years, she was considered 'very lucky' and her workmates were envious when they saw her off. But life in Britain was not easy. Her husband turned out to be a violent drunk who also took drugs. Moreover, he did not follow any studies at all. She took many strenuous jobs to support them both, and found time to bear two children, hoping all along that he would change. He did not. Eventually she succeeded in disentangling herself from him, and set about raising her two daughters by herself.

Cynthia Abraham is now, in her middle age, an immigrant single mother with two young children, who lives in a council house in a low income neighbourhood. On the face of it and by the sort of criteria imposed by the welfare authorities, hers has all the makings of a problem family. Yet a closer look shows her to be an adequate parent, a good neighbour, and a good co-worker at her job. Despite the obvious drawbacks of her

[1] To be 'called to the bar' is to have achieved the status of barrister in the British legal system. The same system pertains in the British Commonwealth and ex-Commonwealth countries.

situation, Cynthia is able to maintain confidence and manage a decent livelihood for her small household in the metropolitan inner city.

Cynthia regards separating from her husband as 'the most traumatic experience' she has ever had. The thought of divorce does not come easily to an African housewife in Britain;[1] the idea of struggling on her own in a strange country without the support of her relations is frightening enough. Isolated in a strange land she would be likely to bear the bitterness of an unhappy marriage in the belief that only changed circumstances had caused the problems and that things would be all right 'back home eventually'. Cynthia is typical in this respect. It was not until her husband's beatings became frequent and dangerous that she finally turned to an uncle living in Britain and discussed with him the possibilities of divorcing her husband.[2] Her uncle was shocked at first and tried to talk her out of it. It would be bad for the family, he said: she should be a good wife. He changed his mind only when he saw the results of her husband's maltreatment. Cynthia is still apologetic when she speaks about the events leading to the divorce. She insists that she would not have left her husband if she had not feared for her life.

Soon after arriving in Britain she had to go out to look for jobs because her husband could not find anything to do. In her own words, she was transformed 'from a timid African house mummy' into an astute young woman who found out what resources were available to her and learned to use them accordingly. Although she had become the principal breadwinner of the family and her husband had become dependent upon her, even for his pub money, he still beat her horribly when he came home at night after having had a mixture of beer and drugs. Her efforts to get him to change and to resume his studies did not help, even after she got a respected kinsman of

[1] Just as marriage in traditional Africa is a family matter, so divorce cannot be entered into lightly or even privately.
[2] Cynthia felt she needed the blessing of a senior relative before she could act, even though in Britain she is formally a free agent in this respect.

his talk to him.[1] When she finally told him she had decided to divorce him he became very desperate and attacked her violently. At that late stage she learned of the existence of a battered women's home through some friends at her work. She took her children and sought refuge there. With the help and support of this home she set about divorce proceedings.[2]

Cynthia remembers her time at the home 'with much gratitude'. Apart from the fact that it gave her safety from physical danger, she says, 'It gave me back my self-confidence'. She was able to walk in the streets again without the constant fear of assault by her husband. It was also through the women's shelter that she first got to know English women, many of whom she grew to like, who formed the nucleus of the first network of English friends she has had in Britain.

The divorce court ruled that her husband was to pay a monthly sum of fifteen pounds for the upkeep of his children. The court further decided that he could only see his children at the discretion of his wife because of his sustained violence towards them. She exercised this right to the full by refusing to let her daughters have anything to do with 'such a man'. He seems to have made no attempt whatsoever to see his children; he certainly never paid any money for them. Cynthia was badly shaken when some items of furniture were taken from her flat while she was out at work soon after the divorce. Suspecting that he had duplicate keys to her flat – he had surrendered his pair to her at the order of the court – she had a new lock installed. Since then there have been no further losses and nothing else has happened. She does not know where her husband is living now, although she suspects he is somewhere in the London area – she jokes that not even the taxman seems to know where he is!

Her only contact with him after the divorce was through letters in which he threatened to have a higher court reverse the

---

[1] Again, the intervention of a senior kinsman was the first and last resort.
[2] Information from her workmates led her to the refuge; information from the refuge led her to the divorce court. In this process she had neither the advice nor the backing of her family: she had moved into another network.

rule as regards his children. To her relief, no summons came. Soon however, letters from him took on a more sinister form: he threatened to take the children 'by any means possible'. Cynthia was so frightened of this that she instructed her children not to open their door to their father. The children are always careful to enquire who it is at the door before opening it to anyone.[1] (The fear of losing her daughters is so profound that Cynthia was initially reluctant to take part in the neighbourhood survey: 'I thought they were still after my children'.)

JOBS

Cynthia left shool at 16 and had had three jobs before she came to Britain fourteen years later. During the same length of time in Britain she has had twelve short-term jobs or temporary assignments.

The jobs she held in West Africa were better jobs, in the sense that they were more prestigious, although her jobs in England have obviously been better paid.[2] Nevertheless, she recalls wistfully how happy she was as a junior officer in the Workers' Brigade. This was established at a time when her country had just received independence and was still a prosperous nation. It was a paramilitary organization whose official function was to work on the so-called state farms. With a large budget, its members dressed and drove around the country in style. The Brigade attracted a lot of school drop-outs with political contacts, although their offices had, in many instances, agricultural skills as well as political merits. Cynthia's duties as a junior officer required her to visit many rural areas to check the supplies of local branches. As a result she met many local politicians, some of whom were to assist her when she later applied for a passport and an exit permit to

---

[1] Communication with the ex-husband is now very rare, but past experience continues to affect the household's present behaviour and expectations.
[2] There are many ways of assessing the value of work.

leave for Britain. She recalls that she was young and attractive then, and very much in demand as a woman.[1]

Of the two other jobs she had in West Africa, the first was as a sales assistant in a shop. She describes it as a temporary position she took after school while looking around for 'something more suitable', although she kept this position for a year. The second job was for her more significant. It was a position as an agent in charge of sales in an oil factory. Her duties there were similar to those in the Brigade, including 'treks' to rural areas to check sales of factory products. She had a jeep with a driver at her disposal and a relatively free hand in allocating her working hours. She says she would have stayed in this job if it had not been for some personal difficulties she had with one of the assistant managers of the factory.[2]

In England Cynthia took many jobs to keep her family going.[3] In the beginning most of these were temporary assignments which she heard about through friends and acquaintances.[4] There were about a dozen of these. Others were more permanent, lasting usually for at least a year. The first was at a Battersea laundry where she washed and ironed clothes. It was a pleasant enough job, she says and she left only because it was poorly paid and the hours too long.

Then she took a job with an electrical components firm in Hammersmith, where she printed serial numbers on the finished products before they were packed and taken out of the factory. She remembers it as a well-paid job but she had to leave it because she had just moved with her family to Battersea and found the commuting connections with the factory rather tedious.[5]

---

[1] An organization 'officially' constituted to manage economic resources (in this case farming) inevitably has an 'unofficial' spill over effect on non-economic resources, such as the status and privilege increments described.
[2] Reasons given for quitting a job only rarely include dislike of the work itself.
[3] 'To keep her family going' = to ensure its survival.
[4] All these information sources were locally based.
[5] Hammersmith is only a few miles away, north-west across the river Thames, but has no direct public transport connections with Battersea.

She next acquired a position in a knitwear company in Southfields.[1] It was a job in which she was happy, knitting and mending clothes with a pleasant team of English women. She kept this job for three years, only losing it because there were no vacancies when she returned after the birth of her daughter. She had only two months of maternity leave, after which she moved in and out of many odd-jobs, leaving the baby with a neighbour whenever she went out to work. Her next job of some permanence was as a maid in one of the fashionable hotels near Marble Arch.[2] It was a very demanding job, 'physically very hard'. She soon found the strain of working unusual hours while nursing a baby too much. The hotel offered round-the-clock services for their guests and sometimes it fell to her to iron clothes in the middle of the night. After a year her health failed her and she quit the job on the advice of her doctor. Eventually she heard of an opening for a packer in a biscuit factory in Middlesex.[3] She applied for and got the job, a position she still holds today.

Cynthia regards this job as the best she has ever had, apart from her years with the Workers' Brigade. She commutes daily for about two hours from her home in Battersea but does not find this in the least inconvenient. What she likes most about the job is the team of people she works with. This comprises ten women – all white, except Cynthia and one West Indian. They function as a self-contained group which works 'harmoniously at its own pace'.[4] They are required to pack a certain

[1] Southfields is south of Battersea and deeper into the London Borough of Wandsworth.
[2] Marble Arch is a central landmark in the West End of London. It is further away than Hammersmith but, being in the centre of town, is easier for access from Battersea.
[3] Middlesex is an area to the north-west of London. This job is further from home than any she has held before. But it is on the railway line from Clapham (adjacent to Battersea and quite close-by) and can be reached in one direct run. It is also possible that Cynthia's satisfaction with the whole work situation makes the place feel 'closer'.
[4] Having control of time on the job is said to humanize even the dreariest of industrial tasks.

number of boxes per day, but because they do not have any difficulties in achieving the stipulated quantity they enjoy an unusual autonomy in their section. They 'look after each other'. The team has on some occasions been able to cover up for a member who needed to go out on some errand or came late to work by punching the card of that person, and still meeting the team's expected level of production. Cynthia thinks it likely the management are aware of such activities, but turn a blind eye[1] because they are satisfied with the output of her team.

To their workmates in the factory, Cynthia and her team are often jokingly referred to as 'the crazy women'. They often joke with the men who have been longest in the factory and somehow seem to have won a position of respect for being able to match the bawdiest of them in trading invectives. They are admired for being crazy with words.[2]

It is a very exclusive group. An attempt by the management to introduce a new member into it failed miserably. This woman was in fact from Cynthia's home region in West Africa. She stayed for a period of two weeks during which the team's rate of production fell. Just at the point when the management were beginning to wonder if they had made a prudent decision, the newcomer quit her job altogether. She simply stopped coming to work. Cynthia and the others felt bad about this; they feared that the cold reception they had given the woman had cost her a job. So after some period of brooding, they decided together that Cynthia, being a fellow countrywoman, should try to find out what had caused the woman to quit. To everyone's relief it turned out that the real cause of her departure was a family crisis which had made her too upset to work, and had no connection with the factory.

---

[1] 'To turn a blind eye' = deliberately not to notice. The management's attitude in this respect is an informal bonus no less valuable than the chance to 'fiddle' a few pieces of timber or a bit of extra money.
[2] No doubt a lot of this verbal exchange is aggressive but it is made inoffensive by its standardized or ritualized form (Radcliffe Brown 1952).

Looking back, Cynthia says they found it hard to accept 'the poor woman' because she was 'not one of us'.[1]

PEOPLE

Cynthia describes the people that she and her children know, and on which their household depends, in distinct and separate sets. Although her contacts are varied and wide, they are composed of networks which do not extend into one another. Each interactive set seems designed to reinforce a particular identity. For example, despite the closeness of her team at work, and the excellent relationship the women enjoy within it, they do not seem to visit each other at home.[2] None of them has ever called on the Abrahams in LARA. Another interactive set is composed of the many Africans who drop in to see Cynthia on Saturday afternoons. These visitors do not know any of her workmates, nor are they acquainted with the 'English' friends who 'drag her out'[3] to the pub on Sundays.

It is only during the weekends that Cynthia is able to entertain her friends and to relax with her family. Friends usually start dropping in around 11 o'clock on Saturday mornings. Her daughters are already watching the children's programmes on television. There is a palatable aroma of African cooking in the air, and Cynthia alternates between rushing to answer the door and dashing in and out of the kitchen. She always starts

[1] In this context Cynthia clearly identified with the work team, and felt no solidarity based on her ethnic origin. Her workmates sent *her* to find out what had happened because they assumed she would be most acceptable to 'another African'; they could assume ethnic identity was important because they had no other knowledge of the woman. Because they knew so much more about Cynthia, her 'African-ness' was only an incidental feature, one aspect of her whole person which was recalled and brought into play when this situation made it relevant.

[2] It may be important that they live far away from each other.

[3] 'To drag her out' = to persuade her, to insist that she goes with them.

preparing food on Friday evenings after coming home from work, and counts on having enough to feed the many guests who come to call on her every weekend.

None of the Saturday guests has been formally invited. They are all from Cynthia's home country in Africa. On 'an ordinary Saturday' there are a young airline employee accompanied by a newly-arrived soldier who has come to London to serve in some capacity or other in the Embassy; two young men, former residents of Battersea, now living in Bristol; a next-door-neighbour, an architect working for the Ministry of the Environment; and three women also living in Battersea who have dropped in to plait each other's hair.[1] Aside from these, a dozen or so Africans arrive during the course of the day, chat for a while, receive a drink of vodka or sherry, and then leave.[2]

Drink flows freely in this house; many libations are poured.[3] Vodka is a favourite, usually neat. Cynthia serves African food – 'proper food' – around 1 o'clock. There is always enough to feed everyone present, probably eight or ten people at once. Those who know each other eat from the same bowl, and those who come alone have their own bowls of food. Everyone eats with their fingers, in the 'proper' way, all the while praising Cynthia for her remarkable ability to make African dishes out of English ingredients.[4] Sometimes a 'genuine' dish that has been brought from West Africa by one of the airline employees is shared too. After the meal the guests sit around talking in

[1] It has long been fashionable for West African girls and women to wear their hair plaited in narrow rows close to the scalp, sometimes with beads woven in. The style has lately been taken up by non-Africans, black and white, in London. Plaiting the hair in this way is a sociable process because someone has to do it for you, and it takes as much as four or five hours to finish. If it is done expertly and very tight, the braids can last for a fortnight or more.

[2] Several of these people live locally, but they are defined by ethnic origin not by local residence.

[3] A libation is alcoholic drink deliberately spilt, usually on the ground, as an offering to ancestral spirits. Like toasts in Europe, libations in Africa are made for good luck, health, prosperity, etc.

[4] Food and the 'proper' way of preparing and eating it are among the most powerful of ethnic identity symbols in every culture. The fact that these people are away from 'home' and are also eating and drinking *together* this way gives the occasion special significance.

groups or listening to 'Highlife'.[1] Cynthia continues serving drinks and encouraging her guests to 'drink like true Africans' – a hospitable evocation by which she means they should quaff without flinching enormous quantities of vodka from tumblers, even though she herself drinks little. There is a striking contrast between the European clothing of the guests and the way they sit around bowls of food, eating with their fingers in the traditional manner. The comfortable force of such simple words as 'drink like true Africans' underlines their sense of belonging together. Yet although they are 'being African', eating African food and listening to African music, the conversation is about life in London: difficulties with a local landlady, the cost of running a car and parking, whether or not the council is going to put another West African family in the vacant basement flat in Cologne Road, and so on.

By 6 o'clock the guests begin to leave. Cynthia then tidies up and supervises her children's supper to make sure that they too get 'proper food' inside them. 'You can't live on fish and chips' she explains.

The only white person who regularly drops in to see the Abrahams during the Saturday meetings is 'Uncle Bill'. Uncle Bill is retired and lives on the ground floor of the same house and 'is more or less a member of the household'. The children call him 'grandfather' and he is extremely fond of them. The younger girl is so fond of her 'grandfather' that she imitates his style, even down to his diction and accent, which is markedly Battersea.[2] Uncle Bill often collects the children from their West Indian childminder across the road and gives them supper before their mother gets home from work.

[1] 'Highlife' is a popular modern dance rhythm in urban West Africa.
[2] Grandparents provide an important ethnic identity focus for their grandchildren (see Epstein 1978). 'Uncle Bill' is not the child's real grandparent and the identity he represents is local rather than ethnic, but her feeling for him and the fact that she learns and imitates his culture echo the 'real' pattern exactly. Even family relationships are social; they do not depend on genetic links. There is no 'blood bond' but the little girl is his grandchild none the less.

Uncle Bill represents another interactive set made up of residents of LARA. Most, but not all the members of this set are white, but either way, origin and colour seem to be irrelevant. The keynote is an identification with Battersea: Cynthia, along with others in the area, believes for example that most street crimes in Battersea are committed by 'lads who come over from Fulham or Brixton'.[1] These local friends drop in on Sundays and try to persuade Cynthia to go with them to a local pub. And if nothing else in on she is glad to 'follow them' there.[2] Many of the other residents that the family has got to know over a decade or so in Battersea could be added to the edges of this set. These are people whose familiar faces and occasional unplanned meetings with Cynthia, reinforce her sense of belonging in the Battersea locality which she loves so well. In this category she includes the butcher at Clapham market who saves favourite pieces of meat for her; persons she meets at the advice centre; members of the church she attends occasionally; the regular washer she meets at the laundrette; and the women who call on her to sell dresses and cosmetics during the weekends. 'There are others too' she says, but does not specify.[3]

TIME

Cynthia takes her job seriously and retires early as a rule, so as to feel refreshed during working hours. She goes to bed at 8.30 p.m. on weekdays, and her day begins at 5.30 a.m. when she rises, and dresses herself and her children. Breakfast is light, consisting of tea for herself and cereals for the children. At 6.45

---

[1] Fulham and Brixton are inner-London districts which adjoin Battersea to the north (over the river Thames) and east respectively.

[2] 'Nothing else is on' = nothing else is happening, a London phrase. 'To follow them' there means to go with them, in West African English. It is typical of Cynthia's speech that both kinds of idioms should be used in one sentence.

[3] Merely recognizing others and being acknowledged by them confirms her local identity.

she leaves her children with the childminder across the street and hurries to catch the train which leaves Clapham Junction at 7 o'clock. It is scheduled to arrive at Middlesex around 8 a.m., and she then has a 20-minute walk to the biscuit factory.

Her working day begins with the operation of a machine known as 'O Boy' which is used to seal bread. She does this on her own until 9.30 when she goes off to have breakfast with her team. Breakfast lasts until 10 o'clock and then all of them pack together until the lunch hour at midday. After lunch they resume packing with the aid of different machines which the women on the team operate between them. This goes on until closing time at 5.00 p.m. Cynthia then catches the train at 5.30 from Syon Lane in Middlesex and arrives back at Clapham around 6.30 p.m. She always goes straight to the childminder and, even if the children have already been taken home by Uncle Bill, she spends some time with the childminder to find out how the children fared during the day, what food they had been given, what activities they did, and so on.[1] She then goes home and supplements whatever they have had to eat with some 'proper food', reads to them, puts them to bed, and retires herself. So the weekdays pass.

Weekends, as we have seen, are quite different. Cynthia does her shopping on Saturday mornings and buys enough to last the week except for vegetables and 'daily' groceries which Uncle Bill buys for her while she is at work. He even remembers to purchase such items as cigarettes for her so that she never runs out of them. She in turn does Uncle Bill's laundry and cleans up his flat once every week.[2] The children are involved in all these activities and assist their mother by constantly running out on divers errands for her and her guests. This is an important part of their training as 'African' children.

[1] Her relationship with the childminder is 'warmed' by these conversations. Cynthia would not leave her children with 'a stranger'.
[2] Cynthia does not say 'He does this for us and we do that for him'. The exchange of tasks, etc. is generalized rather than specific (see Sahlins 1974). Each assumes the help and support of the other in the ordinary idiom of family life.

CRISES AND CELEBRATIONS

The same crises come up in any discussion of the household's livelihood: Cynthia's divorce and her sojourn in the battered women's home. She survived these crises because the many people she knows gave her access to the resources she needed, and her resolution to manage on her own encouraged her to take up and organize the options she had. Information resources have been crucial, especially during her job- and flat-hunting periods. Virtually all the jobs she has had she heard about through friends, and it was also through friends that she got to know that such things as a home for battered women even existed. Cynthia realizes how important her contacts with people are, both in emotional and practical terms. She is a nice woman: people like her and she is glad to be liked. She puts a lot of energy into being sociable, even exchanging pleasantries with people in fleeting encounters in the street. Each time she goes shopping in Clapham she stops and talks to many people in the market. She was not surprised when one of them, a white Englishman, told her of an address where she could buy palm oil extra cheap. She followed up the tip immediately and bought a gallon, sharing it generously with the interviewer who was along on that occasion.

Cynthia will always remember how she got to know Uncle Bill. She had just left the women's home and moved into the street.[1] She was 'still a stranger' when one day her younger daughter did not come home to tea. She spent almost an hour looking for the child without success. When she finally went to a neighbour to call the police, the neighbour suggested she try Old Bill's place. She went there and found the old man surrounded by half a dozen children eating cakes and drinking tea, while Uncle Bill played them songs on his piano. Her daughter was among them. The child became so fond of the old man that she would go to see him every-day. Uncle Bill, perhaps because he has no kin of his own, became 'part of the family'. He has keys to the flat and often takes his meals there.

[1] She says she moved into the street, not the area. Local identity seems to begin at that level. For some people it hardly extends beyond it (see Wallman *et al*. 1982: Chapter 5).

There is a long-term mutual regard between them of the type 'common amongst kinsmen'. For example, after returning from the battered women's home Cynthia was depressed and worried about her family in West Africa. She has tried hard to 'save money to visit', but her jobs paid so poorly that she has been unable to make even a dent in the cost of such a trip. Her friends knew of her plight. One day when she returned home from work, she found an envelope stuffed with £200 and a note from Uncle Bill telling her to go and buy a ticket 'home'. She declined the offer, quite overwhelmed by his kindness. He insisted, and when she would not accept, went and bought an air ticket in her name.

A similar spirit prevails in all Cynthia's relationships and she is generous in her turn. She gives people food and drink and friendliness without anticipating any gift in return. Sometimes no doubt, some of them take advantage of her generosity: asked one day 'Why do you think so many people are visitors in your house?' it transpired that one of the locally based African visitors 'only drops in when he has no money to go to the pub', and that he leaves as soon as her supply of drinks is exhausted. She had never wondered why and in what circumstances he came to her, nor did she feel misused by his motives. It is more important to her that her home should be a focus of warmth and hospitality for her African friends 'in the African way'.[1]

Although Cynthia considers herself a Londoner, and her children are British citizens, her greatest effort is to try to instil West African values into them. She says despite their British background they will always remain Africans, and must therefore be trained in the African way. They will, for example, be rebuked when they stretch out their left hand to receive something from a grown up,[2] and they are not allowed

---

[1] She is assessing the relationship in affective terms; its economic dimensions are not relevant to her.

[2] In traditional African symbolism, the left hand is associated with and used for unclean tasks of all kinds; the right hand for eating, greeting, and showing respect.

to raise their voices to anyone older than they are.[1] As for herself, Cynthia is fairly satisfied and happy with her life. She is resigned to not completing the GCE[2] courses that she began in the hope of gaining an academic qualification with which to return to Africa. She hopes her children will attain the goals she once had. Although she lapses into pidgin English when telling a story related to some comical aspect of African life, she also makes a point of correcting her older daughter whenever she makes a grammatical mistake, adding, as though to soften the disapproval, 'If you want to get anywhere in life you must speak correctly'. The younger girl is however allowed to speak her Battersea English, usually with the comment 'well that girl is going to become a real Battersea woman'. That too is a source of pride.

Cynthia has no plans to remarry, although she has a romantic attachment to a man living in West Africa (but not in her natal country) whom she has not seen in two years. They write to each other regularly. She has his photograph on the mantelpiece, and talks about what a wonderful man he is. Her family write regularly from West Africa, as does her younger brother who lives in the United States; she is very fond of her brother. Her more immediate plans, however, always centre on Battersea. She quotes Uncle Bill saying 'We in Battersea have always been different'. For both of them, and in spite of other loyalties and other ties, membership of the locality is the overriding focus of their identity.

[1] Respect for anyone of an older generation is enforced more strongly in modern Africa than in modern Europe.
[2] GCE = General Certificate of Education, normally taken at Ordinary (O) level at age sixteen, and at Advanced (A) level at about eighteen for those seeking entry into university.

The Charleses

Olive Charles is a black woman in her mid-forties. She lives with three of her four sons; the youngest at home is a toddler, the eldest is in his teens. They have a two-bedroom ground-floor flat in a recently converted Victorian house. Olive got the flat through the LARA Housing Action project.[1]

She spent her early childhood in a mainland town in central America where her father was employed as a foreman at a wharf. After he had inherited a plot of land six miles outside town, she moved with her parents and the rest of the family to this village.[2]

She came to Britain in 1962 to join her partner Kenneth – a distant cousin – who had left the home village for Britain six months earlier. Because she was not sure what their chances would be in Britain, Olive left their 2-year-old son behind in the care of his grandparents. She had intended to send for the child as soon as they got themselves a bit settled in Britain, but domestic problems and financial difficulties never really got sorted out. The boy has grown up in the Caribbean and still lives there.

Olive's relationship with Kenneth became strained soon after her arrival in Britain, but she did not finally break up with him until her third son (now 9 years old) was born. For some

---

[1] As an area resident of more than ten years, Olive was formally entitled to a share in the housing resources the HAA provided (pp. 7–9; see also Wallman *et al.* 1982: Chapter 4).
[2] Both of these settings contrast very starkly with the inner-London environment.

years after that she worked to support her family, but after she was made redundant in 1973, various social services officials advised her to withdraw from the labour market and to stay at home to deal with the rearing of her children herself.[1] For years she was alone with the two children.

Nowadays Olive has a steady friendship with Roderick, another man from 'home'. He is the father of her youngest son. While he gives the family financial and emotional support and spends much of his time with them, regulations laid down for 'welfare' recipients[2] and the financial obligations he has towards his former wife and his children mean they cannot really set up house together to build a more permanent relationship.

JOBS

Olive went to primary school and a domestic science school in the West Indies but has no formal qualifications. This and her immigrant status have combined to restrict her to unskilled jobs in Britain. None the less, she sees herself as being better off here. All she did before she came was help her mother at home because jobs were so hard to come by. 'There was no prospects at all.' This was the main reason for her coming to Britain in the first place.

She arrived without definite employment prospects in Britain either. For the first few months she tried without success to find work through people Kenneth knew. She then registered at a job centre. It took another two months before the job centre found her a job as an auxiliary worker in a small restaurant in the centre of London. Her tasks were to supply the

[1] At the time of these interviews Olive had been unemployed for five years. She 'would have given a lot' not to be dependent on government welfare but has no option if she wants her children with her: this well-meant advice from 'the social services' put her squarely into 'the welfare trap'.

[2] 'Single mothers on welfare' are by definition without a male partner. A woman with a partner is formally disqualified from single mother's allowances, no matter what the economic circumstances of the relationship.

kitchen workers with commodities from the storeroom and to make tea and coffee for the customers. This job involved shiftwork: she had to work seven days a week either from 6 a.m. to 3 p.m. or from 3 p.m. to 12 noon. She left after half a year because of the long working hours and the difficulty she had getting transport back to Battersea after evening shifts. Anyway she found the job physically very tiring and the people she worked with 'didn't grow friendly at all'. More important she had another job to go to, again in central London, in a bakery in Soho. She had found it with the help of a next-door-neighbour who worked there.[1] He both told her about the vacancy and recommended her to his employer. The job was similar to the previous one – she worked as an auxiliary and made tea and coffee for the managers and office staff – but the working hours were more convenient. That was the main attraction of it. However while she was working there she had a miscarriage and her doctor advised her strongly against any work that involved lifting. She told her employer and asked to be transferred to a lighter job, but 'He didn't want to know;[2] just sacked me on the grounds of unfitness for the job'. As the workers in this workplace were not unionized, Olive was in no position to fight the boss's decision.

When she felt stronger she registered again at a job centre. They did try to be helpful, she says, but all the jobs they had needed skills and experience which Olive did not have. After three months' searching she got work in the city through a woman who had a room in the same house.[3] The woman told Olive she was leaving a factory job in Blackfriars and encouraged her to apply. The job involved polishing and checking ashtrays, Olive found it extremely boring: 'You had to sit all day on the same chair, polishing ashtray after ashtray.'

[1] Local information leading to jobs outside Battersea is a characteristic Battersea pattern. Olive's access to it is an indication that she had by this time 'become local' (see Wallman *et al.* 1982: Chapters 6 and 8).

[2] 'He didn't want to know' = he would not discuss it; did not want to know her side of the story.

[3] Again, the local information network succeeded where the job centre could not.

The work conditions were also unpleasant. The only positive feature of the job was that it offered ample overtime opportunities[1] and so she stayed at it for more than a year.

Around the time she left, other important changes were happening in her life, good and bad. On the good side, she gave birth to a third son; on the bad side her problems with Kenneth became so serious that she decided to leave him temporarily. She managed to rent a room in the LARA area in a house owned by a woman from another part of the West Indies. Olive knew her from the time when they were both living in a different part of Battersea and she looked after Olive's second son.[2]

Again, Olive put off leaving the factory until she had arranged a new job, and she used her local contacts instead of official channels of information: a neighbour told her there was a vacancy for a domestic help in one of the senior citizens' homes near Wandsworth.[3] Her work consisted of cleaning the rooms of the residents, helping them in various areas, and assisting in the kitchen. It was just the kind of work she had hoped to get when she first came to Britain. The working hours were convenient and she had 'a friendly feeling' with her colleagues and superiors. As she described it, 'The job was very nice. Most of the other ladies[4] were coloured and although we had problems with some old people who objected to being helped by coloured people, the work atmosphere was very nice.' She worked in this home for over eight years. Then a

---

[1] 'Overtime' is time outside normal working hours. It is usually paid at a higher hourly rate than the normal and, when available, offers even unskilled workers the chance to earn 'extra' money. Overtime rates are calculated on the assumption that some hours are valued more highly and so worth more than others (see Wallman 1979b: 12).

[2] Olive was in Battersea all along, but her entry into the LARA area dates from this time.

[3] Wandsworth here refers to the old Metropolitan Borough which, like Battersea, became part of the much larger London Borough of Wandsworth in 1965.

[4] It is customary in England to refer to unskilled domestic workers as 'ladies' – charladies, tea ladies, cleaning ladies, etc. If the usage was once ironic no irony is intended by it now.

reorganization programme resulted in a number of redundancies and Olive, having a comparatively short length of service, was one of the people laid off.[1]

By this time she had two children to provide for. Having no job and no other means of financial support, she turned to the social services for temporary assistance. She also tried to register at the job centre.[2] Her situation was complicated by the fact that her childminder had moved out of the area and it was hard to find a replacement. It was this combination of circumstances that made the social services officials, as well as those at the job centre, advise her to take on the care of her children and to stop looking for employment.

Since 1973 Olive has been out of work, relying for income on supplementary benefits and other subsidies granted within the British 'welfare' system. She operates occasionally in the so-called informal economic sector by selling handicraft items to friends and acquaintances.[3] She has mixed feelings about her present situation. Her youngest son is 2 years old. For the first time she is able actually to see one of her children grow up: 'This is a completely new experience for me. My first son was still very small when I left for England. Three months after I had the second I went back to work and in the case of the third it was only six weeks. I didn't have much time for them. I'd bring them to a nanny early in the morning and when I came back home in the evening, I had to do housework. I never witnessed them trying to walk or talk. It was like they could

---

[1] 'Laid off' = sacked, dismissed from a job – it may be because of redundancy but without official redundancy rights. These depend on how the dismissal is officially classified. Many establishments use the principle 'last in, first out' when they have to get rid of staff. Olive thinks 'it's probably fair'.

[2] In order to register at a job centre one must be 'available to work' immediately. Technically it is not possible first to get a job and then to make arrangements for children, etc.

[3] The economic gains are negligible, both because Olive charges very little, and because she is reluctant to charge friends at all. A long-standing English resident says Olive insisted on giving him an item he wanted to buy because he had helped her get her flat. In his view, 'She owes me nothing; that place is hers by right.' In hers, 'it was good to be able to give something back for a change.'

suddenly walk and talk – an automatic thing – not something to learn.' However she feels isolated by not going out to work, and finds it hard to cope with 'the negative attitudes' some officials and some neighbours express towards welfare recipients. Her financial position is not really different. As an unskilled worker she was badly paid and her earnings were similar to what she receives now. As she puts it, 'It was struggling when I was working, and it's struggling now. I'm just stuck.'

A feeling of not being able to change her situation shows in Olive's view of job opportunities. She would like to take on a job as a domestic help in a school or nursery as soon as her youngest son reaches school age, but she thinks her chances of finding any employment are slim. A job centre would define her as too old and inexperienced, and the many years at home have reduced her chances of hearing about vacancies through informal channels.[1] She realizes in any case that a job would not end her dependence on supplementary benefits.[2] She would only qualify for low-paid jobs which still would not enable her, as a single parent, to support her family. Officials from the social services always tell her that taking a job would not be worth the effort because she would still have to ask for financial assistance. Their view is not encouraging either.

TIME

Since Olive is not involved in wage employment, her daily work consists of a variety of activities connected with managing her household, relating to her children and Roderick and other people she knows, and pursuing her own hobby interests as best she can.

[1] Informal information moves on informal social networks and depends on casual interaction, gossip, encounters in the street, etc.
[2] 'Supplementary benefits' are State payments made to supplement the wage or pension incomes of households in special need.

Weekdays are largely structured by the school obligations of her children and household tasks. Olive gets up at 7 a.m., wakes the two older children, and prepares breakfast. After they have eaten together and the children have left for school, she goes back to bed or starts with small domestic chores. Around 10 o'clock she wakes up her youngest child and spends some time with him. The rest of the morning she cleans the house and does the family wash. Olive has no access to a vacuum cleaner or washing machine, so these ordinary tasks take up a lot of time. She uses the laundrette occasionally, but most of the time she washes by hand at home. In fact she does not like laundrettes 'because you never know what kind of people have used the machine before you. All sorts of people go there and they're often not very clean. The dirt stays in those washing machines and it gets into your clothes.'

The way she spends the afternoon varies: at least twice a week she goes out shopping; the other afternoons she either does chores round the house, watches television, or spends time on her handicraft hobbies. She always shops locally, using the whole range of local shopping facilities – the small corner shops, the Arndale centre,[1] the market, and shops at Clapham Junction. She goes there on foot, but sometimes comes home by bus if the load is heavy. 'It's only a couple of stops so it's no quicker by the time you've waited.' As she normally takes her youngest son with her, this means an ordinary shopping outing may take the whole afternoon. In any case shopping is for Olive a social activity as well as an economic necessity. She meets local residents, acquaintances, or friends on the way and she occasionally stops at a friend's or a neighbour's house before returning home. Shopping is one of the few opportunities she has to interact with people outside her small household, as friends or neighbours rarely visit her during weekdays because of work commitments.[2] Whatever she does

[1] The big shopping complex that is about thirty minutes' slow walk away.
[2] The structure of time is crucially different for employed and unemployed people (see Jahoda 1982). In effect Olive's friends who have jobs have timetables that do not match hers.

however, Olive makes a point of being at home when the children get home from school. This is the time when she sits with them and asks about their day at school.

Olive is the person who always prepares the main meal. Cooking is one of her hobbies so she likes doing it. Preparing food is also an affirmation of her ethnic identity; 'to cook', as she sees it, is to make Caribbean dishes which require fresh ingredients and take up more time than the quick pre-packed food 'they', the English, eat.[1] While she prepares the meal the children hang about in the kitchen to help or talk to her, but the family does not always eat together: there are times when the children take their food to their room or sit in the living room watching television while they eat.[2] After the meal and during the early hours of the evening the two older children often go out. They are active members of the local clubs and very much involved in the LARA neighbourhood. Olive spends her evenings watching television, doing handicraft, or baking – sometimes in the company of Roderick, sometimes alone – while the toddler sleeps. This is her 'free time' until the family goes to bed.

Sundays are somewhat different. Olive is a Catholic and whenever circumstances permit it, she attends morning Mass with her children. After Mass she spends some hours on domestic chores while the children play, read, or watch television. Sunday dinners are a social event when the whole household eats together and sometimes there are guests.[3] Sundays are on the whole 'relaxing' days. A lot of time is spent watching television with the children and Olive likes to involve them in baking 'good things' with her.

The time of the year makes a big difference to life. During the winter Olive spends much time inside the house and has

---

[1] Like Cynthia Abrahams (pp. 80–1, 83), Olive considers that only ethnic food is 'proper' food for her children. No doubt their sense of identity as well as their nutrition is at issue.

[2] They tend not to talk while they eat; the TV is an alternative to conversation for the Charles household like most others.

[3] On these occasions the TV is switched off.

little contact with other people. As a result the days seem long and she feels isolated. In the summer the neighbourhood comes 'alive' and the street and common gardens are local meeting places.[1] So during the summer she spends much more time with other people: she participates in holiday pro-grammes for local children, is active in other local activities, and the people she knows tend to visit her more frequently. On summer Sundays she takes the children out on short trips or to visit her relatives.[2]

Of course the fact that Olive is a single parent restricts her social life all year round. Her financial situation does not allow her to buy time-saving household appliances so household tasks take up a lot of time. She also does not have a partner with whom she can share domestic chores or participate in social activities outside the home, for although Roderick spends much of his time with her and the children, he is not seen as a permanent household member. While he does undertake household repairs and sometimes look after the children, and the like, Olive perceives him as a guest she cannot impose on, not as a husband who should share domestic responsibilities. The same applies to 'leisure' time; she feels he has the right to lead his own social life and should not be restricted by her family demands. As one of the children is too young to be left alone or even in the care of the other children at home, Olive's opportunities to engage in social activities outside the house are very limited.

PEOPLE

The three children with her form the focus of Olive's life (she tries 'not to worry for' her first born in the West Indies.) They

---

[1] In working-class London, most extra-household social life goes on in public spaces outside the home and is therefore affected by the weather: sociability rises and falls with the temperature.
[2] Some are her own cousins, and some her ex-partner Kenneth's kin. All are in London, some in Battersea.

give her life a meaning and their needs take priority over hers, 'At the moment my children are more important than myself. I've had my time. I had a very good life when I was young. Until my twenties I had everything I wanted – nice clothes and parties – and my parents paid for it. Now it's the turn of the children.' She thinks of them as an emotional support. Even on the practical side they are 'good': the two older boys help her with the shopping and they look after their small brother when necessary.

The upbringing of all three of them is Olive's central concern. She believes in strict education through which children learn to respect the authority of elder persons. She says it is the lack of discipline and authority in British society as a whole and consequently in the schools that is to blame for some of the problems she experiences in bringing up her children. She regrets the way school teachers and community and social workers explain bad behaviour of children in terms of lack of money, or 'disadvantage', because this means they interfere with parenthood too much.[1] She says, 'Parents are no longer even allowed to punish children the way they see it right. If you slap your child and you can see some traces of it, social workers or even the police are informed and appear straight away at your doorstep. They don't blame the child, but the mother and the house, and the broken family. Nobody considers the child might be just bad.'

When she talks of these things, Olive remembers how much she misses the practical help of her mother. Both her parents are still alive but they live in the West Indies. She has not seen them since she left for Britain nearly twenty years ago, and she doubts that she will ever have the money to visit them or pay for their trip over here. Despite the distance they have remained very close. Olive keeps regular contact through letters and she tries to send them money from time to time.

---

[1] In the official cognitive system, black children tend to be categorized as 'disadvantaged'; those who manifestly are not, will not be counted as black (see Wallman 1978a). Olive experiences this classification as a criticism of her parenting, not as a justification for access to official resources.

Even in absence her mother is a source of emotional support. Olive finds it 'helpful' to write to her mother about problems and she 'takes a certain strength' from her mother's sympathy and advice. Her six sisters and her brother are also 'close' to her, but 'no one is nearly as important' as her mother.

Olive's relationship with her eldest son who lives in the Caribbean is problematic. She writes to him occasionally but he rarely answers her letters and news about him comes through letters from her parents. The boy seems to be closer to his father than to her; Olive accounts for this by observing that Kenneth has had the finances to visit their son and she has not.[1] She can understand that her son feels deserted by his mother but still finds it hard to deal with emotionally. There are moments when she is openly bitter about it: 'He only knows me when he needs money'.

Of her kin in Britain, Olive regularly visits three cousins with whom she is 'close' who live elsewhere in London. She has also relatives in Battersea who are Kenneth's kin.[2] Of them all she used to be particularly close to his sister, but since the separation from Kenneth she has lost contact with them. No one planned it that way: 'I suppose it got awkward' she says. So although they live in Battersea, even within walking distance, they are perceived as 'distant' kin – indeed they appear on the network map in similar categories to a number of 'distant kin' in the Caribbean. Both sets are part of Olive's social universe, but they now have no significance to her household's livelihood.

In terms of numbers, most of the people on Olive's network map are not related to her in any way. Nine people form the core of her non-kin contacts: her present partner Roderick, two English women friends in LARA, a couple in Battersea, a couple of Southfields, and a couple in Tooting.[3] Roderick is a

---

[1] She implies a connection between geographic and affective closeness in this case which does not apply to her feelings for other absent kin.

[2] Olive calls her affinal relatives 'family', not 'in-laws'. She lost 'family' when she parted from Kenneth.

[3] Southfields and Tooting are south London districts not far from Battersea.

source of friendship. He also gives her some financial support and does 'jobs around the house'. In all these ways he has 'lightened' her life.[1] The couples in Southfields and Tooting have been her friends for a long time; all four people are from her home village and they all went to school there together. The other four core members are also from the Caribbean, but Olive did not know them before she came to London; three are former neighbours and one is her present neighbour.

Her network of contacts of course also includes people she feels less close to and sees less often than the central nine. Most of these she met through neighbourhood organizations and members of her household. Some are friends or the families of friends of her sons; others she has come to know through Roderick. One of Roderick's friends is a regular visitor on Sundays. He is the godfather of her youngest son; once he helped her with redecorating her flat. Although she does not call any of these people 'close friends', some of them, in particular her local English contacts, have been crucial sources of support in times of crisis. For example, some of her English neighbours helped her stay in the area when the Council 'pressured' her to move out. It happened when her landlord received a compulsory purchase order from the local council because he 'wouldn't' improve the bad housing conditions of his tenants.[2] The council offered her 'alternative accommodation' in north Battersea. Olive knew she did not want to leave the area but had no idea of her rights in the matter. One of her English neighbours then told her how she might oppose the Housing Department's offer. This happened at the time when several residents started to organize collective oposition to the council's plans for the area which eventually resulted in the declaration of the HAA. Neighbours have also informed her of

---

[1] i.e. he has lightened the burden of chores and lightened the heaviness of her heart.
[2] People are not officially allowed to live in sub-standard conditions. If a landlord cannot or refuses to improve them, a 'compulsory purchase order' can then be served on him by the local government authority. Either way, his tenants 'for their own good' must move.

her eligibility to social benefits[1] and on several occasions have taken care of her children.

Still further 'out', Olive is 'friendly with' people from the neighbourhood that she sees outside her home. After all, she has been living in the LARA area for over ten years and knows many of its residents. She meets them while out shopping, attending meetings in the community centre, or helping out in local activities. Sometimes she meets former work friends when she is out shopping at Clapham Junction, so she feels she is still 'friends' with them too. Various people connected with public services and other organizations are perceived at about the same level of distance: she is 'in touch' with the teacher of her older son. She also has connections amongst members of the Catholic church in Wandsworth and speaks warmly of the parish priest: she finds it easier to talk to him about her problems than to a social worker or any other 'official' because he keeps their discussions to himself. Over the years in Battersea Olive has come into contact with hospital personnel and people working in the DHSS[2] and other social services departments. She remembers each of them and notes them on the network map, but the relationship with each is only single-stranded: it has no significance once the problem at issue is solved.

In the category of people Olive 'knows well but hardly ever sees', there are very few entries: some old school friends, a former landlady, a former childminder, and her first partner, Kenneth. She has kept in contact with the latter because of their children; the two older boys spend some of their holidays with him and he visits the family on rare and special occasions. He used to buy the children clothes but now that he is unemployed this support has ceased. Olive says she feels no bitterness against him.

---

[1] State benefits are not offered; they must be *claimed*. People who lack information about claims procedures or their rights to claim cannot receive benefits. Many millions of pounds worth of benefits go unclaimed every year.
[2] DHSS = Department of Health and Social Security.

NEIGHBOURHOOD

The local community defined in terms of the LARA area is an important feature of Olive's life. It is the focus of her daily social interaction and provides many of the resources necessary to her household's livelihood. Although most of the core members of her network live outside the LARA area, she knows many LARA people and regularly relies on them for various kinds of help.

Her objection to the Council's plan to move her family 'out' to north Battersea, her involvement in various local activities organized by the Residents' Association, and the fact that she is a street representative show that she has strong ties with this neighbourhood. Her children too are involved in local activities and 'at home' in the area. Olive says herself that the neighbourhood has helped her bring them up, look after them, stop them doing wrong, and the like.[1] But her relationship with the Residents' Association itself is not without conflicts. She thinks that 'colour difference' has become more relevant since LARA achieved its main aim:[2] too many discussions at the association's meeting are centred around 'coloured' residents. People complain that coloured children dominate the youth clubs, nursery, and holiday programmes and so 'they' benefit most from the community's facilities. 'They' are also blamed for the damage in the community centre. But what distresses her most is the attitude of the white English involved in the association. She feels that they 'want to run the place as they think it right', but do not themselves participate or let their children participate in local social activities. They 'only want to organize':[3] the majority of residents who attended an international evening held at the suggestion of the white English were black. As for herself, sometimes even she feels

[1] In this respect it is like a village 'at home'; there it is normal for any local adult to reprimand and even to discipline any local child who misbehaves.
[2] i.e. the declaration and implementation of an HAA.
[3] This attitude and/or Olive's interpretation of it may be functions of the categorical 'disadvantage' of blacks in the white English view (see p. 96, n. 1).

like an 'outsider', one of 'them' despite her thirteen years' residence in the area and her active involvement in the neighbourhood.

Olive's own problems affect her view of other people so she may not have interpreted the white English view completely correctly. None the less the way she perceives the situation is real in its consequences: since she now feels less accepted on the grounds of her ethnic origin she has become less active as a street representative and attends fewer local meetings. Her lack of participation in turn perpetuates the idea that 'we', the English, have to do all the organizing, because 'they', the non-English, are passive and not interested.[1]

WELFARE AND DEPENDENCE

The fact that Olive's household depends for economic support on supplementary benefits and other special 'welfare state' allowances, affects more than the economic aspects of her life. Her income is similar to that of a low-paid worker and through careful budgeting she can make ends meet. She has even managed to acquire some luxury goods by cutting down on things like visiting, drinking, parties, and clothes for herself. But 'apparently you're not supposed to do all right': even managing, 'getting by' has led to criticism. Some of Olive's neighbours, she says, cannot accept that she has a nice flat and can 'afford luxuries that should be beyond the means of a person on welfare'. Social service officials 'are just the same': they all think one should be able to *see* that a person lives on social security payments. She feels she is expected to justify her expenditure to others all the time.

Although in a welfare state people's basic needs are formally defined as rights, officials who deal with welfare recipients seem to define the welfare provisions as favours you can only

---

[1] We should notice, however, that some white residents who were actively involved in the beginning have also now retreated from LARA (see Alice Kelly, p. 160).

have if you have been good.[1] Thus Olive has the impression that these officials do not tell clients about all the provisions available under the welfare system,[2] and that they resent being asked for more information on the grounds that the client is planning to 'take advantage'. She is also sensitive about the checking procedures of the officials; she experiences their visits as forms of 'spying' and indirect control; they come to check on her, to express their approval or disapproval of the way she manages her finances and organizes her household, and she knows their approach to future assistance will depend on the assessments they make during these visits. They make her think she has to answer to them for all her actions. Most painful to her was the response of social services officials to her last pregnancy. On the advice of one of her English neighbourhood contacts she had applied for financial assistance to buy baby clothes, etc. A visit from an official followed and during this visit she was asked whether she had considered an abortion. Olive says 'they' really meant she had no right to have another child.[3] Similarly, being on supplementary benefits interferes with her relationship with Roderick. While she does not think in terms of legal marriage, she would like him to move in with her and become a full member of the household. But if he did she would no longer qualify for supplementary benefits and other grants,[4] and he does not earn enough to support her family as well as the family of his ex-wife. Effectively it is state regulations concerning financial assistance that prevent her stabilizing her domestic life.

These regulations are mediated through the woman Olive refers to as 'my social worker'. Although she views her present social worker as a nice person and responsive to her needs, she

[1] The criteria used to distinguish deserving from non-deserving claimants are necessarily those that define the boundaries of 'the moral community' (see Flett 1979: 143).

[2] Formally speaking, it is not the job of the State to offer help, only to respond to claims (see p. 99, n. 1).

[3] Again, local information gave her access to resources. Olive distinguishes very clearly between official help and neighbourly help. Her resentment in these matters is against officials and her dependence on welfare, not against the white English in general.

[4] i.e. she would no longer qualify as a single parent (see p. 82, n. 2).

only contacts her when she has no alternative. The reason is not the social worker as a person, but the standard lack of continuity in social worker/client relationships, and the lack of confidentiality: 'I don't like the way everything is written down. These reports aren't treated as private information and everybody who's working there reads them. You never deal with the same person twice down at the office. Every time they ask you the same questions, again and again, even when you know they've got all the answers written down.' These problems and constraints have the deterrent effect that Olive thinks 'they' intend: she only asks for additional financial support[1] if she desperately needs it and can find no other solution, and she does her best to avoid calling on the social services for help of any other sort.

CRISIS

Olive's network includes neighbours, family members, fellow West Indians, and officials, all of whom are, on the face of it, potential sources of support. In actual situations however, they are not equally appropriate options; they are all potential resources, but they are not all resources of the same kind; some contacts are more useful for particular purposes than others. The steps Olive took to deal with one crisis situation indicate the relative importance of kin, ethnic, local, and social services resources and her reasons for choosing one kind of resource in preference to another.

The crisis at issue came up when Olive was told she must undergo a serious operation. As a single parent her main problem was to find homes for her three children while she was in hospital. For a number of reasons she 'didn't even consider asking' her relatives living in London. First, they all have large families and fulltime jobs, and are 'fully occupied with their own lives'. Second, her two older boys attend local schools and since these relatives live outside Wandsworth, the journey to and from school every day would be long and expensive. Third

---

[1] In the form of the various supplementary benefits available to people in special circumstances.

(an afterthought), Olive is not all that comfortable with them and is not keen to ask them any favours. Fourth, and perhaps most important, she had options: in previous similar situations one of her local English contacts had looked after the two older boys, so she turned to those neighbours to see if they could do the same again. They could not, but after discussion and with their encouragement, another local English contact volunteered to accommodate the older two. This left only arrangements to be made for the youngest child. He was at that time 18 months old and still demanded a lot of attention. In his case Olive's first choice was one of her 'ethnic' contacts, a close friend from the West Indies now living in the Wandsworth area. Although this friend worked, she was prepared to make special work arrangements so that she could look after Olive's child. The problem seemed to be solved and Olive was pleased. Then shortly before she had to go into hospital her friend had a crisis of her own and found she could not keep their arrangement. Olive then went, in some panic, to a succession of other friends, but all of them had work or heavy family commitments. Finally she had no alternative but to contact her social worker. The social worker approached the local community worker for information on possible local foster parents. He recommended a local English family which turned out to be willing and able to help out by giving the small child a temporary home.

In all aspects of this crisis situation Olive's local contacts were of prime significance as a resource. It has to be added that in her search for help she was to a large extent constrained by work and family commitments of her friends and relatives, so her reliance on local and social services contacts was partly out of choice, partly out of necessity. In relation to her two eldest children local help was her first choice and, at least at one remove, was available. For the care of her youngest son she preferred a close friend, but when this option was closed to her she approached the social worker and the community worker.[1] They in turn used official information sources to give Olive access to a different set of local options.

[1] The community worker's particular job is to match local need to local resources in this way.

Coping with shopping
(*Photo:* Gina Glover –
Photo Co-op)

Local shop/cafe
(*Photo:* Sandra Wallman)

Typical LARA streets
(*Photos:* Sandra Wallman)

Back gardens
(*Photo:* Sandra Wallman)

Northcote Road market
(*Photo:* Sarah Saunders – Photo Co-op)

Childminders' support group
(*Photo:* Gina Glover – Photo Co-op)

Women boarding a bus in south London
(*Photo:* Corry Bevington – Photo Co-op)

5 Two West Indian Households

The Ellison and Irving households are only categorically alike. They have little in common apart from the fact that they both belong in the British population category 'West Indian immigrant' – although of course, like all the cases in this book, they have comparable incomes and live in the same inner-London neighbourhood. As it happens, the parent members of both households were born in the Caribbean, and all or most of their children are native English citizens who have spent all their lives in Battersea, but the 'West Indian immigrant' category lumps them all together willy-nilly. In both popular and official British classifications, non-white British residents tend to go on being identified by others as 'immigrants' no matter where they were born or how they identify themselves.

In fact these two households differ very sharply in respect of *identity*. The narratives that follow make three points plain: (i) identity (pp. 38–40) is not fixed by skin colour – black households may identify themselves as belonging with white households in the LARA area and may include whites within their household systems (see also the Abraham case in Chapter 4); (ii) ordinary people, whether black or white, have a number of identity options open to them, that is these two households can identify ethnically, locally, or in terms of their various occupations; and (iii) none of the options excludes any other — it is both possible and normal to combine identity resources in different ways for different purposes.

All these points apply equally in both cases, but the balance of their identity investments is very different. The Ellisons overall are locally involved and the Irvings are absorbed by the ethnic community centred on Matthew Irving's church. Relatively speaking, the Ellison household is *localist* and the Irving household is *ethnic*. There are other differences which run parallel with the identity contrast: the Ellison parents are young people and the Irving parents are in their late middle age; although both couples have been in Battersea for a similarly long time, the period covers all the formative years of the Ellisons (Cliff and Annette were both very young children when their separate families settled in London), but only the mature adulthood of Matthew and Joyce Irving. At the same time the kin and friends of the Ellison household live nearby, many of them in the small LARA neighbourhood, while the Irvings' most important contacts are in Matthew's church congregation, which is scattered across south London, and the West End workplaces of his grown-up daughters who still live at home. Predictably therefore, the 'close' networks of the two households have a different geographic spread and they get their *information* and support from different sources. Less predictably however, Annette does most of the planning and negotiating for the Ellison household, even in the public sphere – that is, she is its resource-keeper although Cliff is the main wage earner – and virtually all inside decisions affecting the Irvings' livelihood seem to be made by Matthew, even though the household's money economy depends most crucially on the grown-up Irving daughters, and occasionally on the State. These division of labour styles go against the classic view of West Indian family patterns: the literature leads us to expect the more traditional/ethnic household – the Irvings – to be the more matri-centred of the two. No one household feature accounts for the reversal, but each household's style does turn out to fit the personalities involved and to match the employment options and strategies of household members. In any case, the objective is not to find out which features of each household are the cause and which the effect of its style or its 'success'. The point is that the differences that make the real difference between one household and another are not always visible.

The Ellisons

Cliff and Annette Ellison are both in their twenties although he is the elder by seven years. They are both of Catholic, West Indian parentage, but come from different Caribbean islands. Neither attends church frequently or keeps in touch with family in the Caribbean. Cliff arrived in Britain at the age of 12; Annette when she was 5. Most of Cliff's schooling has been in this country, and he did the best part of his growing up in Battersea with his parents who still live nearby. He wants to remain in the LARA area. Annette is less keen on the place but the nursery school is an important attraction. She would at least like to move to a different street.[1] Many of the houses in their street are in bad repair and it strikes her as not particularly friendly. She came to Battersea to be with Cliff, having grown up in a more suburban part of south London where her parents and many of her school friends still live.

Annette and Cliff had one child at the time of the LARA survey, and were expecting another during the period of these interviews. The second child, like the first, was delivered at the nearby women's hospital, the South London Hospital. Annette was well pleased with the treatment she received there when the first was born. Before the second child arrived, she and Cliff talked a lot about the effect it would have on their lives. Annette was working as a helper at the LARA nursery

---

[1] Annette's attachment to the nursery school and her dislike of the street the Ellisons live in are themes that recur throughout their story.

school which her 2-year-old son attended and was concerned whether she would be able to continue there once the second child was born. Will the nursery school be able to take the new baby as well as the 2-year-old, or will she have to make other arrangements? They also made practical preparations, such as redecorating their flat and converting the room right at the top of the building to make more space. By the time the later interviews in the series took place the second child was born and the changes it brought were beginning to show. Cliff seemed more overwhelmed by new responsibilities than his wife. He often had to take care of the elder child while Annette fed or changed the baby. At the same time he felt under such financial pressure that he took on extra overtime work to cover his commitments. Annette was better able to take the birth of the second child in her stride. It had been a difficult pregnancy; she had suffered from jaundice, which had meant a number of extra visits to the hospital before the confinement, and she was visibly relieved that it was all over and she had produced a healthy baby despite the medical complications. From her point of view the birth of the first had been a heavier responsibility. They were living with her in-laws at that time and she had been isolated and miserable. This time they were settled in their own flat so she felt more in control of the situation and more confident about her circumstances.

According to Annette, the months when they lived with Cliff's parents for lack of alternative accommodation were the most difficult of their marriage. Annette and her mother-in-law never get on too well with each other anyway. It was a great relief to her when she and Cliff got this flat in LARA through the Housing Action office.

Annette's involvement in the nursery school, and in LARA generally, meant that Cliff assumed she would be more closely involved in the interview series than he would, and besides, he was at home less often than his wife. Most of the interviews were conducted only with Annette, but even when he was present Cliff was much less talkative than his wife. Except for the descriptions of Cliff's jobs therefore, this is Annette's view of their story.

JOBS

Cliff took a six-month training course in sheet metal work when he left school, some thirteen years ago. It was a government training course and he got a certificate at the end. The careers office of the local education authority then helped him to get his first job, as a sheet metal worker, in an engineering firm just around the corner from his home. He worked there for four years and was then made redundant.[1] Throughout those four years he carried on his training through part-time study at a local college, but he never completed the course and received no further qualifications. He found his work in the engineering firm rather boring. He had to take a round disc, about an inch or so deep, and then try to make a square out of the disc, by carefully chipping away at it. He had to be careful not to damage his eyes as he chipped away. Even the machinery he had to use was dangerous and he had to be careful all the time. Cliff never had an accident at work himself, but others did, and he had to be continuously on his guard.

After he was made redundant he found himself another job as a sheet metal worker. This too was in south London but much further afield and he had long journeys to and from work every day. That job was more interesting however, and he would have stayed there if he had not been laid off[2] after two years. But from then on he decided against factory work. He did not like being indoors, always being in the same place all the time. In particular he did not like working with machinery during the summer months because it got unbearably hot. Instead he went after a job as a driver: he knew all it took was a clean licence.[3] The job centre[4] sent him to a firm in Brixton

---

[1] Officially this means that the job no longer exists, that the work, not the man, is no longer necessary. It has nothing to do with the skill or behaviour of the worker. Officially too, the man is entitled to a compensatory redundancy payment.

[2] See p. 91, n. 1.

[3] A 'clean' driving licence has no driving offences recorded against it.

[4] One of the few differences in the job-seeking patterns of West Indian and English south Londoners is the greater likelihood that West Indian men will call in at the local job centre when looking for work and may even report, as here, that they got a job by doing so (see Wallman *et al.* 1982: Chapter 6).

which rented out dormobiles[1] and he was given a job as cleaner and driver. He liked it although the pay was not good; in the beginning it was something different. He had to clean out the dormobiles after they came back from renting, and to demonstrate the cars to new customers. There were perks:[2] he was allowed to keep any money he found when he cleaned out the vehicles. 'It's surprising what people leave in rented cars sometimes! They don't check them before they give them back.' But the occasional 'bonus' did not make up for low wages and once the novelty wore off, after about a year, he left to take up his present job as driver with a security firm.

He had applied for the job after seeing an advertisement in the newspaper. He still likes it; it goes on being interesting. He likes the fact that he is not always in the same place; he likes moving about. Every Monday he goes to Bracknell; today he has been to Oxford; at least twice a week he goes to Windsor.[3] He does not like driving in London because of the traffic, and to avoid the worst of it he makes an early start every day, usually leaving home by about 4 or 4.30 a.m. He likes the freedom of driving. On the road there is nobody to tell you what to do. As long as he does the job, he can plan it as he likes. He could finish the day's work early if he wanted to because he makes such an early start, but he prefers not to; such a practice could so easily be abused. Instead he delays his return to the depot. When he finishes around 11 or 11.30 a.m. he comes home to have a bite to eat, visits a friend, or does some other business. He then checks in at his depot around 1 o'clock, a more appropriate time. If he is asked to do a special job and cannot leave Oxford or Windsor till about noon, he goes straight to the depot when he gets back to London, still finishing work by about 1 o'clock. Some of his mates take much longer over their jobs and do not finish work till about three in the afternoon.

---

[1] Large, camping-out family vehicles.
[2] 'Perks' (perquisites) = unofficial, sometimes illegal extra gains on the job probably condoned by the employer within informally agreed limits.
[3] All these places are within a hundred-mile radius of London.

He says he still likes working with the security firm, but is no longer satisfied with the pay. When he first started there he had been earning well, but his earnings have stayed more or less the same. Anyway they have certainly not kept up with inflation. He takes home a bit more than when he first joined, but feels it is not enough in comparison with everything else. The firm is mean[1] when it comes to money. He has never had a Christmas bonus from them.[2] Once they gave him a gift token which he could exchange at an off-licence[3] for a bottle of wine, but that is all. In his view such a large company could do more for its workers. As it is they look after other people better than their own![4]

So again he is seriously considering leaving his job. He does like the work, but it is no good if it does not pay the bills. Now that they have two children the bills seem to be coming in much thicker and faster than ever before. Again he is looking for a job with better pay. He still wants to avoid factory work and is keeping an eye out for other driving work. But as he does not have a heavy goods vehicle licence, only an ordinary licence, the choice is very limited.[5] He is considering applying for a job as a bus driver. He knows it involves shiftwork, but thinks he might like that. Yes, he did say that he does not enjoy driving through London, but maybe it will be different driving a bus.

Annette studied at college after leaving school. She says she was lucky really. One of her teachers at school taught at the college and had been allowed to take along some of her school

---

[1] 'Mean' = stingy, ungenerous.
[2] It is customary for some employers to give their employees extra money as a present at Christmas, especially if the firm or a particular worker in it has done well during the year. In many cases the presence or absence of a bonus has nothing to do with productivity. Cliff makes no mention of it here.
[3] 'Off-licence' = a shop selling alcoholic drink but not to be consumed on the premises.
[4] 'Their own' indicates that he identifies with the firm. He is saying in effect that we, the workers, belong to them, the company.
[5] A heavy goods vehicle (HGV) licence would allow him to drive transport and container trucks as well as cars.

pupils to study in her classes at the college. In this way Annette was able to attend the college without paying for tuition, although of course she would have had to pay examination fees if she had stayed that long.[1] She took typing and secretarial courses at first, then some classes in accounting. She found her studies difficult however, and when her teacher left the college after a year, Annette lost her enthusiasm for the course. She kept going to classes for a while, but left the college before she took the exams. Anyway most of the other students were much older than herself and she felt a little out of place.

When she left the college Annette took a job as an accounts clerk in a printing firm in Streatham, about ten minutes' walk from where she was living at the time, although she later moved to Catford. Her parents lived in Tulse Hill, where she had grown up, but she had moved away from home when she went to college.[2] She found the job in the printing firm rather boring. She had to record the cheques that the firm received in the ledger book and worked in a room all by herself, with no one to talk to. The manager and owner of the firm was very posh[3] and always talked about where he had been dining out the previous night, usually at expensive restaurants, with champagne suppers. His wife always wore matching dress, shoes, handbag, and hat. But the manager was considerate towards his staff; in the hot summer of 1976 he used to bring round ice creams, cold beers, and cold drinks to them. He was good that way, even though he was tightfisted[4] when it came to paying wages. Annette did not get on with the rest of the staff, however. They were much older, some of them had been there for a long time, and could not get used to having a younger person around. She left the printing firm after working there for eight months. She said she left out of boredom, but there were other things happening at the time:

[1] Examination fees in state run colleges are paid to a central authority and are not subject to the discretion of the college staff as Annette's tuition fees were.
[2] All these places are in the inner south London area.
[3] 'Posh' = colloquial in London for fancy or snobbish. The word derives from letters used to indicate cabins best placed in relation to the sun on ocean liners travelling to India: that is 'port out, starboard home'.
[4] 'Tightfisted' = mean or stingy as Cliff complained before.

her first child was born in November that year.[1]

When their son was 9 months old Annette began work in the LARA nursery school. By then she and Cliff had moved into a flat of their own in LARA and the LARA community centre was just beginning to operate. Annette used to pay the rent to the housing office[2] which is just next to the nursery, and one day she went into the nursery to ask about putting her son on the waiting list for a place in nursery school. By chance she found out they had a vacancy for a nursery helper.[3] She worked there for nearly two years, until the birth of her second child. The nursery staff are all young, one or two of them are married like herself, but most of them are single. She says she gets on well with all of them. She really enjoyed working there, and feels it is like one big family. She thinks that there can be few nurseries that offer as much to the children. The children can get their lunch at the nursery and have a rest in one of the little beds, and there are washing and drying facilities for the children's clothes. Even when the children start infant school they can still carry on using the nursery for part of the day. She liked working in the nursery school very much. Now that her second child is born she worries that the nursery will not agree to enrol the baby into the nursery along with her elder child and she will have to give up the job. Seeking alternatives she has asked various of her friends whether they would be willing to look after the baby during the day, but in the end none of them has been able to take on such a commitment. Some of her friends with children in the nursery have found fulltime jobs for themselves in the meantime.[4] Annette says firmly that she

[1] Presumably she was bored all the time but the decision to leave was sensible in view of her pregnancy. She does not say so, but it is likely she would not have left at that time otherwise. The change in her personal life precipitated a change in the domain of work.

[2] This involves a regular visit once a week so the housing staff and the tenants get to know each other well. A local housing office of this sort was one of the early demands of the foundation members of LARA (see Wallman *et al*, 1982: Chapter 4).

[3] Information was locally based and casually, even accidentally acquired.

[4] Since all these women are of similar age and life stage, they have similar obligations and timetables and cannot readily stand in for each other. This is a practical constraint which rules out the use of support or help which may appear (on a network diagram for example) to be abundantly available.

does not believe in childminders and would never give her child to somebody she did not know.

TIME

Annette does most of the housework, but on weekends Cliff helps with hoovering, polishing the furniture, shopping, and the washing up. Since the birth of their second child, Cliff has taken on far more responsibility for looking after the first, now $2\frac{1}{2}$ years old. He fetches him from nursery school at 5 p.m., feeds him, baths him, and puts him to bed. On weekdays Cliff leaves home so early he cannot help with the children in the morning, but at weekends he spends much of his time with them. He gets the boy up on Saturday mornings and generally looks after him for the rest of the day – sometimes 'with only one eye'[1] while he does chores around the house; at the same time Annette takes care of the baby and does the rest of the housework. Together they like to visit friends at weekends, usually in the daytime so that the 2-year-old is reasonable and they can show off the newborn baby.

On one weekday in May Cliff went to work at 4.30 a.m. and arrived back home at 1.15 p.m., having finished his job for the day. His wife got up at 7.30 a.m., made herself some tea, had a bath, and shortly before 9 a.m. got her elder son up and prepared him for nursery school. By 10 a.m. he was safely in the nursery and she had set off shopping with her baby and a friend who lives in LARA and has a baby of the same age. They walked with their prams to the Arndale Centre where Annette exchanged a pair of shoes she had bought for the toddler the week before and did some other shopping. She was back home by 1 p.m., fed the baby and settled him as Cliff came home. While he went out to the shops, she began cooking the evening dinner. She was still busy in the kitchen when Cliff came back about 2.30 p.m. The baby was in his cot in the living room and the television was on as usual. They watched it together from about 3 o'clock until Annette went to fetch the child from the nursery at five. They had dinner at 6 p.m.,[2] and Annette

---

[1] 'With only one eye', because he is doing other things at the same time.
[2] This is 'dinner' because although it is eaten in the evening when others have 'tea', it is the main meal of the day. On a different work schedule 'dinner' would be taken in the middle of the day.

washed up while Cliff put the elder boy to bed. Annette then went out on her own to visit the friend she had gone shopping with in the morning. Cliff watched television at home until he went to bed at 11.30 p.m., interrupting his viewing once to feed the baby at about 8.30. Annette came home at 9.45 p.m., bathed and fed the baby and put him to bed. She too went to bed at about 11.30 p.m.

PEOPLE

Annette has few relatives in this country and no contact with relatives in the Caribbean where she was born. Annette's parents live in Tulse Hill where she grew up. She sees her mother at least once a week and sometimes at weekends. Her mother finds it difficult to come to visit her in Battersea, and usually it is up to Annette to go to Tulse Hill. Sometimes Cliff drives her there at weekends and they all go together as a family.

Mother and daughter have not always got on so well; relations between them were strained while Annette was going to college and when she started working. But since she became a mother herself and particularly since she and Cliff moved into their own flat, the two women like to see each other.

Annette's mother has told her a lot of extra things about looking after children,[1] like putting a silver necklace round the baby's neck to steady his head and stop it rolling about too much. She tried it out on her first born, and from the time he was given a silver necklace he was able to keep his head up. Her mother also told her to give the child a coin as soon as his first tooth grew, in order to make his teeth grow nice and strong.[2] Annette finds it 'interesting' to learn these things from her

[1] 'Extra' to the normal English instructions which both black and white English mothers receive from the hospital, the health and welfare clinics, and from each other.
[2] Babies of course learn to hold their heads up and can develop strong teeth without these precautions being taken. Annette's mother knows that as well as she does, but both of them are sufficiently identified with the Caribbean to feel good about the symbolic value of old customs and will do them 'just in case'. Some say part of their original function was to provide an opportunity for the display of wealth or thrift in rural communities with limited scope for conspicuous consumption of any kind.

mother, who learnt it from hers, and so forth – 'all the things we used to keep in the Caribbean'.

When Annette was in hospital at Hammersmith during her second pregnancy because of jaundice, her mother would visit her there and she saw her father quite often as he worked nearby. Annette also gets on very well with one of her sisters, the one who is married to an Englishman and has a baby nine months older than Annette's second son. This sister lives outside London but comes to see her about twice a month. The two sisters are 'very close' to each other, and in complete agreement about their dislike for the third. Annette sees her other sister no more than a couple of times a year although she lives not far away from the parents' home in Tulse Hill. There is a brother too. He lives at home with his parents so Annette runs into him[1] quite a lot, but she does not feel the relationship is important to her.

Annette sees very little of her former schoolfriends. Before she moved to Battersea she maintained contact with a number of them and saw some at least once a week. Since the move to Battersea and now that she has children she sees all but one very rarely. This special friend had been at school with Annette's sister, but was Annette's close friend from the beginning and is now godmother to her older son. Annette sometimes envies her friend's life. She has a very good job with the BBC; and although she has been 'going out with'[2] the same bloke 'for yonks'[3] she says she is not yet ready for marriage. She even goes out[4] on her own without telling her boyfriend because she feels they should each go their own way and lead their own lives. Annette also goes out on her own sometimes, to visit friends or her parents, but she always tells Cliff where she is going.

Most of Annette's current friends are women she has met since moving to Battersea. She often sees the two friends she made in the maternity hospital during her first confinement. A lot of the women she had met then were also having a second

[1] 'To run into' = to meet in passing without planning it.
[2] 'Going out with someone' is like the American term 'going steady'. It implies the same degree of intimacy and commitment.
[3] 'For yonks' = forever; for a very long time.
[4] 'To go out' here (unlike 'going out with' above) means only to go out in the evening, to the cinema, to visit friends, or even to parties and the like.

child round about the same time as herself, so she could brush up their acquaintance at the antenatal clinic.[1] Her two good friends from the hospital live only a short bus ride away from the LARA area. One of them was born up north in Blackpool and is due to move back soon because her husband has been offered a job there. The other is one of the people Annette approached when she was trying to find a childminder for her baby so that she could go back to work. But this friend's husband will not let her make job commitments. Annette thinks he stops her 'because he is Italian'[2] and does not want to risk his wife making more money than he does.

Annette also has two close friends living in the LARA area. One of them she met through her in-laws, when the woman lived next door to them. Now she has a little baby the same age as Annette's and lives nearby. When Annette talks of leaving her flat to move to a better street in the area her preference is for the LARA street where this friend lives.[3] The second LARA friend is another person she approached when looking for a childminder. She had met her through a workmate at the LARA nursery who had herself met her as a fellow worker in a different nursery. This made her doubly eligible to look after Annette's baby but she had in the meanwhile found a job as a telephonist and receptionist and was too busy to take it on. Some of Annette's friendships depended even more directly on contacts at work. While she was working in the nursery school, two of her workmates would often come over to her flat for dinner or tea breaks. One of them lived near the Arndale centre, and the other in Northcote Road, both places a bit too far to go for a quick break. Now that she is at home fulltime she sees them hardly at all.

[1] This can be described as an age set or cohort effect (see Wallman *et al.* 1982: Chapter 7). The women are of similar age and go through life cycle events at about the same time – all governed by the current norms of family planning, etc.

[2] Annette here exposes the English person's stereotype of Latin men: they are thought to be sexist, concerned with masculine display, and keeping their women in place. Presumably if her friend's husband had not been Italian she would have found some other way to account for his behaviour.

[3] A 'better street' for Annette is a more friendly street; the street where her friend lives is therefore 'better' by definition. Local identity in this area is most sharply focused on streets (see Wallman *et al.* 1982: Chapter 5).

Annette is also quite friendly with some of her in-laws. One of Cliff's cousins often comes from Mitcham[1] to visit them. They see less of his wife because she has a small baby and is less mobile. Annette regularly sees Cliff's aunt who lives in Stratford[2] and comes to visit his parents at least once a week and usually stops by[3] the flat to say hello. It was this aunt who took care of Annette's elder child when she had to go into hospital for treatment during her second pregnancy, and again when she went into the maternity hospital for the confinement.

Apart from her spell in hospital and her attendance at antenatal and postnatal clinics, Annette has few contacts with the statutory services. The health visitor comes round every three months or so to check on the development of the older child and to make sure he has been properly immunized and vaccinated, etc.[4] but Annette usually goes to the health clinic for check-ups rather than wait for the health visitor to come to her. Her main contact with other official agencies is through her residence in the LARA area and through the activities of LARA. It was the LARA housing office that originally allocated them their flat and Annette pays the rent there every week. Her work in the LARA nursery school has brought her in touch with other area residents and has drawn her into activities organized by the Residents' Association. She is not, however, active in the LARA organization itself.

Cliff, by contrast, has little to do with LARA activities, but is much more strongly committed to living in the LARA area than his wife. He grew up in the area and his parents still live in it. Most of his relatives live outside the LARA area, but somehow all of them are frequent visitors either to his parents' house or to his own flat.[5]

[1] Mitcham is further out in south London, but not in the 'inner city' ring.
[2] Stratford is quite a long way off in the East End, which is across the river Thames but still within inner London.
[3] 'To stop by' = to visit briefly, probably, as here, on the way to somewhere else.
[4] This is a standard National Health Service procedure following the birth of children in local hospitals. Health visitors usually work out of or in co-operation with locally based doctors and follow up households registered on their lists of patients.
[5] For Cliff, kinship and locality overlap in the area; for Annette they do not.

He feels closest to two of his brothers and sees one or the other every day. One is married with two children of his own, and lives on a big council estate in Battersea. The other still lives with his parents. This younger brother, a cousin, and a friend are now helping Cliff to redecorate the flat. The cousin and his friends are in a government training scheme as part of the Youth Opportunities Programme for school leavers.[1] It seems to consist of redecorating houses for old people, so they are practising in their spare time.

Cliff has three other brothers who live abroad. The eldest is in Canada and he has not seen him for years, the other two are in the armed forces in Germany so he only sees them when they come home on leave. He feels closer to the two locally based brothers than to his parents, but closer to his parents than to other kin. He sees his father frequently and his mother almost every day, often driving her to the hospital in Fulham where she works. He is fond of his mother's sister, the aunt who helps Annette out with the children, and sees her regularly when she visits his mother in the area. He feels particularly close to an uncle who lives in Balham[2] and manages to visit him about every two weeks. He has 'numerous' cousins whom he sees from time to time but only two stand out of the crowd: the one who is now helping to redecorate the flat, and one living in Mitcham, married with a young baby, who comes to visit him once or twice a week.

Apart from his brothers and his cousins, his closest friend is a former schoolmate who grew up in the same street and now lives outside the LARA area but just a few minutes' walk away. This man is at home in the household, 'a friend of the family', and Cliff sees a lot of him. He has two friends who do live in the LARA area, but his relationships with them are rather different. One is also a friend of his parents and is someone he has known ever since he came to live in the area as a child. The man now lives with his family in the same street and they often

---

[1] The Youth Opportunities Programme (YOP) is one of a number sponsored by central government to ease the effect of unemployment. The idea of YOP is that youngsters leaving school at least get paid work experience usually for six months, even if there are no jobs for them to take up afterwards.
[2] Balham is in south London, nor far from Battersea.

meet, as neighbours or at his parents' house. The other he talks to regularly whenever they meet in the grocery shop or are waiting for the bus on their way to work in the morning. He has never been to this man's house and meets him only in passing, without planning it.

He likes some of his workmates. Outside working hours he only sees them when the workplace darts team plays on Wednesday evenings. It is a friendly place but he does not get on with the works manager and this, along with the need to earn more money now that they have a second child, is why he is actively searching for a new job.

NEIGHBOURHOOD

Annette and Cliff had moved into Cliff's parents' home in the LARA area when their first child was born. They lived in one room for most of the time and Annette had felt very isolated and restricted living with her parents-in-law, but by moving into an HAA they knew they stood a better chance of getting proper accommodation.[1] They would have to wait a long time to be allocated a council flat in the normal way; they would not even have been eligible until the birth of the first child and would then have been on the housing list for ages waiting for a vacancy. Living with Cliff's parents in the area they were able to contact the HAA housing office in January, when their baby was 2 months old, and were allocated a flat two months later, in March.[2]

Both of them are really pleased to have a flat of their own.

[1] Initially the Ellisons were involved in the local system only through connections with family. It is characteristic of the area that access to one kind of local resource allowed them to 'become locals' in every sense quite readily.
[2] In terms of the official system, residents in an HAA have priority in access to accommodation refurbished in the HAA project. Once existing residents have been suited, vacancies go into the general borough housing pool. The possibility that non-locals would then move into the area has been a source of some anxiety to LARA as a whole. Both the strength and the content of this anxiety demonstrate local identity very clearly (pp. 7–9; see also Wallman *et al.* 1982: Chapter 4).

Annette says it has made all the difference in her social life because she can now invite anyone she wishes and do whatever she likes in her home. They spent time and money on the flat in anticipation of the arrival of their second child. Nevertheless, after living in their flat for a year and a half they have some reservations about it. Annette feels a bit closed in and is tired of going up and down the stairs with two small children. She would like to live on the ground floor and have access to a garden so the boy could go out to play a bit and have more room to run around. In any case they do not get on with the downstairs neighbours. Whenever anybody calls, the 'old hags' peep out of the door or the window to see who it is, always asking questions and pestering visitors, always wanting to know who is coming or going.[1]

Annette feels quite strongly that she would like to move out of the street altogether. Many of the houses in the street are in a bad state of disrepair. Only two at this end and two at the other have been done up so far. Anyway there are not enough young people with kids around and she does not know any of the neighbours to talk to. She would prefer some other part of LARA, maybe the street where her friend lives, where there are more young couples with children; and it would be good to be rid of[2] the old hags downstairs. Cliff is less bothered than his wife about the kind of street they live in, perhaps because he already had close kin and close friends in the area when they moved in and has less need to make contact with his immediate neighbours. He has no involvement with the Residents' Association as such, and leaves his wife to deal with 'those sorts' of local issues, but he definitely wants to stay in the LARA area: after all he has lived here ever since he can remember. Annette on the contrary is glad of the opportunity to be involved in LARA itself. This is not the area in which she

[1] There are a number of reasons for this new dissatisfaction. Their needs have changed since the new child arrived; they have got used to having a place of their own, and they have had time to discover that the neighbours interfere with their autonomy. In any case they want to continue to better themselves – Cliff at his job, Annette at home.
[2] 'To be rid of' = to get away from.

grew up so she now lives some distance from her former schoolfriends and her own mother. Because the LARA nursery school has brought her into contact with other mothers in the area, and has provided an important focus for her social life, the idea of giving up her job in it distresses her. She is not sure her feeling of belonging will continue if she is not actually working there.

CRISES

Cliff's family helped out in a number of ways in the crises surrounding the births of their two children. After the birth of the first the couple lived with his parents for seven months before moving into their own flat. The first four were specifically aimed at securing the right to be rehoused within LARA ; after the flat was allocated they stayed on another three months so they could save money to buy furniture for their new home. The hospitality of Cliff's parents gave them the right to a flat, but it was up to Annette to contact the statutory services and the housing office of the HAA in order to secure the flat itself, rather than through the intervention of her in-laws or her husband.

Annette's illness during her second pregnancy was another crisis. She had been sick a lot and had hardly eaten anything for weeks. In the sixth month it turned out she had jaundice and some problem that required a blood transfusion. She attended the general hospital in Hammersmith once a week till they found out what the problem was, and then went in for a week's observation and treatment. Eventually they traced the illness to her reaction to the anti-sickness tablets she had been taking. Since then she vows never to take medicine to relieve pain or headaches, even though she still suffers from migraine from time to time.

While Annette was in hospital for treatment her eldest son was looked after by Cliff's aunt in east London. The first time he stayed away from home he had missed his mother and was quite angry with her when she first came out of hospital. But he seems to have enjoyed playing with his cousins. He began to talk much more clearly, and when he returned to the nursery school he knew how to hit back when he was being pushed around. Cliff took a week off work to look after him when the baby was born so the child only had to stay with his great-aunt for a few days. Anyway the boy was used to staying there by then and was quite happy to go.

The latest anxiety is the need to find someone who will look after the baby during the day so that Annette can return to work at the end of her maternity leave.[1] The nursery school does not normally accept children under the age of one and is afraid of creating a precedent by letting Annette bring her baby to work.[2] She is adamant that she will not take the baby to a childminder she does not know, so she has not contacted any of the statutory agencies or locally registered childminders.[3] She has asked some of her friends who stay at home to look after children of their own but none of them can help her: they have part-time work which takes them out of the home, are about to move away from the area, or have husbands who would disapprove of them earning. Their family resources are no more useful than the friendship network.[4] Her own kin live too far away; and on Cliff's side the only eligible woman living locally is his mother and she works part-time in a hospital some distance away. There is no real crisis while Annette's maternity leave lasts, but the issue looms unresolved on the family's horizon.

---

[1] Women are not normally paid wages during maternity leave in Britain, although they may be entitled to state benefits of one kind or another. Maternity leave means only that the job is 'held' until the leave period is over. If it is not taken up 'on time', the woman loses her rights in it altogether.
[2] This is a household crisis, but not as an economic problem. Annette's contentment is more vital to the household livelihood than her small earning from the nursery job; much of that anyway will go to paying any person who looks after the baby.
[3] Registered childminders are officially recognized to have space, hygiene, and social facilities in their homes which are adequate to the care of a specified number of children. Some childminders are women at home who look after their own child or children anyway. Not all childminders are registered. Some are said to avoid it only because they dislike formal involvement with officialdom of any sort.
[4] It is only in practical terms that the Ellisons' kin and friends are ineligible to help. There are numerous people whom they feel close enough to, and who would be reliable enough to be entrusted with the baby's care.

The Irvings

Matthew and Joyce Irving have seven children. Three of them live away from home, but a nuclear family household of six is still large by LARA standards.[1] Matthew and Joyce are both in their fifties. They have lived in Battersea since 1954, when they immigrated from Jamaica. They brought Alice and Mary with them, one a baby and one about ten at the time; they are the eldest of the seven and although now grown women still live at home with their parents. The two youngest, Keith and Thelma, now in their teens, also live at home. The three 'in the middle' live in London but away from home. These last five were all born in LARA.

Matthew is a Pentecostal minister and very much in charge of his family and his congregation. He describes himself as 'patriarchal'. His status in the church necessarily affects the lives of all the family, and he expects them to conform entirely to the rules of Pentecostalism. Church meetings take place in the home on three evenings a week, and parishioners 'are free to call' there when they need advice or help from the minister. Sundays, and much of Saturday, they all spend in the church nearby and the whole household is closely involved in the 'spiritual side' of the church as well as its day to day organization. The involvement of the three women, Joyce, Alice, and Mary, is essential to it. Matthew believes that women should 'show themselves; come out and do things' and

[1] Only 26 of the 446 household units contain six or more residents; most of these are collectives or extended families.

this principle is particularly relevant in the church, where all the women members are encouraged to play an active role. Indeed it is necessary that they do so, as the great majority of the congregation consists of women and children. 'Male persons' over the age of about twelve rarely attend. But the Irving household, including the one boy still at home, is united by its members' religious activities and is a close and affectionate family. The absent children seem to have left home initially because they had 'independent ideas' which got in the way of them conforming to the strict moral and behavioural code that Matthew and Joyce have laid down. They do not talk of being disappointed in these children: in the course of the interviews they referred to them hardly at all.[1]

The Irvings moved into LARA one year after their arrival from Jamaica. They now own the house they live in and feel settled in it. Matthew grew up in a devout church-going family and had been working as a self-employed farmer before emigrating to Britain. They came here hoping 'to improve life and get a better job' when things were economically particularly bad in Jamaica.

Matthew only became a minister six years ago, after he was 'called to help people', especially the young. He was, and is, especially concerned about black youth in this country and much of his work focuses on helping youths and children to 'keep out of trouble' and 'get along' in this society. He much admires the LARA community centre – it is one of the best he has seen in London — but fears it came into existence ten years too late: that many youths are already in trouble, 'troubled in spirit'. It also concerns him that the centre is used predominantly by black youngsters living in the area. He would like to see a better mixture of black and white using the place. His own church is harassed by youths and he makes sure to be around during Saturday choir practices in case 'rude boys come and disturb them'. He is also aware that the police harass these boys and even respectable members of the black community; both he and his eldest daughter have on several

---

[1] The Irvings talk of their six-person household as 'the family'.

occasions been stopped and even charged by the police without justification.[1]

Although Matthew's church is small, forty to fifty members, they regularly participate in joint services with other churches. Part of the church's strength lies in the fact that several people have been healed during services – 'we wouldn't worship Him if it wasn't proved! It has to be proved. The Bible is dead without works.' Matthew's main ambition is to expand his church (he would like to get money from the community to help in this) and above all to see its influence grow.

JOBS

Matthew left school in Jamaica at eighteen, Joyce when she was two years younger. Matthew's work experience in Jamaica consisted of farming and some carpentry. After coming to England in 1954, he had a succession of manual jobs, followed by several business enterprises, the last of which failed. He then became a minister of the church.

The first job he took on coming to London was in a cabinet makers' firm.[2] This job lasted only six weeks as it was poorly paid, at £5 a week. His next job was on a building site, as a labourer. This was better paid, but physically so hard that he had to leave after two weeks. Next followed a series of jobs with British Rail at Clapham Junction: carriage cleaning at

---

[1] London's blacks have suffered inordinately from a revival of the ancient 'sus' laws by which a police officer has the right to stop and search citizens 'on suspicion' that they are involved in or planning a felony. 'Sus' was most often applied to young men; hence Matthew's particular distress when he and his daughter are stopped.

The resentment felt by innocent people interfered with in this way was fired by the first sparks of 'the Brixton Riots' in 1981 and set good citizens too against the police (see Scarman 1982).

Note that Matthew was complaining about 'sus' more than two years before these events led to modification of the law and an official change in Metropolitan Police tactics on the streets.

[2] A 'cabinet maker' does skilled and often intricate carpentry and woodwork, usually making furniture, etc. to order.

£15 a week, portering, sorting parcels, and working in the cleaning shed washing down carriages (he says he enjoyed the carriage cleaning especially). In the second phase Matthew was a self-employed shopkeeper, first with a general store and then, by 1961, a butcher's shop. These were in different premises but both in this neighbourhood. Matthew is proud of being 'the first coloured man to have a butcher's licence in Britain'. He adds that his shop was the first butcher's shop to be owned by a Jamaican in London.[1] But in 1963 the Irvings sold the shop and returned to Jamaica with the idea of settling back there again. They tried to re-establish themselves in farming but did not succeed. Anyway Matthew was unhappy 'in himself'. He felt like a stranger and missed being in London and having a 'settled mind and settled home'. In 1965 they re-emigrated. Back in Battersea they opened another shop, this time in the food importing business – mostly food from Jamaica and Nigeria. It survived a number of years but cost the Irvings a very great deal of money by the end, and in 1972 they went out of business. During all this time Matthew had been a member of a large Pentecostal church and had become a preacher within it. In 1975 he diverged from its doctrine and took a group of the congregation with him to form his own church.[2]

As a fulltime preacher, Matthew has no steady income of his own. He has been looking for other work without success (possibly a combination of his lack of formal qualifications and his age)[3] and only applies for social security 'when things get just too hard'. In the meantime the household depends on the wages of the two elder daughters, both well-educated and personable women, who have good jobs in central London in

[1] With these firsts Matthew follows an important precedent in Battersea's history (see p. 7 and Wallman *et al.* 1982: Chapter 2).
[2] A dispute over doctrine is invariably the justification for forming a new church, whether or not social tensions and personal crises or ambitions have played a part (see Calley 1965).
[3] Matthew is too old for the casual manual jobs that are sometimes available, and all his skills were learned on the job, as a self-employed man, not in any college or apprenticeship scheme.

the West End. The congregation contributes towards the running costs of the church by paying the weekly rent of £9 for the church hall (leased from the community), and for petrol for the two vans that are used to ferry the congregants to and from their homes and to transport them on church outings. Because Matthew is a self-taught mechanic he is able to do most of the repairs himself. He still hopes to find some employment which will 'ease me up' while he continues working for his church.

During the twenty-odd years of his time in Britain Matthew has shifted his working energy from the lowest strata of the formal industrial labour market through upward-striving business ventures into the independent and 'informal' sector. His two daughters, on the other hand, have firm careers and he is very keen that they should stay in the formal work sector.[1] He encourages his other children and the younger members of his congregation to succeed at school and at work and to conform to the mainstream in these areas. He describes his present situation as a result of his coming to know immigrants like himself. The church had always been an important part of his life, but he turned to it at a time of crisis – that is when his most ambitious project collapsed. Although he was already a preacher in the church, it was soon after this point that he concentrated on it in a 'professional' way and gained the support of a section of the congregation. He refers to this move as 'being called'. He also refers to his concern with the fact that 'he saw a lot of people in trouble'; that children of West Indians felt they should be getting equal rights in Britain and were being denied them. His own experience of set-back in this country led him to identify with the frustrations of others more sharply.

He could not have made the decision to become a fulltime preacher if he had not owned his own home and had a stable and supportive household behind him. It is his wife Joyce and the four children at home – the older girls especially, but the

---

[1] In these times the best off households are those which can spread their energies over a number of domains of work, and can keep a foot in both formal and informal sectors (see Wallman 1979b: 17–19).

younger children too – who are his primary source of support and his most crucial resources. They all play important roles both at home and in the church. His parishioners are supportive in another way. Although they rely on *him* for spiritual guidance, he depends as much on them: without them his 'mission' would be impossible and his status in the community shaken.[1] Matthew has good contacts with white people in the locality but his world and his work centre around that section of the West Indian community that forms his congregation.[2]

TIME

In relation to the time he spends doing practical things, a lot of Matthew's time is 'just with people'. (Anything up to ten hours a day.) Much of it is spent with the members of his congregation, somewhat less in the narrow circle of the household. Joyce, however, spends a great deal of her time (around eight hours a day) on housework, shopping, and cooking. Matthew never cooks or helps cook; he says 'I'd only mess it up' and makes a point of staying out of the way when Joyce prepares food. Joyce and Matthew spend time together when visiting others, and on those rare evenings when there are no church meetings (which usually last about one and a half hours) at home. But most days Matthew is in and out of the house – 'looking at the garden', visiting, or repairing the vans. Joyce sometimes helps as a workmate with these repairs when Matthew cannot manage alone. Reporting the

[1] This reciprocity is an important element in the success of Matthew's congregation.
[2] The two spheres are very separate: many of the Irvings' neighbours do not seem to know the extent of their church activities. The church is not relevant to them so they have no reason to pay attention to it. On the Irvings' network map, church and local contacts are distinct.

distribution of tasks neither of them noticed Joyce's work on the vans.[1]

During the week the household as a whole comes together only at breakfast time. This is an informal but substantial meal cooked by whichever of the women gets up first. Just after eight Mary and Alice leave for work; then Thelma and Keith go to school and Matthew and Joyce get on with their respective tasks. Matthew does his study of the scriptures and preparation for church services and meetings in the morning. In the afternoon he visits congregation members or the teachers of children who are in trouble at school; when there is an evening meeting (on Tuesdays, Wednesdays, and Fridays) he does not, of course, go out.

The evening meal, prepared by Joyce in advance, is taken in shifts: Matthew and Joyce eat at about 4 o'clock (their only meal), Thelma and Keith when they return from school at around 4.30; and Mary and Alice as soon as they get home at about 6.30. During the evening the latter read or watch television and make sure that the former do their homework. Nobody goes to bed later than Matthew who likes to be asleep by 11 o'clock. He would not go to bed while any member of his household was out.

Joyce shops locally two or three times a week, taking perhaps an hour to do so on foot, and Alice and Mary drive to Brixton on Saturdays in the van to do 'a large shop'.[2] The laundry is also done in sections: Joyce does some at home by machine, Thelma does some at the laundrette, and Mary and Alice do their own washing at home by hand or machine. The survey reported that 'not more than five hours a week' were spent doing washing, but adding up the separate amounts of time spent on it by each of Matthew's womenfolk, the total is much higher.[3] All the women do some ironing sometimes, but Joyce does some every morning, possibly for around an hour.

[1] Man's work done by a woman is not valued in the same way; and work which is not conventionally valued tends to be unnoticed, invisible (see Wadel 1979).
[2] 'A shop' in this usage = a shopping expedition.
[3] There is a lot of 'invisible work' done in this household (see n. 1).

The cleaning appears to be done mainly by her throughout the week.

The fact that this is a large household with virtually three different age groups contained in it encourages a division of labour into pair groups for the performance of particular tasks. Although Mary and Alice mostly work together, since they share the same timetable, jobs may also be done by Joyce and Mary, Joyce and Thelma, or Alice and Thelma. Keith being the only son in the house, does least. He, like Matthew, never helps cook, but he helps his father with carpentry and maintenance around the house ('man's work') when necessary. The household does not have a lot of labour-saving equipment, only a hoover,[1] a washing machine, and a freezer. The fridge is broken.

Sundays are different. Prayers are held with the whole family at 8 o'clock, then those who are not fasting have breakfast together. One or two are likely to be not eating; it is unusual for all of them to sit down together on Sunday morning. Alice and Matthew then collect church members for morning service at 11.30, while Joyce and Mary make lunch. Alice takes Sunday school at 11 o'clock along with other adults. After the service she and Matthew take the congregation home and then the whole household has lunch and relaxes until it is time for evening service at 6 o'clock (Joyce and Thelma clear away lunch.) When the service is over at around 9 o'clock, Matthew and Alice again drive people back to their homes. In the church itself, Alice may lead prayers or testifying, Mary plays the electric organ, Thelma plays the guitar, and Keith sings. The music is strong and beautiful: neighbours say they sound like a professional group. But it would not occur to them to perform anywhere else.[2] In fact any form of social life outside the home or church is discouraged, even for grown-up members of the household. School friends are welcome in the house, but anyone who is not known to

[1] 'Hoover' is the brand name of a vacuum cleaner, but is commonly used, as here, as a generic term for vacuum cleaners.
[2] Music is for praise and fellowship, not for commerce or entertainment.

Matthew and Joyce 'may be a bad influence'. Even Alice's social life is confined to home, and she functions as a second mother to the younger children. The restrictions against 'outsiders'[1] or outside influence in effect turn the family in on itself for recreation and friendship, and this closeness is reinforced by Sunday worship and all church activities. A church convention, for example, involves daily services for several days at a stretch. No one complains about these obligations or the lack of 'modern' standards of freedom for younger family members. All six members of the household operate as a team in relation to and in dealing with the outside world.

PEOPLE

Family and ethnic community networks overlap to a very large extent: family life is dominated by the church, and the church membership is entirely Caribbean. The whole household goes to all the church services; church meetings take place at home; parishioners visit the minister at home. At the same time, the younger generation's social contacts are restricted to the home by household rules which are based on the church's moral code. This does not strictly apply to the work acquaintances of Alice and Mary, because their work is in a different domain, but it limits their scope to working hours. Their home and work networks are entirely separate.

Members of the family living elsewhere in London visit the household from time to time, but they do not appear to play an important role in its general livelihood. Matthew has a brother and a sister living in Clapham whom he sees 'maybe every month' and Joyce is 'quite close' to a niece living in another part of London. Both have a few cousins living 'around England' and many living in Jamaica – Matthew puts the

---

[1] 'Outsiders' are not defined by ethnic or local criteria, but in relation to church membership and religious observance: on this basis blacks who do not conform to Pentecostal conventions are no more 'inside' than ordinary whites.

figure in the hundreds! Joyce also has four brothers in Jamaica, and Matthew has a brother and a sister there, and another sister living in Boston, USA. Matthew and Joyce 'keep up a correspondence' with all their brothers and sisters. Both sets of parents are dead.

The three children who live away from home get the occasional visit from Joyce alone, but see everybody at the house when they come every month.[1] Two of them fall into the category of people that Matthew finds difficult to get on with (they are entered in the lower triangle of the diagram, along with certain members of the church from which he split off).

The household's most constant and significant relationship is with Matthew's congregation, numbering forty people, about twenty of whom are children. The other big group is made up of Keith and Thelma's school friends, numbering around ten, who visit the house regularly. Matthew's (and to a lesser extent Joyce's) casual acquaintances consist of another hundred or so church members from other churches, local community workers (around thirty), past business contacts, and people from local social security and medical services. In Jamaica he also has 'hundreds' of friends from past church congregations apart from relatives mentioned earlier. Of all the groups mentioned, the only one that Matthew wants to distance himself from is that of past business contacts; and the one he wishes to enlarge is that of his own congregation. It is from this group that he derives his status, his identity, and ideally, his livelihood. Any other family interests are over-shadowed by the church, yet the household is 'wholeheartedly' involved in it. The dominance of church activities gives cohesion to the household and largely determines the organi-zation of time. The centre of activity shifts from home to church and back to home but is irrevocably fixed in either one or the other. By contrast, local contacts in the LARA area have little significance.

---

[1] These visits are scheduled in advance; Joyce's visits to them on the contrary, happen when she has time, or is 'worried for them'.

6 Two second family households

The Rapiers and the Kellys are couples of similar age, and each has two young children at home. Both partnerships are second marriages for the women, and both Edith Rapier and Alice Kelly also have adult or near adult children who are the product of their first marriages. None of these children has ever lived as part of the second family unit. At this stage they are dispersed at different addresses but mostly within the south London area, geographically quite close to their mothers' homes.

The marital history of the two women is also remarkably similar: both were first married very young and had a child by the time they were nineteen, and each left the marriage to escape their husbands' violent abuse. [So did Cynthia Abraham and Olive Charles (Chapter 4). Domestic violence was not one of our selection criteria (see Chapter 3), and is not a feature of any of the present cases; but the fact that the women of four out of eight 'ordinary' households suffered it, implies an appalling frequency of the experience.] Both women describe their second husbands as dependable, quiet, not very sociable – all characteristics that appear to stand in contrast to the first partners, and to counterbalance the two women's extrovert personalities.

A census enumeration would record two points of difference between the households: the Rapiers live at the same address as Bruce Rapier's father so the household unit would be counted as an extended family of five against the Kellys' nuclear four; and Brian Kelly shows up as foreign born because he comes from Eire. Neither of these features has the significance one might expect. The younger Rapiers have such limited contact with the elder that he is no more than peripheral to the household system. He does share in (indeed he owns) the household's housing resources, but the three generations only rarely 'eat from a common pot', spend little *time* together and do not seem to *identify* with the same people or the same pursuits. Brian Kelly's ethnic origin is not a distinguishing mark of his household and has no apparent effect on its livelihood overall. This a-ethnic stance is a consistent characteristic of Battersea residents, and it may be that Brian would more often identify himself and be identified as an Irishman if he lived somewhere else (see Chapter 1). Here, however, the Kellys are no less 'local' than the Battersea-born Rapiers.

The most profound difference between these two second family households is in the extent of their involvement with the two women's first families, and in the sheer numbers of kin incorporated in each household system. The Rapier household barely includes its co-resident father/father-in-law, and although Edith sees her grown-up daughters regularly, she identifies more strongly with neighbourhood interests and local people and participates more keenly in community activities than in her first family's affairs. The Kelly household by contrast is crowded with Alice's 'big' children every day. They organize their cooking, washing, and shopping in common, look after each other's children, and spend every important or ritual occasion together. Although they live in different houses, many of their *time, information,* and *identity* resources are pooled in a single household system, and Alice acts as resource-keeper for the whole lot.

Corollary to this, the core Rapier and Kelly households differ in the extent of their commitments to the LARA area: the Rapiers would never think of leaving it; the Kellys sometimes talk of moving 'somewhere better' on the grounds that the street they now live in is 'unfriendly'. It is true that Bruce Rapier was born in the area and Brian Kelly comes from Eire so the two men might well have different feelings about the neighbourhood, but it is their south London-born wives who decide the social scope of the two households. Through Alice, the Kelly household's most important connections are independent of its geographic location; wherever it was it would remain the focus of a large number of her kin. The Rapiers' most important connections were established by locality in the first place, and, because ties of locality are not as transferable as ties of kinship, depend more obviously on the household continuing to live where it is.

The Rapiers

The Rapiers have lived in Battersea practically all their lives. Bruce Rapier was born in the LARA area itself, in fact in the very house where he now lives. Except for a short time in his childhood when he lived with his parents in his father's original home in north London, he has spent all his thirty-eight years within the range of these few streets. His wife Edie ('my real name is Edith'), is his elder by a couple of years. She too was born in Battersea, and although she has been married before and has moved house several times in her life, she has never left the area. The Rapiers live in the house with their two children, a girl of 11 and a boy of 4, and with Bruce's 74-year-old father who owns it. The old man occupies only one room upstairs and lives virtually separately from the family. He comes down regularly one evening a week to watch television with the rest, and is visited by them regularly once a week in his room.[1]

Edie's first marriage was 'terrible'. She still has nightmares about her first husband. When things became unbearable with him she took their two little girls and moved out to live with her 'nan'.[2] For months Edie's nan looked after her great-grandchildren so that Edie could continue working. She met Bruce in that period, but the husband still would not give her a divorce; her and Bruce's first child was born before they were free to get married.

[1] They are one family but arguably two households under one roof.
[2] 'Nan' = working-class London term for grandmother, most commonly the mother's mother, used talking to her or about her.

The daughters of the previous marriage are now grown up and living away but they make sure they see Edie regularly, either at her home or theirs. The unmarried one lives locally; the one who is married with two small children lives in the East End. Although she sees them a lot, Edie looks after her two grandchildren very little, 'but not for any special reason'.

She does however look after two local 'coloured' children along with her own every day after school. Edie met both mothers at the LARA community centre where she works part-time in the nursery. Most of her social life stems from here. She is keen to work, but only within school hours; she wants to be at home when her children are there so they have 'a better time' than the older ones did. Childminding at home does not keep her away from her children[1] – although one of them 'isn't particularly keen on it'.[2] She is paid for looking after the two children until around 6 o'clock; she did not ask for the money, 'it was offered'. Edie is also a parent-manager at the local primary school and has been instrumental in getting the first West Indian parent-manager elected. It is 'such a mixed-race school' she thinks all groups should be involved.

Edie left school at fifteen without qualifications; Bruce stayed on until sixteen to get his O levels. Bruce's father left school at fourteen and later took an engineering course in the evenings; afterwards he worked as a dairy-produce store-keeper and is now retired. Bruce himself is a clerk in a building society. He is not involved in the community activities – he leaves that to Edie. He is a very quiet and seemingly passive man; while Edie is outgoing and increasingly gaining confidence in herself through the encouragement of her aunt[3] and her involvement in community life.

Most of the activities in the house go on in the one front room: watching television, washing the children, eating meals, hobbies, visiting, etc. Generally a warm, affectionate, and relaxed atmosphere prevails.

[1] This non-economic appeal of homework or outwork must account for women's apparent willingness to be underpaid or not paid to do it.
[2] The child gets on badly with one of the two visitors.
[3] This woman is in fact Bruce's aunt. It is as though the closeness of the relationship converts her from an in-law into a kinswoman.

JOBS

Bruce Rapier is still in his second job since leaving school at the age of sixteen. Edith Rapier worked in her girlhood in a factory and now works as a volunteer in the local community nursery.

Bruce's first job was as a sales assistant for Philips Electrical Company. He found the job through the Youth Employment Bureau, straight after leaving school in September 1956. He worked for this firm (based in the West End) for eight and a half years, only leaving to get a better paid job. He remembers precisely the date when he changed jobs: 28 February 1965. His second and present job is working as a clerical assistant for a large building society. He has no plans to leave as he enjoys it and gets on well with his colleagues. He has worked there now for fourteen years and intends to stay until retirement – he is already looking forward to that! He got this job through an advertisement in the Evening News.[1] He did not get married for some years after changing jobs but those years coincided with a crisis in Edie's life and the start of his relationship with her.

Edie's first job was several years after she left school, since she married for the first time when she was very young and had her first child when she was nineteen. Her second child was born two years later. When it was only a few months old and the marriage had broken down altogether, Edie took a job as a packer in a Battersea biscuit factory while her nan took care of her children. Her nan's neighbour found the job for her and she was very happy there, enjoying the social life with the other girls. She worked there for eight years, until 1967.

All this time she was trying without success to get a divorce from her husband and worse, he took the children to live with him. However by 1965 she had met Bruce and he helped her through this time of crisis. In 1968 they had a child, and finally managed to marry in 1971. In 1973 their second child was born and Edie only started work again in 1978 on a part-time basis. She was on the LARA committee and got the job through

[1] Both of Bruce's jobs he heard about through formal and impersonal information sources.

another committee member, although she had to be voted in by other local inhabitants.[1] She would like eventually to get a job in the primary school where she is a parent-manager, possibly with some training first. Again she says she wants a job this time that leaves her free outside school hours to be with her children.[2] Anyway, 'I've seen too much of that latchkey business round at the community centre'. There are some problems in her personal relationships with fulltime members of staff, but she is not often concerned. Generally, Edie sees herself becoming 'more aggressive' over the years. She stands up for herself in her job; Bruce does not, she says, 'He's just a misery!'[3]

Bruce's job at the moment means a lot of travelling, as he has to travel to the south coast daily from Clapham Junction, but he does not mind; it is a temporary situation while he is on 'relief'. He says the hours are not flexible but there is no trouble if he is late. He works with four other people, but his particular job, that of assessing mortgage applications, involves him dealing with the public most of the time, which he enjoys. He has only the manager above him, so he does not feel much pressure in his work. He says there is a very good atmosphere at work and he enjoys it. A good day for him is one where he solves problems. The one thing that irritates him is ignorant customers![4] He has friendly relationships with his colleagues, he is even 'concerned about them' but he does not socialize with them outside office hours. At work he belongs to a staff association run by the building society as a whole, but does not feel it to be very effective. Bruce generally accepts things the way they are: the house they live in, the job he does for a living, and the way his family life is structured. He is without ambition in his job, enjoying the type of job he has but looking forward simply to the day when he can stop going

[1] In contrast to her husband, Edie has found all her jobs through local and personal connections.
[2] i.e. with this batch of children. She had little time with the daughters of her first marriage when they were small.
[3] This is affectionately said. It implies that Bruce is over-serious, earnest perhaps, not that he is unlikeable. It is commonly used in London with this meaning.
[4] 'Ignorant' can also mean badly behaved. It is not clear what he intends here.

there. Any push for change comes from Edie. She does not see herself as 'working' at the present time, 'Housework isn't work!' Her other jobs are work, but not 'proper' work.[1] She, having had factory work experience (in the 'formal' sphere), now involves herself very actively in community organization: in the nursery (some of it paid), running jumble sales, minding children on a regular basis (also paid, although she did not really expect it), and serving as a parent-manager. But Edie has definite plans for the future: she will get some training to be able to work as an auxiliary helper in the primary school.

Bruce's hobbies – gardening, rug making, and doing jig-saw puzzles – seem likely to occupy his interest increasingly, along with bringing up his children jointly with his wife. Edie however, is keen to expand and consolidate the working sphere of her life, always, of course, keeping up the level of input into the home and children that she has at the moment.

TIME

Bruce and Edie organize their time very consistently. Weekends always follow the same pattern in terms of visits and tasks, and weekdays, although for Edie somewhat more variable, have a strong similarity to each other. The allocation of tasks in the family is divided basically between Bruce and Edie. Their little girl helps with some household tasks such as cooking, but is still considered too young to do much, and their son is discouraged altogether from cooking for the same reason. Bruce's father lives separately from the family, washing 'his own bits' and preparing his own food. He occasionally helps out by cooking the evening meal when Edie is too tired or is working. The household owns a hoover, spin dryer, fridge/freezer, sewing machine, and hand and electric tools. They also have a washing machine, but it is not working. They have no car.

[1] Housework is widely undervalued (Oakley 1974). Since it is not defined as work its economic value tends to be invisible, even hidden (Wadel 1979). Similarly Edie dismisses the part-time work she does in the 'informal' economy. It is not 'proper' work. She does not identify herself by it nor does she give herself credit for doing it.

Bruce and Edie co-operate in running the home, but they do not appear to *share* tasks. The main meal washing up, for example, seems to be done entirely by *Bruce* both in the week and at weekends (taking him about $3\frac{1}{2}$ hours a week.) Edie does most of the cooking since she makes the evening meal for the family and lunch for herself and her daughter. She says she spends very little time on cooking (around $2\frac{1}{2}$ hours a week). Bruce cooks lunch on Saturdays. What they do share is the care of the children, at least during the hours that Bruce is at home. (He never goes out in the evenings.) Playing with the children, talking to them, and reprimanding them, joking or watching television together – these 'tasks' they share 'equally'. During the week, Bruce gets up first, has a quick breakfast with the family and leaves for work at 8.15 a.m.; he does not arrive there until 9.45. (Bruce spends about 15 hours in the train each week.) Edie then takes the children to school and shops at the local shops, mainly the local grocer. (She shops daily and spends 5–6 hours weekly on this.) She then either washes clothes (by hand, taking about 5 hours a week) or cleans the house. She has lunch with her daughter when she comes back from school, and then continues the housework, hoovering, tidying up, and doing the beds. (Edie does not call this work, but it adds up to 22 hours per week!) At 3.30 p.m. she fetches her own children along with the two that she 'minds'. The children then watch television or play in the street. When the two charges have been fetched by their mothers, Edie cooks dinner which they eat as soon as Bruce gets in at about 6.30. If her next-door-neighbour, Jane, is away, Edie now goes round to feed Jane's cat. Bruce then washes up and everyone watches television together, unless Edie is due at a community centre meeting. (The children watch up to 3 hours of television daily, Bruce and Edie a good deal more.) Alternatively the children play until their bedtime at 9 o'clock, while their parents knit, sew, or do other hobbies until they go to bed at around 11 p.m.

Every Saturday all four of them go shopping at 9 o'clock. When they get home at 10 a.m., they go straight upstairs to Bruce's dad's room and spend three-quarters of an hour having 'a cup of tea and a chat' with him. When they go back downstairs the children again watch television, Bruce pays bills and washes up the breakfast dishes, while Edie goes to visit Bruce's aunt in Wandsworth, with whom she is very close, until lunchtime. Bruce cooks and washes up the lunch dishes. On Saturday afternoons they all go to visit Edie's father and mother, who live north of the Thames, about half an hour's drive from LARA. This visit lasts through into the evening. While the two men play darts, Edie and her son help or entertain his nan: Edie washes up for her and the little boy reads aloud. His sister entertains herself. When they get home, Bruce's father makes his weekly visit downstairs to watch 'Match of the Day' with the rest of the family until bedtime.

Although Bruce does certain tasks around the house, he is defined (only) as the breadwinner, responsible for paying all the bills, and Edie is the housekeeper. Neither the hours she puts in at home, nor those at the community centre are really considered to be work. The money that Edie earns is used only to supplement the housekeeping money or to buy clothes, which are seen as an extra.[1]

As a couple, the time they have together is predominantly that spent with the children, watching television, following their hobbies, or visiting their relatives. The main focus of their life could be said to be their children, for although Edie has interests and friends outside the home, they do not have any activity in common apart from this.

PEOPLE

The Rapiers filled in their network diagram with unusual precision; most people were given their full name and relation to the family unit, and the size of all groups was indicated. In terms of numbers the 'map' is weighted on the side of kinship, but as regards 'closeness' or intensity of interaction the picture is different. Edie's acquaintances outside the family and inside the community are numerous, and important to her, and Bruce is distant or estranged from most of his kin.

Although his father lives upstairs, Bruce says he sees him

---

[1] The man's work in the domestic sphere tends to be undervalued or invisible, just as is the woman's work outside the home.

only once a week. When Bruce's brother comes to see the
father once in a while, both Bruce and Edie avoid him. (He is
unhesitatingly placed on the diagram in the triangle for
ambiguous or difficult relationships.) When Edie goes to see
Bruce's aunt, Bruce never goes with her her. Edie is very fond of
her; she also got on very well with his uncle before he died – he
used to sing to her, she says. Bruce's father himself is very
isolated; he has few visitors and hardly ever goes out. Edie
says, 'Bruce's dad won't go anywhere', although he does spend
Christmas Day with one son and Boxing Day with another;
'Mind you,[1] he spent this Christmas with his daughter.'

Bruce visits Edie's family every weekend and speaks well of
them.[2] He also has a sense of being close to some of his
workmates. During the period of the interviews a young
colleague at work died and he grieved for days. Bruce seems
also to value the day-to-day contact he has with the general
public in the course of his work. It is in the sphere of work
where he feels he exercises his sense of judgement.[3]

Edie, although she values contact with her family a lot, has
not found that her own eldest daughter has turned to her for
help with her grandchildren. But in that time of crisis when she
left her husband, Edie did not turn to *her* mother either; it was
her grandmother who took her and her daughters in. Anyway
she is not 'all that close' to her daughters now. After all they
lived away from her and with their father for part of their
childhood. Edie talks most about the younger of the two and
spends most time with her. She does not yet have children.
Sometimes she asks advice about handling her bloke.[4]

Bruce and Edie themselves, in times of present crisis, depend
first on their neighbours, Angus and Sue, for help; or on
another neighbour who is also a friend from the LARA
management committee. For example, when the Rapiers' little
boy was in hospital, Sue took over the running of the Rapier

[1] 'Mind you' = but on the other hand, however, even so.
[2] It is as though they each feel closer to their in-laws than to their own kin.
[3] In the observer's view he is quite a different person in each sphere.
[4] 'Bloke' = man. But used in the possessive – 'my bloke', 'her bloke', etc. –
refers to a steady sexual partner. Sometimes a husband in the legal sense, but
not here.

household so that Edie could spend maximum time with her son; and when Bruce once fell ill in the middle of the night, it was Angus who drove him to hospital. Edie has a key to Angus and Sue's house and counts on making telephone calls from there, since the Rapiers have no phone of their own. In exchange, Edie looked after Sue's baby for a whole year while Sue was working and sometimes takes in washing for her even now.[1]

Edie has very friendly relations with the local shopkeepers, particularly with the grocer just across the main road which borders the LARA area. She does not mind that it costs a little more to shop there because she likes the fact that she can share a joke and get a bit of special attention. She gets given free biscuits, saved bread, or sugar in times of shortages and, most important, goods on credit. She has been going to the same shop for twelve years and has no intention of changing. At Christmas the grocer always gives her presents for both her children and she might even give him one back.[2] He sometimes jokes that her kids are his!

Edie is very much involved in the running of the LARA community centre. She is a member of the committee and a nursery helper. Even so she is very critical of it. She says that there is a power struggle going on, 'a lot of bickering',[3] a tense atmosphere, and 'no-one helps me from the nursery' (saving of course, the second neighbour, who is also on the committee and does help her out in a neighbourly way).[4] Edie thinks the committee is run 'undemocratically', that the chairman does not share information with all the members and puts everyone's back up. She is in the process of forming a support group for the nursery consisting of two parents, two helpers, and two

---

[1] The exchange is not symmetrical at this level: Sue might look after Edie's baby but would probably not offer or be asked to do her washing. Some tasks remain class specific and the two women are of different class background.
[2] The fact that she even considers reciprocating makes this more than a narrow customer–shopkeeper relationship.
[3] 'Bickering' = petty argument.
[4] i.e. she is not seen as a committee member when helping, only as a helpful neighbour.

people from outside the nursery. They want to 'shake up'[1] the place and work out what activities they could develop.

The same keenness shows in her participation in community activities of all sorts. Edie has made innovations in her term as a school governor – she instigated the election of the first West Indian parent-governor – and in many situations she supports others and puts her energy into bringing about change. She looks after other people's children and helps to organize communal events. In all this her kin are of only minimal support — social more than anything else. For example, her sister visits her occasionally, bringing Edie's teenage niece along. Edie says the girl 'doesn't do anything indoors'[2] for her own mother but 'she will give me a bit of help when she's here'. Edie's emotional support comes from the members of her small household. She gets practical support and access to certain superior resources, such as transport and a telephone, from her neighbours, and her father-in-law will cook the occasional meal. Support of a different kind, but no less essential, is given by friendly local shopkeepers in the form of credit and other favours.

Bruce being a solid husband and a stable father to her children, gives her the support she needs to go out into the world and play an active role. He, for his part, finds his greatest social satisfactions at work. At other times he is content to stay at home and experience local life vicariously through his wife. Although it is probably true to say that the wider family network provides an anchor of stability to both of them, in terms of day-to-day interaction and the ordinary business of livelihood it is not the principal source of support. As a household they are thoroughly integrated into the local system, and the integrating force is Edie herself.

[1] 'Shake up' = make drastic changes.
[2] 'Indoors' = in her own home, at home.

The Kellys

According to the survey, the members of this household are Brian Kelly, an Irish-born man, aged 42, his English-born wife, Alice, the same age, an 8-year-old son, and a 5-year-old daughter, both born in London.[1] The son has a slight physical disability which leads neighbours to identify him as the family's 'problem'. But in a more complex picture of the household, and one drawn from inside rather than outside, the child's stigma is not a central issue.[2]

Alice has been married before and had given birth to nine children before her marriage broke down. After fourteen years of conjugal life, family problems including the violence of her husband, led her first to a mental hospital and then to a friend's house.[3] She never made any conscious decision to leave her family and start a new life. Events and emotions just built up until she realized she could neither go back nor take care of her children. No one actually accuses her of having abandoned her children, but the guilt of it still haunts her. The fact that some of these children have lately shown her recognition, love, and affection has been a source of immense happiness.

However the existence of two families in close proximity (all in riverside south London) is not entirely without

[1] In this case the difference between the census-defined household and the complete household system is unusually marked.
[2] The categorical definition 'family with a handicapped child' does not take account of the many other features by which the family identifies itself.
[3] Alice does not talk of looking for help or support in all those years. She 'just soldiered on' until she broke down altogether and had to be hospitalized.

problems. Brian dislikes the frequent and lengthy visits of 'relations' he is not particularly close to, and keeps out of such family gatherings. Alice often feels pulled apart by her two families, and tries hard to keep a balance between the two. So, for example, against her own wish to keep her daughter Esther and Esther's two babies for the night, she asks her to leave so that Brian will not be disturbed. He is quiet, she says, and a bit withdrawn; he would not necessarily even show he was upset. Compromises and considerations like these underline Alice's special position in the extended family group. In the small Kelly household she is the main resource-keeper, manager, and spokesperson. Consequently she played the main role in our interviews.

Family, close relatives, and two friends are the most important people in Alice's life. To escape from loneliness, sadness, problems, and herself, she calls on her daughters, her friend Sheila, her uncle Jack, or her mother. Furthermore to make work less boring, she is looking for a firm that will 'take on' both her and Sheila.[1]

Alice does most of the routine housework with those of her daughters who live locally; they bring their washing once a week so that everything is put in the washing machine together. Mother and daughters go to the market together so that large quantities of food can be bought at low price and shared out.[2] Alice is very seldom alone in the street. If she is not pushing a pram with a grandson or a push-chair with her own youngest girl, she is giggling with her friend Sheila on the way to the job centre. At home, at the risk of annoying her husband, there are always some members of her first family, their boyfriends, their kids. Alice herself grew up surrounded by relatives; apart from her parents and brothers and sisters, her uncle Jack and his wife and child lived in the same house, and her mother's parents lived in the house next door. As long as the maternal grandparents were still alive the whole family gathered regularly and kept in very close touch. From the time

---

[1] 'Take on' = hire. Apparently the kind of job and the conditions of work are secondary considerations in the search.
[2] All this takes careful organization and is supervised by Alice herself.

they died Alice felt 'the family' drifting apart.[1] But recently everybody seems to need and want a reunion, and this pleases her a lot.

Cuddled by grannies, aunts and uncles, as well as her own mother and father, and especially loved by her uncle Jack who was the one she could go to when punished by the others, Alice is providing today the same care and affection for her own children and grandchildren. Kids in general are always mentioned in conversation as 'lovely children'. They do not appear as a burden or an obstacle to anything anyone wants to do. Even going out in the evening is not a problem: even the youngest ones accompany their mothers to the disco.

JOBS

Alice took up her present job when Brian became unemployed and she felt it was her duty to contribute to the household income. She considered the employment temporary and saw no interest in it other than the money it brought in. Since she had no school qualifications but had done 'the odd job' before, she went to the local job centre and asked only for 'a job'. She was offered a fulltime post as a canteen worker in a local Metropolitan Police Station.[2] She accepted it and was given a few weeks' training in what she considered she already knew only too well – washing up, preparing sandwiches, serving food, etc. The working hours were too long and inconvenient for her. She left home at 6 a.m. so her husband or one of her elder daughters had to prepare the children for school; and although she was back in time to collect them from school, she was 'too tired to be much use to anybody'. Nevertheless, working at the police canteen 'wasn't a bad job; all the girls – we were three white and five coloured – were friendly, the

[1] 'The family' extends to 'everybody' who is related in any way. It includes all the kin she grew up with as well as her husband(s) and children. Alice never uses the term to refer to the Kelly household specifically (compare p. 129, n. 1).

[2] The Metropolitan is the London police force. Policemen and women are assigned to particular local areas for long periods of time. Alice therefore knows the members of the station well enough to make the job sociable.

place was nice.' The boss lady did not allow them to eat or drink anything without paying and was very strict with the employees, but Alice was not unhappy. When Brian eventually found a job and there was no real need for her to work, she chose to keep a part-time job in the same place. Even now she is not seriously thinking about changing but 'it would be more fun' if she and her friend Sheila were employed together.

She did not remember or did not want to talk about previous jobs; they were all temporary, unimportant, and simply a means of making a bit of extra money. She is always happier at home with the children and Brian's employment is much more important for the family's income, but he never talks to her about work. She only knows about it when there is a problem – like him being laid off,[1] or the possibility of redundancy.[2] She does not worry about him too much. He is very skilled, serious, and capable. He will always get a job.

TIME

Alice now has a half-day job, her husband Brian works fulltime, and both children are at school. Alice's day starts at 6 a.m. when she gets up, prepares breakfast, and packs lunch for Brian. The couple have breakfast together and then Brian goes to work. At 8 a.m. she wakes up the children, gives them breakfast, waits for the school bus to take her son off to his special school, then walks her daughter to school nearby.

At 9.30 she leaves home again for the police canteen where together with the other employees she prepares the food, serves lunch, and washes up.[3] She picks up her little girl from school and they are back home by 3.30 when the school bus brings her little boy back. Around that time, Alice's older daughters come in with their babies and boyfriends; the house

---

[1] See p. 91, n. 1.
[2] See p. 113, n. 1.
[3] 'To wash up' = to wash the dishes – plates, cutlery, saucepans, etc. (i.e. the washing up) after a meal.

is full of children until Brian gets back and the tea[1] is ready at around 5.30. Then the daughters and friends leave and Alice and Brian and their two children have tea and watch TV together. After tea Alice washes up and puts the children to bed. She and Brian go to bed not much later, at around 9.30.

The weekend is different. It is also spent with the family but there is more time for everybody to be together. Alice's big daughters with their families and friends are in the house for most of the time. Brian remains in the background, listening to music by himself – he has a record player in the upstairs front room which is kept specially clean and tidy for him; or fixing the house; he has quite a few tools, such as an electric drill and sander, saw, hammer, screwdrivers, etc. and does a lot of decorating and small building works in the house.

On Saturday, Alice and the whole family, that is *all* her children, go to the market in Clapham Junction where they buy in bulk and share out. This keeps the cost down for everybody. When they come back they all help with the housework. In the home there is a vacuum cleaner, electric iron, washing machine, and spin dryer. Alice's daughters bring their own washing and ironing and everything is done communally.[2] They prepare tea for everybody and after that all of them, including the children and grandchildren, (but usually excluding Brian) go to a London Transport disco somewhere in south London.[3] They meet friends there, dance, enjoy the music, the jokes, raffles, and 'all the fun of the fair' until about midnight when they go back home. Sundays are more restful; sometimes Alice goes to the pub with her husband, where they meet his friends. She says, 'They never understand how me and Brian can be married to each other.

---

[1] 'Tea' in this usage is the evening meal whether only bread and tea or a cooked dish is taken. The equivalent meal is called supper in middle-class households, although even there children might be given 'tea' as a meal when they come home from school. 'Tea' for the middle and upper classes otherwise is a light snack taken at 4 o'clock.

[2] In all these activities however, Alice is the central figure, the resource manager for them all.

[3] Presumably one of the family works for London Transport and so has access to discos organized by and for their employees. They would not normally be open to the public.

We're so different. He's so quiet and I'm always excited. I like a lot of people around, and a bit of noise!'

PEOPLE

In the interviews with Alice, the main topic was her family; her parents, grandparents, uncles, aunts, sisters, and her own children were always mentioned with love and affection. She has no qualms about a Christmas gathering of the whole family. In particular, she never speaks of children as requiring hard work or being too much responsibility.

From her first marriage Alice has two sons and seven daughters, with ages ranging from 12 to 24. She seems to get on better with the girls, especially those who have children of their own.[1] One is 18, and has been married for a year. She has a baby boy, and is expecting another baby shortly. Another is 19 years old and lives with her boyfriend. She too is pregnant. The eldest is 24; she has been separated from her husband and works as a housekeeper. The second eldest daughter is 22 and still lives with her father, but has plans to leave home and get married soon. The three younger girls – aged 17, 16, and 12 – are also living with their father. So is the younger boy, now 14 years old. The other boy is 21 and married but he remains 'rather distant'.

The two girls mentioned first live locally, within the LARA area; they spend a lot of time at their mother's house and help with her younger children. Their partners are also welcomed there, particularly the steady boyfriend of the unmarried one; he himself comes from a family of eleven children. The eldest daughter lives in Kent,[2] but visits her mother every fortnight; 'she is the first and the closest'.

But even those who are still living with their father are slowly getting close to Alice again. The one who is arranging to marry has asked her to get involved in the wedding prepara-

[1] Apart from the extra bond of the grandchildren, it may be significant that the daughters who have children no longer live with their father.
[2] A county outside London to the south-east but within commuting distance for some.

tions; in the past she would only visit her mother very occasionally. Alice sees the rest of the children when they choose to visit her. She is very pleased to see them 'whenever'[1] and to know they want to see her too, but she will not force herself on them.

Alice's own mother lives in Dorset. Some time ago she started working in a big hotel there, liked the place and stayed. 'She's had a tough time . . . separated from my dad with six children to support.' Alice is the eldest, then come three brothers and two sisters. Her 'baby sister' is her favourite; she used to live with her husband and two children in the same house as Alice in LARA but she chose to be rehoused by the Council outside the area[2] and Alice does not see her that often since she moved. The other sister lives out of London, Alice does not remember the name of the place; they have not met for three years. But she is expecting to see her at the upcoming wedding.[3]

Of her brothers, one is in Australia but has kept in touch with the family, and one lives just outside London but has cut himself off from them.[4] Alice went to his wedding and was the only one of his relations there. Not long ago he wrote to invite her to his house and she was very pleased. The third brother, the youngest, has always been the 'naughty one'. When Alice sees him they always end up arguing and fighting. He once beat her up so Brian does not let her see him any more.[5]

Alice's father lived in south London after his divorce, and he used to visit her very frequently. Then he remarried. Alice thinks his new wife does not want him to see his sons and daughters. They lost contact when both families moved to new addresses and 'she wouldn't know where to look for him now'.

---

[1] 'Whenever' used by itself like this implies anytime; whenever they like.
[2] People entitled to public housing have some amount of choice in the matter of where and what that housing should be, especially if they are good 'normal' English families (see Flett 1979).
[3] The wedding of Alice's 22-year-old daughter.
[4] The contrast between the geographic and the affective closeness of Alice's two brothers shows up very plainly on the network diagrams and justifies taking both meanings of 'close' into account.
[5] Alice says this with some pride. Brian is not only non-violent, in contrast to her first husband, he also protects Alice from the violence of others.

The uncles and aunts on her mother's side also used to be close to Alice but since her grandparents died, she has only seen them at weddings and funerals.[1] The one exception is uncle Jack who shared the house with Alice's parents when she was growing up. He has only one son. He has always loved Alice a lot and always been her favourite uncle; now she still feels just the same when they are together. When she was in hospital having an operation and felt lonely and miserable, it was uncle Jack she phoned. Another time when he went to see her in the maternity hospital after the birth of one of her children, the nurses had mistaken him for her husband, so close were they together.

In contrast to all this, 'Brian doesn't seem to have a feeling for family'.[2] Alice is amazed that he has not seen his mother, who lives in Dublin, for many years and that he does not seem to worry about it. He has been away from Dublin for twenty years himself.

Apart from family, people Alice has met, but 'wouldn't call friends' are mentioned occasionally in conversation; women she has met in maternity hospitals, neighbours, people at work. Only two friends, Sheila and Joy, are close to her. They take part in the family outings and often visit her house. Alice has been in touch with the social services, the housing department, and the job centre on various occasions and does not seem to have any difficulty relating to officials or claiming her rights. At the time of the interview it was the International Year of the Child and she was hoping to get a free holiday for her children from the local social services. She is confident in her dealings with them. She has already managed to get into council accommodation through the HAA allocation scheme,

[1] Grandparents are often the kin-keepers for their grandchildren; when they die the family constellation is likely to change. The description of contact 'only at weddings and funerals' here means little or no contact. It is a way of saying they are still related.
[2] Family is used here again in the widest and most general sense. Clearly Alice is aware that Brian has a feeling for his wife and his own children.

and to move again a few months later when a better house was available.

NEIGHBOURHOOD

Alice has been living with Brian and their two children in the LARA neighbourhood for about ten years. They moved from one road to another, and then back to the first. She seems to know 'everybody' in the area. She shops locally, sends her kids to the local school, and occasionally uses the LARA centre for various social activities. On top of that, her cheerful and talkative personality give her ample opportunity to meet everyone. Nevertheless she sees no particular reason for staying in the area and would like to move out to 'somewhere nicer'. It is not easy for her to define what she means by that. She does not know much of London outside the south-west corner and has hardly ever been out of London itself. 'But somewhere nicer' would certainly be in Wandsworth,[1] and probably in a street with 'nicer' people.[2] Schools or other amenities were not taken into account.

But if this neighbourhood is not 'nice' enough, it is quite convenient; she shops regularly at the Clapham Junction market and shops, buys bits and pieces at the small grocery on St John's Hill, and for very special buys goes to the Arndale centre in Wandsworth. Alice has never gone to the West End for shopping;[3] she does not really need to go there for anything.

On the whole Alice seems to know the neighbourhood and the people living in it very well, and she knows how to benefit from the resources offered locally. She is aware of activities that take place at the community centre, and of the services

[1] Wandsworth is the large Inner London Borough of which (since 1965) Battersea forms a part. It is now the effective local government unit for the allocation of housing and other official resources. Battersea no longer has political status in this sense (see Chapter 1).
[2] Again the first level of local identity is with the street (Wallman *et al.* 1982: Chapter 5). It seems the ideal place would be the same but different, local but 'better'. In Alice's view the 'niceness' of people is not predictable on the basis of their colour or ethnic origin.
[3] The West End is the fashion, theatre, and tourist centre of London.

offered by the Council. She is a member of LARA and reads the *Echo*.[1] She was one of the first street representatives for LARA, but has kept out of the association over the last few years.[2] She does not participate in organizing any of the social activities and uses the centre as she would use any other place; she sometimes goes to the disco evenings, but usually prefers to go elsewhere.

CRISIS

The greatest crisis in Alice's life so far has been the break-up of her first marriage and the separation from her home, husband, and children that it caused. Alice does not talk about the details of the situation but says she stayed with friends for a while. These friends do not appear on the network diagram – maybe because it is seven or eight years ago and a lot has happened since. But it is surprising that Alice did not 'turn to her relations' for help since she categorically filled in the inner and most supportive circle of the network chart with kin. Of course, some members of her family may have been away from London at that time, but the majority of them have never left south London. It is not that she did not seek her family's assistance for practical reasons: she did have a choice, however limited, in the resources available to her at the time of that crisis. It is as though she preferred not to go to her close relatives in the terrible state she was in. Alice is normally an extrovert, cheerful, chatty, easy-going person; this is how she likes herself and how she likes other people to see her. Specifically she sees herself as the central focus and support of the widely extended family. She organizes weddings, offers her house as a meeting place for all her relatives, enjoys inviting and entertaining them there. This one-sided pattern seems to have made it impossible for her to ask them for help when she was desperate for it.[3]

[1] The Residents' Association's monthly newsletter.
[2] Alice is one of a number of people who were involved in the founding of LARA and the battle for a HAA but have pulled away since (see Olive Charles, p. 105).
[3] It may also be that the family was too close, too much involved. When finally Alice just could not cope she surrendered herself to the impersonal hands of the health service and went into hospital.

7 Two typical English households

The Bateses and the Masons are both young English families who have spent all their lives in south London. The two families must at least know each other by sight because they live in the same set of streets and use the same local facilities, but neither appears on the other's network diagram or plays a part in the other's story. They are presented in parallel to highlight ways in which two households that are superficially so similar can yet be so different. They are the same in terms of south London ethnic origin, age, family size, household structure, income, class, and status. But as much as they match in structural position and material resources, by virtue of the organizing resources we have been talking about, they constitute quite different household systems. Three contrasts make the point.

First, both households have extensive close family connections in the south London area, but kin are a different kind of resource in each case. The Bateses' kin are friendly but not emotionally demanding: although they are sometimes the source of small emergency *money* or useful *information*, they are not much involved in the household system on a day-to-day basis. Pat Bates sometimes gets practical help with the children from her mother but is more comfortable depending on friends and neighbours for both material and emotional resources. The Masons by contrast are thoroughly kin oriented; their livelihood is dominated by close family members who come to the house for talk, comfort, or celebration and prevent them organizing everyday life or having time alone. They recognize that all these kin are in some ways a liability, but they would not or cannot refuse them the emotional support they expect. Anyway, they do get practical help from some of them in exchange: Eileen never needs to ask her friends to babysit. What is more she would not like having to depend on anyone outside the family for anything, and is wary of neighbours who might get too close or intrude too much. The two households' different involvement with their kin is reversed in their relation to the locality: both are locally active and sociable, but the Bateses have long and firm ties with the LARA neighbourhood and *identify* very closely with Battersea and 'Battersea people', while the Masons never talk in those terms and would readily leave Battersea for the sake of a better house and a bit of a garden – as long as it was in the south London area within which both their families live. [A similar complementarity of kinship and locality shows in aspects of the contrast drawn between the Rapiers and the Kellys at the beginning of Chapter 6.]

The second contrast is in the matter of style of livelihood: the Bateses' household is much more easy going than the Masons'. The Bateses too have a sense of family but do not accept the same burden of family responsibility; and they have more friends and consistently more *time* for friends than the Masons ever manage. The two men have similarly different attitudes to employment and unemployment: John Bates does not really mind being out of a job as long as there is money in the house; David Mason hates being on the dole, loves work, likes the idea of being self-employed. The Bateses take life as it comes; the Masons are always striving, defining, and solving problems, testing themselves against obstacles.

Finally, the two households manage *time* in very different ways, both at the level of day-to-day organization, and in their perspectives on the future. The Bateses are resolutely present oriented: they have a regular schedule of tasks, meals, visits, etc. and know roughly when events happened in the short-term past. Pat Bates is meticulous about paying bills when they come in, and manages to save small bits of money each week to cover a specific purchase or an occasion which she and John have agreed is to happen in the short-term future. But as much as they express a sense of control over present time, they neither plan for nor worry about the long-term future.

The Masons are quite the opposite in both respects. Their daily and weekly timetables are much more erratic: although David Mason knows exactly what time certain tasks have been or have to be done at his place of work and keeps to every deadline imposed by the job or his employer, no such control is achieved by the household at home; Eileen tends not to know what time it is now, or was when some remembered event took place, or will be when the washing will be finished, the meal ready, the children asleep; and together they have found it so difficult to save money from week to week that they no longer make any effort to do so: for something big they say they would borrow from kin or from the bank. Against the relative chaos of their day-to-day situation however, the Masons have sensible and clearly formulated plans for the future, and they are readier and more able than the Bateses to visualize how things might be and how they would like them to be in the longer term. In effect the Bateses look after the present and let the future take care of itself, and the Masons look forward to a time when their resources will be under better control.

The three features suit each other very neatly in both cases but as usual there is no simple cause and effect relation between them: they go together only as interconnected parts of each household system. The fact that one narrowly defined household type can accommodate two such different systems underlines the scope of the 'conditions of possibility' described in Chapter 2. And of these two typical households, who is to say which has the more typical livelihood?

The Bateses and the Masons

The Bates household unit includes John, aged 27, Pat, aged 25, and two children, aged 5 and 4. John and Pat Bates were both born and bred in Battersea. Pat is the younger of two children. Her parents have their own do-it-yourself business[1] and recently bought their own home in suburban south London. John is the youngest of thirteen children whose ages now range from 27 to 56. His father died eight years ago; his elderly mother lives locally. John and Pat met in their late teens. Pat was working at a steady secretarial job and John was moving through a series of casual jobs and spells on the dole. They married when Pat was 19 and John was 20, and lived with Pat's parents. Both their children were born while the couple shared the parental home.

David Mason is now 27 and Eileen a year younger. Each is the eldest child of a large family. They have two children aged 5 and 3. David and Eileen grew up off Wandsworth Road, Vauxhall. David's father works as a scrap dealer and his mother as an office cleaner; Eileen's mother is widowed, and Eileen did not mention her father's occupation. David and Eileen met at a disco, then found that Eileen was a friend of David's sister, and that they had friends in common. They went to a lot of dances together. When they decided to marry, both mothers planned a big wedding, which Eileen, very shy and nervous then, could not face. So once they had found somewhere to live, they eloped to Brixton. 'Nobody knew.'

---

[1] A 'do-it-yourself (DIY)' shop, sells the materials and rents or sells the tools needed by amateurs renovating or repairing their homes.

David was then 19, and Eileen 18. They had always planned to have two children and completed their family while they were in their early twenties.

How did these families come to be living in the LARA area? The Masons emphasize that they are not Battersea people. They moved to Battersea when a friend told them of a vacant flat in the area[1] (just round the corner from their present home) and they wanted a flat in order to start married life. Small and damp, the flat was an inadequate home for them once they had a child, and by the time Eileen was pregnant again, she felt she would have a nervous breakdown if she stayed there any longer. The couple had put their name on the council waiting list. They waited five years and got their flat in the end by pestering the council for a place. Meanwhile the HAA was declared, obliging the council to rehouse them in order to improve the house they lived in. Though they wanted a house rather than a flat, Eileen felt she could not face further delay: they accepted an upper storey maisonette. That was three years ago. They have since petitioned the council for a transfer to a house or to the downstairs maisonnette in their present house, which would give them the use of the garden, but without success. Buying a house looks like the answer. David is sure this is wise financially – people at work have convinced him of this – but he worries a bit about the financial commitment. While he reckons he could afford £16–£18 a week,[2] with prices the way they are in the suburban areas he favours (for example, Mitcham), he would probably have to pay at least £20–£24. They hope that a year from now their dream of buying a house will be a concrete project.

In their minds Battersea is just a staging post: 'We never planned to come here, you know', and for most purposes they do not identify with it, describing it as 'a pokey little hole' and professing still to feel more at home round Wandsworth Road. David goes back there to drink. While Eileen speaks more warmly of the neighbourhood than David and has more local

[1] In this way they were drawn into the area by the friend's involvement in the housing information network.
[2] Prices as at 1978.

contacts, through the children's school, the local shops, and the Residents' Association, she still sees it as a block to her aspirations, 'There are some people here who drag the area down. They could turn Buckingham Palace into a slum.' However hard she tries to keep the place clean, these people ensure that it is dirty; for example, people dump rubbish in the area in front of their house, and the council has refused to erect a fence to prevent this happening. The Masons see this as yet more proof that 'They don't do much for you, the HAA'.

Pat Bates on the contrary 'can't understand people who want to leave Battersea'. While John can understand it – 'It's a bit of a comedown after places like Putney'[1] – he shares her attachment to the area. They both grew up just a few streets away from their present home. John's childhood home was razed in a slum clearance scheme a few years ago, and his mother was moved to the nearby Winstanley estate. John speaks bitterly of the council devastation and the enforced emigration from the area.[2] His childhood friends 'have all moved away'. Battersea was a much friendlier place when everyone still lived in the old terraces, and it felt safer too. His mother never bothered to lock her door in the old house, but now she keeps her flat locked all the time; and John will not go on the housing estate without carrying a club 'because of all the attacks you know'. The Bateses' great dane acts as a guard dog for Pat and the children. John attributes rising crime locally to the non-Battersea people the council has brought in.[3]

Until they moved to this place, Pat had lived all her life in another house within the LARA area, as did her mother and her mother before her. John moved there on marriage. To help

---

[1] A neighbouring area, with a middle-class reputation.
[2] In the 1960s particularly, local government policy was directed by central government towards the compulsory purchase and demolition of older inner-city housing. Residents were moved out into new local government developments – often high rise flats.
[3] 'Outsiders' by any definition, are dangerous. True to the Battersea style, John makes no reference to the colour or ethnic origin of 'outsideness'.

the couple out, Pat's parents gave the tenancy of the flat over to them and bought themselves a flat in Surrey.[1] Pat did not realize until later what an enormous sacrifice this was and what a wrench for her mother to leave Battersea. They got their present house by mistake. The council needed to move them from the previous place so it could be rehabilitated and a housing official offered them the Harbut Road house. Housing department officials tried to retract the offer afterwards, saying they needed the house for a bigger family. But Pat's mother had been present when the offer was first made and she insisted that the council could not go back on its word. She claimed that she and Pat's father were also part of the household, and all together they qualified for a house. She won her point and John and Pat moved in with the two children. They knew they might face some ill-feeling but were unwilling to let go of their only chance to get a house locally.

If ties of kinship and long-residence bind them to the area, it is the house that keeps them there. Four years ago they almost moved to a GLC[2] expanded town, in order to get a house. Two of John's sisters and Pat's brother had moved via the GLC to houses and jobs outside London giving John and Pat a chance to judge this kind of move. John saw his brother-in-law with so little choice of employment that he was forced to take a factory job for low wages, while John's sister, working to make ends meet, rushed out to work as soon as her husband got home, so they scarcely saw each other. It did not seem much of a life. John did not fancy starting in a new place, and when Pat became pregnant again and imagined being at home with two babies in a place where she knew no one – 'I'm never much of a one for being on my own' – they withdrew from the scheme. However, if this house had not turned up they agree they would have had to go later anyway. John deeply resents this, 'People brought up in Battersea shouldn't have to move

[1] A county immediately to the south of London.
[2] The GLC (Greater London Council) set up in 1965, owned houses throughout the Greater London area until 1981/2, when most of them were handed over to each relevant local authority. The GLC administration was and still is independent of the London Borough Councils, and of central government, but at the time of writing the latter is proposing its abolition.

out of London to get a decent place.' He is sure there is money at the bottom of it: speculators developed new towns and induced local councils to send people there. If he were a millionaire, he would build little terraced houses on London's deserted railway yards and let people have them at reasonable rents. That is what people want.

With the Masons situated in their small house by the railway line and the Bateses in their upper-storey maisonette, we can next try to place them in their social network.

FAMILIES

When they were shown the network diagrams, the Masons chose to do one each, and the Bateses did one together, saying their network was shared. In practice, husband and wife in both families have different social contacts outside the home: the men have their workmates; the women have the children's teachers, other mums at the school, Residents' Association members, the family doctor, and local shopkeepers.

The Masons' inner circle is entirely kin, except for Eileen's old school friend, Cheryl. It is quite densely packed with parents, siblings, and their children. 'Family's important', Eileen says, 'You have your ups and downs but they're very close. Sure to be important with so many.' Kin are not just felt to be close, they actually live in south London and are frequently seen. But they do not live in Battersea, and they never have done;[1] Eileen's mum, two sisters, and brother live at Kennington and her married sister in Camberwell. Neither Eileen nor her mum has a phone, so her mum will arrive unexpectedly and let herself into the flat with her own key. She comes over about twice a week, and Eileen's sisters visit every other week. Eileen does not get down to Camberwell often, because it is hard to travel on the bus with the kids, but she sees her married sister at her mum's anyway. Her friend Cheryl calls by every Monday, Thursday, and Saturday and they go shopping together at the Arndale.

David's parents live in Norwood with his youngest brother

[1] Kinship and locality ties do not overlap.

and sister, and recently, his divorced brother, Harry. One married sister also lives in Norwood, whilst the other has recently moved to Southfields. They will see a lot more of her now she is nearer and they can meet 'down the Arndale', doing their shopping.[1] David's mum often phones him at work, he runs over to Norwood (borrowing a car from work) quite often, and his family turns up at the Masons' flat when they feel like it – notably when they have problems to discuss. Harry may even arrive in the middle of the night if he needs a place to sleep or wants to talk to them.

David has no close 'mates'[2] and says he never has had. He sees old school friends when he goes back to Vauxhall to drink. He does not go as much as he used to, not since he found he was drinking too much of his wages away. The friends he and Eileen have as a couple live outside London and visit them only very occasionally.

Eileen has met a lot of people through LARA and sees them regularly at the children's school. It has made a big difference to her. Before LARA, she knew only one of them, the woman who lived in the same house (their previous house), whereas now there is always someone to drop in on 'to have a chat and swop[3] problems'. But Eileen is wary. When she used to have a lot of neighbours round to the house, she found 'they tie you down, like kids – you can't get on with things. I'm too much of an active person to like sitting chatting and not getting on with things.' So sometimes she does not answer the doorbell.

Eileen does not depend on her Battersea friends much. For babysitting she prefers to ask her mum or Cheryl. If she has to make a phone call she will search for an undamaged call-box rather than bother a neighbour who has a phone. Her kids are too young to play outside and she does not want to invite local children into the house. Neighbours may 'take liberties' and she could find herself regularly childminding for the whole

---

[1] The shopping (also) has social functions, and the shopping centre is, for some, a meeting place.

[2] 'Mates' = popular term, without sexual innuendo, for friends of the same sex as the speaker. Used talking to or about them.

[3] 'Swop' = exchange.

neighbourhood. If you have to ask a favour you are safer with kin.[1]

The one exception is Cheryl, 'Anyway she's like a sister – only closer.' The two of them went through all the problems of growing up together, and still they tell each other everything. It is significant that what Eileen describes as her nervous breakdown (see p. 177) happened when Cheryl was working abroad. With Cheryl away Eileen had no one to turn to.

David and Eileen both underline the closeness and importance of kin, but they clearly find their big families a strain much of, the time. They are called on to provide – and do provide – a great deal of help, and their families absorb much time, money, and emotional energy.[2] Even Eileen's plans to get her housework done early can be thwarted by 'one or other mum down here, in tears, wanting me to sort out their problems. What they don't realize is that we have got lives of our own'. 'But when it's family,' David adds, 'you've got to get involved. Eileen says "Don't get involved", but you've got to.'

The principal cause of David's mother's distress is his brother Harry who has been in and out of Borstal and prison since he was thirteen, is addicted to drugs and, recently divorced, is living at home and influencing the younger children. The younger brother was recently given a three-month jail sentence, and the police keep raiding his mum's flat. So David has to be the good son, the pillar of strength to his mother. He went with his dad to visit Harry in prison on the Isle of Wight every month, and he is trying to find him a hospital place to be cured of his addiction. Harry is seeking treatment, but as David sees it, the welfare state cannot simply respond. Tooting Bec hospital would not take him unless he was referred by a general hospital; St George's would neither refer him nor admit him for the night, they just told him that if he took any more drugs in the next few hours it would kill him. So he had to spend the night at David and Eileen's. David went

[1] 'Close' means different things. Also, while Eileen says she does not depend on neighbours or identify with Battersea, she is involved with activities in the community centre: 'I get to meet an awful lot of people round there' and 'I'll miss LARA if we move away'.
[2] Objectively it is hard to see the resource value of the Masons' kin.

back with him to the hospital the next day and saw the psychiatrist. He was not impressed: the psychiatrist did not know half the drugs, did not understand the language junkies use, asked Harry the sort of questions anybody could have asked, and seemed more interested in David's feet than anything else (he had come out with no laces in his boots and the psychiatrist kept staring at them). The psychiatrist could not offer any help – just another appointment with a psychiatrist in two weeks' time. But Harry needed help *immediately*. David tried phoning a number that a workmate gave him but they could not do anything; he tried the Samaritans, but they 'hadn't a clue either. It just isn't true that addicts can go and be cured'.

Emotionally, the Masons' relationship with their families is one-sided; they give more than they get. Practical assistance is more reciprocal.[1] The parents willingly babysit; Eileen's mum has even taken the older boy on holiday, and last year's family holiday was a fortnight in David's mum's caravan. David's family helped them move house, pushing their belongings round the corner on a cart. In his turn, David has borrowed a lorry from work several times to help his brother and sister move house or to help his dad with a big load of scrap. Eileen says if you need to borrow, you should borrow from family; and now that David is doing fairly well, his family turn to him when they need a loan.

They have such heavy kin obligations that the Masons have little time or energy for other relationships. Smothered by kin, they nevertheless appear isolated. Neither gets or gives much help outside the family, except for Cheryl of course. Eileen and David look to each other for support, encouragement, and a bit of a push when necessary. They talk things over at night, helping each other find solutions to problems. Their families leave them little time to themselves. Any outing becomes an extended family outing. The two sets of parents both want to see the grandchildren at least once a week, and each set gets jealous if they think the other has the advantage, so Eileen consciously tries to divide the children's time between them.

[1] There is a different balance for different kinds of resources.

The Bateses' network is more crowded than the Mason's: they have more friends and more time for friends.[1] They also have a strong sense of family. Relatives are close by definition: for example, Pat included aunts and uncles that she sees only once a year in the 'very close' circle and John, wondering whether to use the negative section of the diagram for his 'snobbish' step-brother and sister whom he never sees, decided against, 'because after all, they're family'.

Pat's parents are Battersea people, though they now live further out in Kingston; so were her grandparents. John's mum, we recall, lives on the nearby council estate, his sister Helen and her children are now living at mum's, and one of his brothers lives on the same estate. Other brothers and sisters live in various parts of south-west London, except for the one 'housed by the GLC' in Huntingdon.[2]

Mum is the centre of John's family: 'she brought us all up'. She and her husband did not get on. John remembers his father as a remote, authoritarian figure, only intermittently at home. Mum still keeps in touch with all the family. Two of John's brothers who emigrated to Australia when he was a child, write to her regularly, and when they visited for the first time a year ago, they were easily absorbed back into the family. Mum's flat is the family meeting place; all the family gather there at Christmas – however small her flat, she would want them there. John loves Christmas every time, 'It's always one great big family'.

John visits his mum weekly. He sees four of his brothers and one of his brothers-in-law at least as often, and three of his sisters every other week. He keeps an eye on his mum of course, but the old lady – 70-years-old but 'hale and hearty' and still working – does not need much help. If she did, his brother and sister on the same estate would help. (Before Helen moved back there Pat made a point of looking in a couple of times a week to see if John's mum needed anything.)

John enjoys the company of his family and the sense of

[1] Is this evidence of social energy? More friends appears to mean not less time but more densely filled time.
[2] Unlike the Masons', the Bateses networks of kinship and locality coincide.

belonging. They also extend his links with the outside world; he has heard of jobs through his brothers and has got to know their friends. They do not exchange services or money within the family;[1] Pat says the family agreed a long time ago not to buy each other presents because there were just too many.

Pat feels a bit overwhelmed by her husband's enormous family. The first Christmas up there after her normal Christmas with just her parents and brother, she wondered what she had walked into. But she likes them and feels quite close to them. They are not a strain because they do not burden her and John with their problems or with high expectations. Pat found her own parents domineering when she was a teenager; even now they 'insist on helping out'. But now that she is independent of them, she gets on well with them and appreciates their help. She knows she can borrow money from them if necessary,[2] and that saves a lot of worry, even though she has only done it once. Her mother helps her to budget by saving the family allowance[3] for her till Christmas and, as we have seen, her parents helped with housing at every stage, letting the young couple live with them when first married, leaving them the tenancy of their flat, and helping them to secure their present house.[4] When John was unemployed, Pat's mother would bring her the odd bag of groceries; once she slipped a £5 note into Pat's purse. But if their help was unobtrusive, their anxiety was not: 'It wasn't that I minded him being at home,' Pat said, 'it was that my parents were going on about it. Like, "Is he out looking for a job?" and so on. They were concerned about the kids.' When John and Pat got married, John took 'a government job' on the railways because Pat's parents were 'bothered about security'.

Pat and her parents phone each other quite often; her

[1] i.e. they exchange only information and affection. Again, unlike the Masons' pattern.
[2] A different ideology of exchange pertains to the two natal families.
[3] Each mother in Britian, regardless of means, receives a weekly government pension (£3 in 1978) for each child under sixteen and living at home.
[4] The long term planning of the household seems to be covered by the couple's parents. They are themselves resolutely present-oriented (see pp. 200–09).

mother comes down every Friday when they do the weekly shopping at the Arndale, using her mum's car. On alternate Wednesdays they clean her brother's house in Mitcham and on Sundays the three families meet for Sunday lunch at Pat's or her mother's. Pat's mother is the link with her seven sets of aunts and uncles, five of whom live in south London and two on the south coast. Most of them Pat sees only once a year, at a get-together at her mum's.

In the last six months Pat has been in the unusual position of helping her brother. Tony is four years older than she is, lives in the suburbs, and normally saw Pat and John only once a year. Then Tony's wife Ann walked out on him 'just like that'. Ann, who is John's sister,[1] moved back to her mum's with the kids.[2] Tony was shattered: 'he didn't know what to do with himself'. He had made the kids the centre of his life and had not bothered about friends much, so when things went wrong, he turned to Pat and John. He rings them up and comes round just for the company, and he meets his children there on Sundays. Pat makes him welcome. She gave a birthday party for one of his kids, just as she does for her own. She has even spent a Saturday night in the pub with him (leaving John at home with the kids), and was surprised to find that they had plenty to say to each other. John was not keen on Tony before, but things are improving with more contact. Pat was afraid the split between John's sister and her own brother might cause a rift between herself and John, but this has not happened because 'John isn't all that close to his sister'. However, the break-up has reduced Pat's contact with John's mum; since Ann is now living with her Pat feels awkward about going round.[3]

[1] Brother-sister exchange – i.e. Pat's brother Tony is married to John's sister Ann – reflects or effects unusually close ties between kin and in-laws since the two sets of people are doubly related.
[2] Her immediate move home suggests she could depend on the natural support of mum.
[3] In these circumstances some conflict of loyalty is inevitable. It is Pat who is most conscious of it.

FRIENDS

The Bateses list both shared friends and separate friends on the network diagram. Pat goes out once a week with her own friends, and John meets his friend Jim for a drink on Fridays. Pat works with a variety of local residents on the LARA committee (of which she is the youngest member) and having lived in the LARA area all her life, she knows most other longstanding residents. She feels very involved locally – no wonder she 'can't understand people wanting to leave'.[1]

She uses her local network to find work: she puts it about that she is interested in cleaning jobs, and when the LARA secretary is told of 'help wanted', Pat is the first to hear. She belongs to the LARA babysitting circle, who work a 'counter' system, and so depends on neighbours rather than kin for babysitting, even though John's kin are nearby.[2] She and a neighbour share the task of taking their children to and from school. She and John use the community centre for entertainment, and go to the LARA discos, etc. And John got into a job training scheme through one of Pat's local contacts.[3]

Pat contributes a lot locally by her work on the LARA committee, she runs the summer play scheme, helps at OAP[4] dinners (along with John) and at the children's school, where she gives cookery lessons. She lets neighbours use their phone 'anytime' and is generally ready to help friends and neighbours out – knowing they will help her out in return.

CELEBRATIONS AND CRISES

It so happened that both the Bateses' and the Masons' younger child had a birthday during the period of the interviews. How did they mark it? The Masons' boy turned 3; Eileen thinks he is too young for a party, so they gave him a really nice present instead, and some of the family came over, of course. The

---

[1] She sees Battersea as central to her identity.
[2] The Masons by contrast avoid involvement with neighbours.
[3] The Bateses' information network is extensive but centred on the local area.
[4] 'OAP' = old-age pensioner.

Bateses' daughter was 4 and had a proper birthday party. Pat has given the kids parties since they were 2; it is hectic – each time she wonders whether this should be the last – but the kids enjoy it. She had eight of the little girl's schoolfriends round, confining it to schoolfriends to keep the numbers down. John played with the kids, and Pat served a birthday tea and gave each child a present. These are the sort of extras her wages help with. Apart from the kids, Pat's brother, her mum, Jim, and a couple of other friends came to the party and stayed on into the evening, talking over sandwiches and gin.

If this suggests who celebrates with them let us consider who they turn to in a crisis. The Bateses have not been through any crises recently, but Pat insists that she would ask 'any' of her friends for help; she does not single out any one of them. If they needed money to get through, she knows she could borrow from her parents.

The Masons all had flu during the interview period. Who helped? 'No one. You just have to plod on.' Eileen might have got over the flu quickly if she had had a couple of days in bed but 'you can't just go to bed when you've got kids'. As her mum does not have a phone she did not know they were ill until they were getting better and it was too late to help.[1] How had Eileen managed the year before when the children had measles, German measles, and whooping cough in rapid succession? Her friend Cheryl and Lorraine across the road did some shopping for her. Apart from that, 'you just change your routine a bit and then when they're better, you go back to normal. It's just that it gets you down a bit.' She was having to spend half the night in the children's room. David went to them sometimes but Eileen did most of it, he says; after all women cope better than men in a crisis – 'it's their instinct'. Notably the Masons did not call on either family for help.

In both households, the most recent crises involved siblings and our respondents were cast in a supportive role. We have

---

[1] Again the sense that in practical terms the Masons' kin are only liabilities.

dealt already with Tony and Ann's separation and with Harry Mason's attempt to get treatment for drug addiction. The worst crisis lies two or three years behind them in each case: for the Bateses it was John's prolonged unemployment; for the Masons it was Eileen's nervous breakdown.

'That was a really bad time in my life. Everything happened together. And we were still in that awful flat, that didn't help. I was all on my own then, I didn't know anyone round here – I'd worked outside the district and my friends and relatives were outside the district. The kid had reached the stage of driving me round the bend, wanting to go out all the time. I'd worry about going out with him and the baby in case I blacked out, so I'd get myself into a state before I even left home, and by the time I'd got to the top of the road I'd be in a cold sweat'.[1] She would not go out if she could help it; she got David to do the shopping when he came home from work. 'But he nagged at me for my own good – he'd nag at me to do things and because he's strong-willed and I knew he'd win in the end, I started doing things to avoid the friction. So I'd feel a bit independent, that I didn't have to depend on him that day. I'd feel pleased with myself.'

So who helped? 'David helped a lot, he's very understanding and he'd discuss it all with me and push me because he knew I needed pushing.'[2] Cheryl was abroad. Eileen hid her state of mind from her mother and sisters, since they suffer from nerves themselves; 'I think it was looking at them that made me get myself out of it, because I saw what it was doing to their lives. It stopped them doing anything, stuck inside all the time. All that time they wasted.' Practical help came from the welfare officer. Eileen had been in touch with the welfare when her first child was born; 'they're very nice, you can always go in and see them. I don't go down very often, but I feel I *could* go if

[1] Eileen explains this by reference to her own mum who had a nervous breakdown as a young mother of five, 'and really did black out once'.
[2] Eileen limits her dependence on her kin but feels a strong, explicit dependence on her spouse.

I wanted to.'[1] The welfare officer found a place for the child at the clinic nursery, and six months later he was able to start at a day nursery. Meanwhile Eileen began to go to LARA. Things improved.

The Bateses regard John's 18-month period of unemployment as a strain more than a catastrophe. Perhaps it does not even qualify as a crisis for them. There were jobs he could have taken if he had been desperate. How did they cope? Pat had a little cleaning job, and John was on the dole but earned some money on the side at painting and decorating.[2] Someone he knew – not a friend – used to get the jobs and phone John up. He quite enjoyed the work, but it was not like getting a regular wage. They felt the pinch in having no money for extras: most weeks Pat will buy a toy for the kids,[3] but *then* she could not; and John had no money for doing things in the house, so he felt bored at home. Pat's parents helped: 'That's when my mum really helped out. She wouldn't say anything, she'd just creep in with a couple of bags of shopping. One day I knew I'd only 50p in my purse, and after mum had gone, I'd £5. Very sneaky.'[4]

Getting by on the money side did not mean there were no problems. Pat says she did not realize what a strain it was until later. She found she was 'getting ratty' with John and the kids, mainly because they had so much of each other's company. And although Pat's parents helped out with food and money, their anxieties about John's unemployment somehow made matters even worse.[5]

---

[1] Where David's support is affective or emotional, the social welfare is used for practical assistance.

[2] John engages in 'informal' economic activity to make ends meet.

[3] Some would define this frequency as extravagant under any circumstance. To the Bateses a toy is part of the 'normal' weekly budget.

[4] 'Sneaky' = devious. Here it is an acknowledgement of the fact that her mother knew she would have been embarrassed by a direct offer of money and might even have refused it.

[5] On the practical side Pat's parents were a resource at this period; on the emotional side they were a liability.

JOBS

In both families the men are the main breadwinners: both are wage-earners rather than salaried or self-employed and both reckon they get good money. Both have daytime jobs, basically Monday to Friday, with some Saturday overtime. Neither does shift work. David averages £120 a week over the year, with higher pay for longer hours in the summer. John's earnings are more in the region of £80 or £90 if he does a lot of overtime:[1] 'If the overtime is there you do it, because you always need the money.'

Both work for small firms. David is yard foreman for a scaffolding business; John is a wood-machinist in a cabinet making firm. They have both recently moved out of the unskilled category by taking government-sponsored training courses. David trained as a heavy lorry driver and worked for his present firm as a driver before being picked out, over older men, as the foreman. (He fancied taking the bricklaying course but the training was too long for the family to survive on the paltry training allowance.) John did a 10-week course in wooden toy making at the London College of Furniture. He has always enjoyed working with wood; he likes the feel of it. The course taught him how to use hand tools and he subsequently learned to use machines.

Both men seem fairly satisfied and see their present jobs as an improvement on previous ones. Both like working in small firms, where you know all your workmates and the 'guvnor'[2] personally. If you have a problem or grievance you can take it up with the guvnor directly. They contrast this direct contact with the trade union way of handling grievances. Both dislike unions – 'I don't believe in them, they're too powerful', says John – and are pleased not to belong to one.[3] Both like and

---

[1] These figures are for 1978 and were then around the national average. It is likely that neither man's earnings have kept pace with inflation since.
[2] 'Guvnor' is an elision of 'governor' and is the colloquial London way of referring to the boss. As a term of address it is shortened to 'guv'.
[3] Perhaps this is a sign of extra dependence on the guvnor, more likely it shows a standard distrust of large-scale bureaucratic organizations.

rather admire their guvnors who, after several years at their separate trades, have each achieved their own business and are doing well. David's guvnors (two brothers) 'used to work (as scaffolders); now they just do estimates and accounts.' John worked with his boss before. He is a bit of a friend of the family and John was pleased to see him start his own business. The man has been generous to him, especially when a big order came through and when he took time off sick. David's guvnors give him lifts home sometimes in the Jaguar, and offer to help him with house purchase. Both John and David feel that if the firm they work for prospers, they will prosper with it; they value the fact that the guvnors tell them how business is going. They can identify with the firm in a way they could not with the railways or the factory.[1]

John has worked in three different local factories but hates factory work, 'You're not a person, just a number: clocking in, putting your hand up to go to the toilet'. His present job by contrast allows him a fair amount of independence. The guvnor gives him a work sheet with enough items to last several days. He plods through it, largely organizing his own time, and asks for another sheet when he has finished. He hates being rushed because there is more chance of making mistakes.

David enjoys being his own boss, in charge of the yard. Responsible for supervising, loading, and hiring the drivers, he needs managerial ability and good judgement. Each morning he opens up the yard, feeds the guard dog, and phones his guvnor to get him out of bed. He has to make sure the lorries are loaded with scaffolding and dispatched to the work-sites on time. When the drivers come back or phone in for further instructions, he tells them where to go next. At the end of the day he will have the lorries loaded ready and the drivers' routes worked out for the next morning.

If they are asked what they dislike about their jobs, both men say the working conditions.[2] David works mostly outside. The yard in winter is a sea of mud, and he sloshes about in it all

[1] Again the preference for small scale. In this instance it may be the very smallness of the outfit that allows them to personalize it and so to identify with it.
[2] Some evidence suggests that more strikes in Britain are about physical working conditions than about rates of pay.

day. This is when he thinks he would like his sons to have nice, clean office jobs when they grow up. John works indoors. He complains that the workshop is poorly heated and cramped – he has to keep stopping and cleaning up all the time – and the men virtually choke on the wood dust because there are no dust extractors. In fact, speculating about what he would spend his money on if he won the pools,[1] John homes in on dust extractors for the guvnor as his most concrete project.[2]

Both men started in these jobs fairly recently. John about four months before the first interview, and David within the year. Both have long and chequered job histories, which show similarities at several points. Neither of them did well at school and both were suspended before the age of fifteen. Both then got apprenticeships, David in a metal shop, John with a butcher, and realize now that they could have done well if they had stuck at a trade. The school friend who started with John is a manager now, with his own shop, and earns over £100 a week. But John quit after a year, sick of being a dogsbody and of stabbing and cutting himself, and all for £5 a week! David's apprenticeship was equally short lived: he left after hitting his foreman in an argument. Both then went through a string of short-term jobs, preferring those that took them out and about (labouring on building sites, driving), and avoiding factory jobs as far as they could. Both have at some time been sacked for working a fiddle, John for selling railway lines and David for selling towels as a laundry delivery man. 'There's a fiddle in every job', David confides, 'there's always perks.' Then on a note of caution he adds, 'But not in the job I've got now'.[3] Both

[1] Each week millions of people in Britain bet on the outcome of the week's many football games. It is not necessary to know about football to do so. Stories of individuals whose lives have been transformed by enormous winnings are part of British folklore – and are the base of common fantasies about 'suddenly' becoming rich.

[2] Another evidence of his identification with the firm.

[3] 'Fiddles' and 'perks' (perquisites) are morally acceptable forms of illegal advantage. At each level of the occupational hierarchy (in Britain at least) there are loopholes in the system which allow 'good citizens' to profit from cheating i.e. without defining themselves or being defined by others as criminals (see Ditton 1978; Mars 1982). The collusion collapses only if someone 'points a finger'. When that happens the wrongdoing must be punished or the system will collapse altogether (see classically, Malinowski 1926).

had young children to support when they lost their jobs. David who hates to be out of work, resorted to a job on the railway (as a linesman), even though he generally condemns railway work as suitable only for 'thick' people.[1] Meanwhile he applied for a place on a government training course. John was out of work for eighteen months after he was sacked. This period is the recent crisis he and Pat described.

But if their careers have similarities, the two men's attitudes to work differ enormously.[2] David sees himself as a worker; he started by heaving coal through the streets at the age of twelve, and he hates to be dependent on the dole or supplementary benefits,[3] 'For a start you cannot live on what they pay you; second place, it's humiliating not to be able to support yourself or your family.' Although he works 'not for himself but for Eileen and the kids', he recognizes that he would not know what to do with himself otherwise; when he caught flu he was itching to be back at work and returned before fully recovered. Explicitly, he evaluates jobs purely in terms of money: 'you follow the money, you've got to.' A job is a good job if it pays well. Implicitly, other things count, especially being his own boss. Several of his jobs he described as a 'doddle' (that is easy jobs with a lot of freedom). Even if the hours are long, he can pop home during the day and see Eileen and sunbathe. Doddles are good. Some of the things he says reflect the common evaluation of non-manual work as superior to manual, regardless of pay. Sometimes he even envies people with clean office jobs, though his wife insists that he would hate the bitchiness of an office and the feeling of being cooped up. Work is his preoccupation. He has no hobbies and no close friends. Eileen says that even at home all he talks about is work. His description of a day focuses on it:

[1] 'Thick' = stupid, slow-witted.
[2] The existential meaning of work cannot be read off observed patterns of working behaviour (see Wallman 1979b).
[3] The 'dole' is unemployment insurance. To qualify a person must have been employed in insured industry for twenty-six weeks prior to claiming. Supplementary benefits are uninsured social security payments granted on the basis of need alone.

his time chart detailed the activities of the working day, including the phone calls, the cups of tea (and who made them), and the conversations with the boss.

John, by contrast, says he does not like working and does not like talking about work; nevertheless we spent two evenings on his work history. He works because he has to and is quite happy not working if, for instance, he has enough money to do things round the house. 'I don't mind being unemployed if I have something to do. It's just the money I miss. If I've no money I can't work on the house or anything.' When he was unemployed, he worked casually as a painter and decorator, so money was not such a problem as it first appears. If the dole sent him for an interview for a job he did not want, he would mess up the interview or take the job for a week and then drop it. The dole[1] were not really bothered. If they were, he could go on social security instead, where, as a bonus, it was easier to get extra money.[2]

He has clear ideas of jobs he would not take: factory jobs and anything with very low pay – £30 to £40 basic. A job has to be financially worthwhile. Aside from that, 'you've got to be happy at work; its not just how much you can earn.' John knows he gets bored easily; a job has to hold his interest. His description of each of his many jobs was either 'interesting' or 'boring'. As a teenager he would switch jobs for the variety. He likes moving from building site to building site. He enjoys being a delivery boy and meeting different people. His present job is inherently more interesting and leaves him pretty free: he thinks he will stay there for a while. He says he went through a phase of bothering about security, when he was first married

[1] See p. 182, n. 1. 'The dole' is not a person, but the people who distribute it are referred to by their office.
[2] In the form of 'exceptional needs payments' for clothes, etc. John's successful management of his social welfare rights depends on the information and confidence that come from long-standing residence in Battersea and familiarity with the English system. On both counts a new immigrant (of any colour) would be at a relative disadvantage.

and Pat's parents went on about it.[1] When their first baby was due he took up a job as an electrician's mate on the railways, thinking a government job would be more secure. Though 'the money wasn't any good', he stuck it for three years, until he was sacked for nicking[2] railway lines.

Work became more interesting when John joined a toy-making co-operative that he had heard about through a friend of Pat's.[3] It was sponsored by Job Creation.[4] This was how he got into training at the London College of Furniture. He became a group leader, supervising four men. 'To start with, it was all lovely. I was on the Board of Directors. I used to look forward to getting up in the morning. Then after a year, a new manager came and everything went sour. He didn't consult at all. He chopped people down. Before he came, if you had an idea you could try it out. Not with him; he discouraged it. Or he'd buy an idea for two weeks' wages rather than a percentage. He wouldn't even let us take the scraps and sawdust any more.' They were meant to get a big rise. When it finally came, John got less than the other group leader, supposedly because he supervised fewer men. John argued that, as he was training them to use machines, he had the greater responsibility. 'So after a "discussion", I said I was leaving. Very disillusioning.'

Since both men appreciate independence at work, we might expect self-employment to appeal to them. John's guvnor offered him the choice: employee or self-employed; some of the workshop are self-employed. Pat asked her (self-employed) dad, who did not think it was worth it, what with paying an accountant and all that. Besides, Pat prefers to know that the money he brings home is all his, rather than having to put aside tax and not knowing how much. Still, John might do some work on his own account. A friend coming out of the merchant

[1] 'Went on' = nagged, made a fuss.
[2] 'Nicking' = colloquial for stealing in a small way (see also p. 181, n. 3 on fiddling).
[3] Local information sources again.
[4] One of a number of government schemes to combat unemployment.

navy soon is going to set up an antique business. He asked John if he would like some evening work restoring furniture. In Pat's view 'a little would be all right, but he wouldn't want it to take over'.

David's reaction to a similar opportunity is characteristically different: 'Yes, it will take up a lot of spare time at weekends, but I'll do it instead of overtime – better money and tax free.' The opportunity is to do some paint spraying with the bloke who used to live in their previous house. He has done a government training course in paint spraying; someone has now asked him to do some work privately, and he has invited David to help. 'So David's bubbling this week', Eileen observed. A paint job normally costs £200, but the two men will do it for £50 if the customer supplies materials; their costs will be £10 to hire a spray gun for the weekend. Their biggest problem is where to spray; the best hope is a relative who is caretaker in a place where there are lots of big garages. They have already been asked to do a second car, and they may advertise. If it goes well and they get plenty of orders, they may decide to take the risk of going into business. 'Funnily enough', as David says, an accountant contact of his partner has offered him £20,000 to set up a business. David loves the idea of his own business. He does not see much risk in giving up his present job, since he has always got his HGV licence to fall back on.

Opportunities for private work have come through friends in both cases. When we examine how they heard about jobs, we find friends or family were the source in most instances. Of David's fourteen jobs (classing building site jobs as one), only one was obtained through the labour exchange[1] (back in 1968) and two through answering adverts (in 1967 and 1971). Labouring jobs were obtained by asking at the site. David heard of all his other jobs through friends and brothers. The same applies to John. He heard of only three of his twelve jobs through formal channels: one through an advert in the papers, two through the labour exchange. While John was still living

[1] Officially 'labour exchanges' have been replaced by 'job centres' but both terms are still used.

186 Eight London Households

at home, his dad found four of his five jobs. Later, he obtained his jobs on the buses and on the railways through friends already working there.[1]

Eileen Mason had no job at the time of the interview, and indeed has not worked since the first child was born. She regards herself as an independent kind of person and wants more than simply housework and child care. But with David working long and unpredictable hours she cannot take on an evening job or go to night school, and daytime work would mean leaving the children with a minder. She is not prepared to do that. She would leave them with her mum, but her mum is too far away. Even when the toddler starts at nursery she will have only three hours a day free, and there will be the problem of child care in the school holidays.[2]

During the period of the interviews, Eileen and her friend Cheryl started making things in macramé, which Eileen learned at LARA. Suddenly she found new purpose. Selling initially to friends of the family, she and Cheryl plan to have a market stall and later maybe a shop. She likes the idea of her own business, 'you always work harder for yourself', and of providing homework for women like herself who are stuck at home with kids. (She has thought of doing homework herself, but does not know where to look for any; no one she knows knows about it either.)[3] But while she dreams of having a business when both children are at school and she can work 9 to 3.30 on macramé, now she can hardly manage to devote even her mornings to it. It is not the children who stop her, it is the frequent arrival of kin.[4]

---

[1] It is characteristic of the Battersea workforce that most men hear about work from local and informal sources of information – irrespective of the job or where it is based.

[2] Time is a resource which belongs to the household as a whole; the time available to one member is not independent of the time 'expenditure' of another.

[3] Apparently she considers it is only lack of information that stops her.

[4] Kin as liability again.

Pat Bates wrestles rather more successfully with similar but less extreme constraints. John's hours are less erratic, and she seems better able to use her network to find work. Though her children are already at school (or nursery) all day and have their dinners at school,[1] Pat does not seek daytime work because of the problem of child care during school holidays.

Pat does not want to be dependent on anyone except John and she, like Eileen, is unhappy to think of leaving the children with a minder. So she looks for early morning or evening cleaning jobs, often holding two at once. Ideally she sets her own hours. She cleans a shop up the road, has her own key and just pops up there when John is home and the kids are in bed, so that it disrupts their lives as little as possible. She earns £6 for spending half an hour up there four times a week; her morning job brings in a similar sum. She puts it about among her friends that she will clean and hears through them of jobs they are giving up or cannot take.[2] One job came through the editor of the LARA *Echo*, who phoned Pat as soon as the shopkeeper approached her. Pat realizes that she could run several small jobs at the same time, but does not want to take on so much that it would intrude on her time with the children. She gave up one cleaning job because she could not stand her supervisor, and another, early morning job because it left her exhausted in the evening and John complained about her tiredness. One job ended when the couple whose house she cleaned split up. She used to get depressed when she gave up a job and to look round in panic for another, but now she realizes this was silly; she does not *have* to work – they *could* manage on John's wage. What her work provides is money for extras, her daughter's birthday party for instance, and a sense of independence. The knowledge that she is 'chipping in'[3] also

[1] 'Dinner' in working-class English is the midday meal; 'tea' is the evening meal – at least for children.

[2] Membership in the local network is essential for information and for 'references': none of these jobs is formally advertised anywhere, and only someone known to a previous worker is entrusted with access to someone's home or shop.

[3] 'Chipping in' = making a financial contribution.

makes her feel less of a burden on John, 'though I shouldn't feel that because it's his responsibility to keep us'.[1] She was anxious to get back to work after the birth of each child, not so much for the money, 'though it helped', as for the independence. Although John thought she wanted to work too soon, she managed each time to find a shop job locally where she could take the baby with her. Each time she stayed in the job about six months, until the baby became too active.

Both women, as it happens, began their working lives with jobs in banks, Pat in the West End, Eileen in the City. Both did rather better at school than their husbands (Pat got a couple of CSEs),[2] yet had little idea what to do. It was their parents who favoured banking. Both answered advertisements in the paper, and both were recruited to work alongside other school leavers. Their reactions to the job diverged. Eileen found it 'a home from home, very friendly' and stayed until after she was married and had moved house, when the journey from Battersea to the City was awkward. Pat hated working 'among all those silly girls', and with no contact with the public, and left after six months – to her father's disappointment. Though she realizes she could have made a career of banking, she has no regrets. She found a job locally as cashier in a men's tailors. Her next job came from an unexpected quarter: her brother, knowing that she was restless, found her a job in the firm of jewellers he worked for in Hatton Garden.[3] The two of them were not close until then. As secretary/receptionist, she stayed with the firm until she was pregnant and 'very sicky'. She really enjoyed the job.

Eileen moved from the bank to a clerical job in a local factory, but it was not the same. Her 'face didn't fit' and she was dismissed for no good reason. (This, she says, was

---

[1] Even 'modern' English mores are not egalitarian in this respect.
[2] A CSE (Certificate of Secondary Education) in any subject is achieved by examination. The standard is less academic than for GCE (General Certificate of Education) O levels, but CSEs are useful qualifications for unskilled work – or were when unskilled work was more readily available.
[3] In 'the City' – London's central business district, north of the river Thames, but not a long journey to work by Battersea standards.

common among her friends before the legislation against unfair dismissal[1] – especially with girls.) She worked briefly in a dress shop; the trouble there was trying to look busy when in fact she had nothing to do. Her most enjoyable job was as cashier in a betting shop,[2] one of a small local chain. A relative of David's worked in another branch and Eileen decided to ask about vacancies.[3] She described this job as a turning point in her life – it forced her to deal with a great variety of people. Eileen had been very shy, and when she found herself able to cope with lots of people, and with working under pressure, taking bets and paying out winnings, it boosted her confidence. Unfortunately the job lasted only six months; when she asked for time off to visit her grandmother in Ireland, who was dangerously ill, they refused to keep the job open for her. She worked for a while in another betting office which she liked less.

Once married, she could be more picky about jobs. David never tried to push her into working: 'Look around, take your time', he would say. So she demanded that a job be interesting as well as reasonably paid, by which she means paid on a par with people she knew locally doing the same sort of work.[4]

MONEY

Having seen how the Bateses and Masons earn a living, we may consider how they spend the money they earn. Their spending patterns and (in the next section) their time budgets, cover the allocation of two of their most important resources in the business of bringing up a family.

[1] Employment Protection Act (1975).
[2] The bulk of English betting shop business involves gambling on the outcome of dog or horse races, but money can be 'placed on' any current sporting event.
[3] Without the initial connection through David's kin she probably would not have been considered for the job, even if she had heard of it.
[4] Her reference group is specific and realistic. It would not occur to her to aspire to what richer or better educated people earn.

Both families are at the same stage in the life cycle, both have the same sized households, and both have roughly the same housing costs as tenants of the local council. In an objective sense we could say the economic needs of both households are equal. So are their incomes: David Mason earns £120 a week; John Bates brings home £80 to £90, and his wife Pat earns £10 to £15.

David as we have seen, judges jobs by the wages they offer: 'if you can't live up to the standard you want, then that's no good'. The standard is 'whether you have everything you need for the kids and food and a nice home'. The Masons spend at least £30 a week on food. They aim to give the children what they like to eat; if they do not like the food they can leave it and have something else. Similarly with toys and clothes for the children: they do not want the boys to go without or to have to share (and fight) over toys. Though their rent is only £8 a week, having a nice home obviously costs them far more than that: the plush living room carpet and three-piece suite speak for themselves. They go for a fortnight's holiday every July, often camping in Cornwall, last year staying instead in David's mum's caravan near Hastings, this year maybe driving on the continent. They find they cannot save, 'not with families like ours'.[1] There are always birthdays, weddings, etc., and Christmas is a big expense – they have to start early. Since they believe that the family should help each other out, they have lent money to their relatives. With nothing left over from £120 a week, they do not know how anyone can survive on £50 to £60.

The Bateses however did manage on £60 a week when John worked in the co-op, 'He had to put his entire wage packet on the table (for housekeeping) and I had to get the family allowance out to give him for his fares. That was awful. He really got cheesed off[2] with that. Now it's better. But even if

---

[1] Money trickles away on a succession of family events and needs – but it never occurs to the Masons to refuse familial requests or obligations.

[2] 'Cheesed off' = irritated. Similar in meaning to the more common phrase 'fed up'.

he's got £30 left (after the housekeeping) he doesn't keep it all – he'll chip in with things for the kids.' John gives Pat £45 for food, rent, insurance, electricity, phone, and TV. Pat was anxious about getting colour TV at £9 a month instead of black and white at £3, and insists that John gives her £2 a week for it, which she saves, or they would never have the £9 at the end of the month. The rent is £10 a week. She never dips into the rent money, 'It's too dangerous'; but she sometimes 'borrows off the insurance money'.[1]

They went on holiday the year before last and had thought of going away this year, but it was a choice between a holiday and doing up the front room, and they have chosen the latter. They want to knock the living room and dining room together and redecorate, which they have never had the money to do before – Pat's job makes the difference. When they took over Pat's parents' flat, all the furniture came with it, 'so getting new things is to prove that we can do it, we can get a nice place ourselves'. They spent £200 on a new living room carpet, borrowing the money from Pat's dad when they discovered how much extra the HP[2] would be. They repay £20 a month and are more committed to paying 'because it's Dad. If it were HP we might dip into it.'

Pat hates to be in debt 'even though you have to be'.[3] For the first time they are managing to save. Her mum saves the family allowance for her; 'what could you spend £6 a week on? But if I save it all year it will be £300.' It could go on a new living room suite, or on Christmas.[4] They gave up buying presents for all the relatives, 'But just our kids and having a big Christmas dinner for my mum and dad costs a lot. If I had £500 in the bank, I'd happily spend it on Christmas.' While Pat knows she can always borrow from her parents if necessary, now more

[1] i.e. she takes money out of the envelope for insurance payments, expecting to put it back before the payment is due.
[2] 'HP' = hire purchase, i.e. buying something on credit and paying it off, with interest, in instalments. Sometimes called 'buying on the never never'.
[3] It may be the prospect of long-term commitment to impersonal creditors rather than of 'consumerism' as such which she rejects.
[4] Anthropologists talk of a 'ceremonial fund' which even the poorest peasants will reserve for special 'non-economic' occasions and spend, no matter how hard up they are. The notion seems appropriate here.

than ever before she really appreciates having something saved.

TIME

Both couples accept without question that it is the man's responsibility to keep the family and the woman's to care for it. This broadly determines the use of each partner's time. In both families the pattern is that the man works outside the home from morning to evening, Monday to Friday, plus some weekend overtime, while the woman is at home looking after the children and keeping the house. Pat manages to fit some part-time work into her schedule. We shall look in more detail at the division of labour in each household, and see how the basic work of shopping, cooking, washing, and cleaning is carried out.

Eileen reported she had been talking with her friends about how they shared their housework. They concluded that 'when you first get married, your husband really helps you a lot, you share things. Then when you have your first child he does a bit less. And when you have two kids and could really do with a bit of help, he does nothing.' David has his own explanation: 'When we were first married I had easy jobs. The last, say, four years, I've had to work much harder, much longer hours, to get the money in. Like now. Well, you've seen the time I set off (6.30 a.m.) and the time I get back (8.30 p.m.). After that, I've had enough, I'm not fit for anything.' So normally he does very little. (The day of the interview was exceptional because all the family had flu, Eileen was behind with the housework, and David had spent much of Sunday helping.)[1]

In spite of her teasing, Eileen deliberately takes responsibility for everything that needs to be done in the house: 'I do as much as I can, to take as much pressure off him as I

[1] In the neighbourhood survey answers to the question 'Who else sometimes helps?' revealed that it is very common for men to take over household tasks in emergencies or on special occasions – even if they see themselves as 'doing nothing'.

can. . . . His family depends on him a lot, they often ring him at work and ask him to do things. That's why I try not to pressure him too much in case he cracks up.'[1] So Eileen looks after the children, does the cleaning, the washing and ironing, and plans and cooks the meals. David will help with shopping on Saturdays, if he is not working, though he hates to shop – even preferring Eileen to buy his clothes without him – and goes only to help carry things. Alternatively, he will mind the kids while Eileen goes shopping with her friend Cheryl.

Eileen makes contact with the school and the doctor whenever necessary and deals with all the 'clerical tasks', partly because David has problems with spelling. (He went to literacy classes but found he did not get enough attention to make it worthwhile.) So she pays all the bills, fills in all the forms, deals with all the letters that come in, and writes all the letters that have to be written. David, for his part, 'does all the running about'; for instance, he will go round to the off-licence for cigarettes and will run things down to his or Eileen's mum. With access to a phone at work and the boss's car he can make essential calls (for example, to the Housing Department about a transfer), keep in touch with his family, and deliver presents and things to them.

How do the basic chores get done? The household machinery is a factor here. The Masons have an automatic washing machine, a tumble drier, and an iron, so there are no time-consuming trips to the laundrette or wearisome rubbing and wringing. In fact, 'I don't think of washing as work, except for taking it out and sorting it. I'm always doing something else at the same time.' Eileen uses the washing machine every day, doing several loads of washing. She hates ironing because it is so boring; she will stand at her ironing board while the children are playing and while she and David are watching TV in the evenings.[2]

---

[1] David 'supported' Eileen during her nervous breakdown and she worries about the stresses he suffers now. Their concerns are clearly reciprocal but Eileen talks in psychological terms of people 'cracking up' and David in practical terms about their being too busy or too tired.
[2] Time and task charts obscure the social content of work unless 'Who else was there?' and 'What else was happening?' can also be recorded.

Since some badly housed families still have to share a cooker, it is worth noting that the Masons have their own; they also have a fridge but not a freezer, so they can keep food for a few days but they do not bulk-buy perishables. This and their lack of a car influence their shopping. Eileen does the main weekly shop on Saturdays at the Arndale Centre, and if they really have a lot to carry they may take a cab home. But Eileen also shops locally every day, on her own, with the younger child, or with Cheryl.

The Masons rarely eat together. On weekdays Eileen brings David tea and cornflakes in bed before 6 a.m., then makes breakfast for the children at 8 a.m., but has nothing herself until 11 – a cup of tea. Though she makes the pre-nursery child some lunch at 1 o'clock, she rarely eats anything herself. David at work normally does without lunch too. Eileen reckons to spend about half an hour preparing the main meal, which she serves about 6 o'clock; the children eat theirs in the kitchen, while she eats hers from a tray watching TV ('for a bit of peace'). David's goes back in the oven till he gets home at 8.30 p.m. At the weekend of the time budget interview, the family had fish and chips together on Friday evening when David got home from work earlier than usual, a fry-up[1] at Saturday teatime with Eileen's mother and sister, and a Sunday dinner, served at 4 p.m., of chicken, roast potatoes, frozen carrots and peas, with trifle[2] 'for afters'. Again the children ate in the kitchen, while the parents had their dinner in front of the TV.

If we move two streets away to the Bateses, we find them eating a similar Sunday dinner: roast beef, roast potatoes, carrots and peas. It is more of a social occasion: Pat's brother and his children are eating with them.

The Bateses have similar household machinery to the Masons – cooker, fridge, automatic washing machine, iron – and have the important addition of a phone. Pat Bates too

[1] 'Fry-up' = an assortment of meat or eggs and vegetables, sometimes 'leftovers', fried together in one large pan.
[2] Trifle is made by soaking plain cake in jelly, layering it with fruit or jam, and covering the top with custard and/or cream. It is a favourite English dessert, and said to be a fine way of using up stale cake.

spends about half an hour preparing the main meal, which, except at weekends, is eaten at 6 p.m. when John gets home from work. Usually the four of them eat together, unless the children have really been wearing Pat out, in which case she may feed them earlier. She gets breakfast for John and kids at 7.30 a.m., and has a bit of breakfast herself at 9.30, after she has taken the kids to school. John takes sandwiches for lunch and the kids have lunch at school. Friday lunchtime Pat does a weekly shop at the Arndale Centre with her mum who comes down in the car. She gets odd bits of shopping most days on the way home from her job at the Junction.[1] Like Eileen she does the washing at home in her automatic washer, but she uses hers only every other day.

So again running the home is the woman's job. John would cook and shop if Pat were ill. He can cook, she says, if he puts himself out,[2] but she would not ask him to because he is out at work all day. She altered her expectations a bit when John was unemployed, so he did a bit more round the house. It was the thought of still having all the washing and ironing to do when she got home from work that put her off working fulltime to support the family; there is no way John could take all that off her hands.

Pat manages the money: John gives her all the regular sums and she has little envelopes for rent, phone, TV, etc. The rest he keeps and it is up to him how he spends it. She pays the bills. John is not good at sums and he gets confused if she explains the bills and budgeting. As for the tax form, neither of them can understand it, so she gives it to her dad, who has his own business, or John takes it into work. Pat deals with the school, the doctor, and the Housing Department.[3]

Both partners have a recognizable weekly routine. John's job keeps him in the workshop until 5.30 p.m. Monday to Friday. He may go to the pub with workmates on the way home on Mondays and especially Thursdays, as it is pay-day.

[1] There is a large open air market next to Clapham Junction railway station. Both are only a short walk from LARA.
[2] 'Puts himself out' = makes a special effort, suffers some inconvenience.
[3] As Wandsworth Council tenants, they pay rent to, and arrange repairs, etc. through the local Housing Department.

Friday evening he always goes out with his sister's husband. They go 'down the pub'[1] and meet friends, including his best mate Jim. Saturdays he tries to go to his mum's, if he is not working, and Sundays are taken up with Pat's family. If he and Pat go out at all, it is on Saturday night to LARA discos, etc. The rest of the week in his leisure time, he 'potters round the house'. Now he is decorating the living room and restoring an old fireplace which he found in someone's front garden. In summertime they are out and about more. They all go to the pub Sunday lunchtime, or for an hour in the evening; the pub has a little garden for the kids. And they take the kids to feed the ducks in St George's Park. John likes to take the kids out on his own too; 'He's always saying, "Pack the sandwiches", and he's off.' Weekends either way are times to spend with the family – Pat and the kids or their two families of origin.

Pat's weekends are spent much the same way as John's. During the week she works part-time at the Junction every day except Wednesdays, when she cleans her brother's house on alternate weeks. Her mum always comes up Wednesday afternoon and Friday lunchtime, often bringing her friend with her. One of Pat's own friends comes down Tuesdays and Fridays for an hour or two. Apart from that, friends pop in[2] casually, or she calls on them. 'I'm not a loner,' Pat says, 'I'm always with friends.' She goes out with friends one evening a week, and Friday night she stays in on her own while John goes out, 'but we go out a lot together too, socialize together. It's important that, to have a joint life, as well as a bit of independence.'

The Masons' week has a less regular pattern. David gets home late every night but Fridays. Eileen's friend Cheryl comes down Mondays, Thursdays, and Saturdays; according to David, 'she practically lives here'. Eileen goes round the Centre (LARA) a lot, especially in school holidays. Either her mum or David's may arrive at any time. 'Not many days when I get a

---

[1] Always the same one – their 'local'.
[2] 'Pop in' = to visit briefly, perhaps unexpectedly.

day to myself' she says. If David goes out on his own (apart from running things down to his mum's from work) it is to a pub; he has no regular drinking mates and just goes when he is restless. Before he became foreman he used to have a drink with his workmates. Now it 'doesn't happen'. Eileen dislikes pubs – she finds them 'boring' – and does not much like eating out. This is a pity for David who enjoys both. He reckons they have had dinner out about twice in their married life. Over the weekend they recorded on the time clock, a film at the Junction and a Wimpy[1] was their Saturday night out. Most of their time together is spent at home. It is rarely just the two of them, because of their families and the kids. They would like more time to themselves, but 'you can't stop the family coming – they'd be very offended'.

As for daily routine, two days in the lives of Eileen and David, and Pat and John, were described in the time clock diagrams – a weekday and a Sunday. The difference between the weekday and the Sunday shows the tremendous influence of employment on the management of time – and not only for the employee.[2] Eileen Mason for instance, is up at 5.30 a.m. on the weekday; on the Sunday very little happens before noon.

The Sunday diagrams confirmed that neither the Masons nor the Bateses go to church. David identifies himself as C of E:[3] 'I mean, I'm atheist really, religion's never done anything for me.' Eileen believes in God but does not feel that church attendance is necessary. Neither of the Bateses mentioned religion, except to say that they do not want to force their children to go to Sunday school in the way Pat's parents forced her.

The diagrams also illustrate the amount of energy spent interacting with children. While they do the obvious 'work' of cleaning, cooking, ironing, etc. the parents are keeping an eye on the kids, sorting out their fights, making them drinks, washing them, and talking to them. Time is rarely spent alone – even, David says, in the bath. Half an hour on Eileen's

---

[1] 'Wimpy' = an English-style hamburger from a food chain called Wimpy.
[2] By the same token the unemployment of any one member disrupts or destroys the time structure of the whole household.
[3] 'C of E' = Church of England, i.e. Anglican.

weekday time clock is marked specifically 'talking to' the toddler, but she is also talking to him virtually all day as she does housework and shopping. The nature of the work is also affected: she will clear up two or three times instead of once, and the shopping takes an age because all the local shopkeepers talk to her little boy.

This moves us towards a more subjective approach to time. How is time *felt*? There are four different levels: (i) hourly time; (ii) time as something to be consciously organized and allocated; (iii) the passage of time over the years, and (iv) generational time.

On hourly time, watching the respondents complete the time clocks was revealing. Eileen found it hard to remember when she was doing what. She says that she is terrible about time, just never aware of it. Though she has clocks about the house, she never looks at them, unless she has got to go out, for example to collect the elder child from school. She could remember the jobs she had done that day (Sunday) and knows she is 'normally doing half a dozen jobs at once': putting loads of washing in the machine, sorting out the airing cupboard, keeping an eye on the kids, and stopping to take the toddler to the toilet. But she could not remember in what order she had done different jobs or what time it was when she did them. David helped her out by relating her jobs to what he was doing at the time; it was often two hours later than Eileen had guessed. She says time passes not by the hour but by the day.

David is acutely aware of time. Constructing a time clock for Friday, two days previous to the interview, he would say, 'ten past eight, the guvnor phoned; twenty past, we started loading the lorry', etc. He was precise, but not quite so precise, about time spent at home. John's clock presents a total contrast. The hours from 8 a.m. to 5.30 p.m. are simply marked, 'At Work'. Apart from personal differences, these contrasts reflect the varying importance of time to each of them: David has to get men and scaffolding to the right place at the right time.

Both men have jobs that allow them some scope to organize their own work, and both value this. But the women have much greater scope: 'Being a housewife you're your own boss, so time doesn't matter to me. Housework's always there and you do it when you feel like it or when it's needed', says Eileen. And from Pat: 'The housework gets done when it gets done. I'm not one for routines.' Both women spoke explicitly of the management of time, and of the inherent conflicts between the children's needs, their individual needs, and their obligations to cook and clean.

Pat experiences the problem in relation to jobs. She likes to have a job for the sense of independence it gives her; if it starts to get her down or becomes impossible with the kids, she gives it up and finds another when she is ready. But there is a problem of balance: she realizes that she can hear about lots of little cleaning jobs, and it is tempting to take more on, but then she would be rushing from job to job, with no time to herself. Like at the moment, she has got this new morning job: it is done before 10 a.m., she does her housework before she goes out, and then she has got the rest of the day free. The kids have their dinner at school and do not come in till 3.45 p.m., John at 5.45 p.m., and she has supper ready about six. She pops out[1] to do her evening job after supper when the kids are in bed, so that it does not disrupt their lives at all. She is free therefore from 10 till 3, goes out shopping, visits friends, pops up to Kensington sometimes to get things for the kids. She could get a morning or afternoon job instead, but this would be awkward in school holidays. The present way she does not have to depend on anyone except John. She is only careful not to have jobs where she is rushing out just as he rushes in.

Eileen, with a 3-year-old still at home, has less time to herself, and sounds more frustrated. The younger boy is due to start at nursery soon, but 'until he is five, I can only go out morning or afternoon, I have to be home for his lunch. So I can't travel far for work or for learning anything new.' However, this is not getting her down as much as when the elder boy was at this same age: 'At three, he had reached the stage of driving me round the bend, wanting to go out all the time. You just don't know what to do – go out and keep the

---

[1] 'To pop out' = to go out briefly, without having planned it. Pat's use of the term here reflects her desire to show how easy it all is.

kids happy and let everything go to pot,[1] or keep the house tidy and your husband happy, but have the kids moaning. If you haven't got a garden, you're stuck.' A nursery place, procured by a welfare worker,[2] solved that problem. Eileen now finds that the more she has to do the more organized she seems to be, 'The busier I am, the better I cope. If everything is haphazard and busy, I can cope very well with problem after problem. If I'm bored, I can't cope with anything. I like to change my routine – not just the chores, but the people I visit, and the places I go to.' So her approach to managing time is to see how much she can cram into a day. 'For instance, if I've got a lot of bills to pay and it means going to the Arndale and the Junction, and do the housework and do some macramé and bath the kids, I cram it all in, so that the next day I can do something different – woodwork or mending or visit somebody.'

At the time of the interviews, she was trying to work out a new routine that would create time for starting a macramé business. 'At present I try to get the housework done by 12 o'clock. For three days last week I managed it, then everything went wrong. My mum and John's mum both came down and wanted me to sit and listen to their problems and sort them out.'[3]

Time to oneself, time to do one's own chosen work, is precious time, more valuable than the time spent on housework, or, in Eileen's case, in meeting the kin obligations that encroach on it. 'I get very frustrated having no chance to do anything because *I* want to', she complains, and believes her frustration is greater than many other mothers' since she is very independent and wants to do things; 'Achieving things matters to me. Even if it's only a little thing.'

Past, present, future

The passing of time is marked by their movement from one life stage to another – teenager, parent, parent of teenager – and by

[1] 'To go to pot' = to go to pieces.
[2] Eileen mentions the state's help without reference to the officials who arranged it or the family members who failed to help.
[3] Kin in the way again.

the accompanying changes in themselves and in their relationships with their parents.

How do they feel they have changed? David used to go 'pubbing it and clubbing it five nights a week. But you can't do that when you're married.' He used to fight a lot, 'I was a punch-up artist', he tells you. When they got married he quietened down. Eileen, on the other hand, used to be very shy and self-conscious. Her job in the betting office was a turning point, forcing her to be more outward going and to deal with all kinds of people. LARA helped too, broadening her social circle. So did, in a contradictory way, her mother-in-law: 'She interferes, so I became more independent to fight her'. In David's view Eileen had not really grown up when they married, 'She wasn't really mature until she had the two kids.' Eileen attributes this to over-protective parents. Her mother, she says, treated her like an 11-year-old when she was 16 and – even when she had met David – refused to let her go out or insisted she came home early. Eileen rebelled by climbing out of the bedroom window: her mother retaliated by locking it. 'I used to hate her sometimes but we get on terrific now, like a friend. Nowadays I'd go anywhere with her. Once I'd never have gone anywhere with her. I think it's because she's relaxed – because she doesn't have to worry about me any more. Once I was married she let me go.' With the passage of time and her own experience of parenthood Eileen now feels that everything her mother did was for the family's own good: 'We've all turned out quite happy, none of us has fallen by the wayside.'

When the Bateses talk about time and change, they stress the same two themes: changing interests and improved relations with their parents. Pat is amazed at how time passes. She has been married seven years 'but it hasn't felt like a long time. The difference it makes is that your interests change.' Some of her unmarried friends are still rushing home from work, getting dressed up, and going out every night – like they were all doing at 16. She would not fancy it now.[1] As for John, she says, 'Well,

[1] 'Fancy it' = want it. Used also about people with a lighthearted sexual inference.

his old mate Reggie came round recently, and I thought they'd be jarring[1] all evening about old times. But ten minutes and they dried up. They just hadn't that much in common. Reggie was still drinking and drugging and raving it up. And John's not interested any more. That's what seven years of marriage means.'

John looks back on his teenage escapades and calls them 'silly things'. Both he and Pat feel that it is the search for identity that makes teenage rebellion inevitable. His father's authoritarian approach just made it worse. As the baby of the family, he was not treated as a grown-up until he had children of his own.

Pat's parents wanted their only daughter to do well, and showed their disappointment when she gave up a possible career in a bank to work locally as a cashier. Whereas now she can appreciate and accept their help, as a teenager she resented it. Now that she is in her mid twenties, with her own family and her own home, Pat has 'sorted out' her relationship with her mother: 'I can say anything to my mum now, but when I was a teenager she was just in the way.'

Pat talked at length about 'sorting herself out'. She has not been through anything as traumatic as Eileen's nervous breakdown, but she has been thinking about her life and taking greater responsibility for it. The impetus to 'try to sort your life out now before anything happens' was her brother's marriage break-up. 'I hope nothing will happen but you never can tell. John might pack his bags,[2] and if I hadn't thought about it I'd be lost like my brother. . . . If you've got a lot of friends and a bit of independence, you'd be OK. Wouldn't have to rely only on mum.'

If thinking through how she would cope on her own has made her feel more 'sorted out' in herself, she and John are both more 'sorted out' now that he has found congenial work: 'It makes a lot of difference if he's doing something he likes.' Unemployment, as we have seen, meant parental anxiety, too much of each other's company, and no money for extras. A

[1] 'Jarring' = jawing, i.e. talking.
[2] 'Pack his bags' = leave.

previous job had involved carrying six men who did not work properly: 'He'd come home moaning about it. And I knew that deep down he didn't want to go. And there's nothing worse.' In that job all his money went on basics with nothing left over for him. That was hard. 'I used to think money doesn't matter,' Pat remarked 'but I've noticed how we get on better when we've got enough.' The measure of change for John is that he is settled and happy to be so. Pat says 'he's not the only one surprised'.[1]

When each of the four was asked whether they had had a picture, as a teenager, of what life would be like now, John had 'no conception of it; I never thought I'd be married with two kids'. For Pat, 'It's more or less what I expected, except I didn't expect it to be so hard – little rows,[2] money worries, and so on. I expected it all to be rosy. It's only in the last couple of years that I've realized what it's all about – that it's what you make it.' David: 'I always knew I'd get married, because I didn't want to be a bachelor. There's no fun in that, they have no life. You're working five, six, seven days a week, and in the evenings you're in the pub giving the money back, instead of putting it into a nice home. I thought about kids, whether they'd be boys or girls, where I'd live, whether I'd have a car, whom I'd marry, what she'd look like.' Eileen too always wanted kids. She was anxious when they were first married and she did not get pregnant, and then when she miscarried. But they have got what they wanted – two kids – and they are very pleased with their kids. She compares her life with her friend Cheryl's – Cheryl travels a lot, has lived abroad, has had her own flat – but would not swop with her for anything.

There is little need to ask what is the central thing in their lives. All four say children. David insists 'You get married for kids and if you don't want kids there's no point in getting married'; 'We got married for kids. We discussed it all beforehand.' For both couples earning a living and caring for the children structured their lives. As Eileen put it, 'They're dependent on you, so you have to put yourselves out. And you

---

[1] i.e. she is surprised too.

[2] 'Rows' = arguments (pronounced to rhyme with 'now').

organize your time round them – there's so much you have to do for them. Even the type of food you buy is influenced by them. The house is all arranged to suit them; the furniture is even arranged to give them play space.'

All four think a great deal about parenting, how strict to be, how protective, how to comfort, how to reprimand, how to encourage, what treats and outings the children enjoy. Eileen, who criticized her parents for being too protective, found herself wanting to protect her own kids. David wants the boys to be 'tough and strong as boys should be'. He is afraid that if they absorb too much book knowledge, they will not be able to stand up for themselves, although he still wants them to get a better education than he did. He recognizes that if his children were girls, he would be more cautious, 'you have to be very protective with girls'. John, who does have daughters, certainly feels protective towards them. He would kill anyone who laid hands on them. He worries about their safety in the neighbourhood as they grow up and is already talking about teaching them karate and buying them a car as protection.[1] Pat thinks 'John's fears are greater than mine, with having two girls', but she too worries, especially 'about them getting to the teenage stage – getting pregnant and everything'. Recently a neighbour's 14-year-old daughter gave birth prematurely, just a week after telling her mother she was pregnant. Pat wants something better for her daughters.

Do they want their children's lives to be different from their own? Both the Masons do, emphasizing small family size and education. 'Our kids are brought up differently, I come from a big family, so if you wanted anything you couldn't have it', Eileen explained, and David added 'If you had anything, your brother nicked it'. David wants his sons to get a better education, 'so that they won't have to do the sorts of jobs I do; they can get a nice, clean office job, or get a decent trade behind them'. They wanted to send the children to a private school but they cannot afford it.

Pat is not consciously striving to give her daughters a life different from hers. She sends them to the school she went to as

[1] From casual street crime, mugging, etc.

a child – she liked it and she never considered anywhere else – she is bringing them up in the same neighbourhood and has no wish to move, and she can give the two of them the same kind of attention that she received, as one of a small family. Where she is determined to differ is in leaving them free to make up their own minds about jobs.

For both families, many of the explicit decisions they have made about parenting are in reaction against their own parents. David Mason says, 'Well you know what your parents did wrong. So you do it differently.' For both men the biggest difference is to spend more time with their children than their own fathers did. They want to know their children and stay close to them in their adolescent years. David again, 'You have to have a lot of time for kids. That's why we only wanted two – one each, if they both want to talk about things. I encourage them to talk to me – like if they do something wrong, I talk to them about it. Let them know everything's all right. . . . Like I can't sit down and have a conversation with my dad, because I never have. My dad was always up the betting office. My kids, when they're teenagers, I'll have more time for them, I'll take them out more, football matches and so on.'

John Bates loved his dad, although he was rarely home, but he never respected him and never really felt he knew him. He loves to spend time with his kids: 'Some families, the wife talks about *my* kids – he's not really interested. But with us, it's *our* kids.' He and Pat worry about bringing up teenagers. She says, 'It all gets much harder when they're teenagers, you can't just tell them off. I'd like to be friends with them then, but it doesn't work. I've never seen it work.'

Eileen Mason is more optimistic, 'I think I'll understand more (than my parents). That's why I wanted to have kids young, so that I could still understand. I'll go out with them more, so that I meet their friends, I want them to be able to discuss things with me, and if they have problems they'll bring them to me instead of to their friends – friends always give the wrong advice. I want them to know I've been through it all too.

I want them to know I'll blow my top[1] but I *will* help.' Both Masons look forward to having teenage sons and, later, adult sons and grandchildren. Eileen says, 'People I work with, their kids phone them up and they go out together', and David can see himself 'having a pint with them, or going to football matches'.

Both families feel that life has become easier in the last couple of years. Both men have got better jobs, both women have a bit more time to themselves, a bit more independence, now that their children have started (or will shortly start) at school or nursery. They feel better. Eileen Mason has got over her nervous breakdown. John Bates is no longer out of work.

Perhaps it is these changes that make both families happy about the present and, at least in the Masons' case, fairly hopeful about the future. Pat is 'quite happy as I am'. Eileen is 'quite happy about how things are going'. It is not by chance that Pat speaks of the present and of herself, and Eileen implies a notion of progress. This is characteristic of the two women and of the two families. It is in their attitudes towards daily life and towards the future that the Bateses and the Masons differ most markedly: the Bateses are comfortable, the Masons strive; the Bateses are resolutely present-orientated, the Masons look to the future. The contrast is most clearly articulated by the women.

Pat describes herself as 'very day-to-day'. She is happy. John is in a good job. She seems able to take things in her stride,[2] organizing her time and the family income so that everyone's needs are met. She is the family's resource-keeper. Coping with daily life is not a problem for her. She sees herself as impulsive and as not doing jobs in a logical order – but she does get things done. John's daily life seems pretty much to take care of itself. He is more methodical than Pat, a perfectionist at jobs like decorating and woodwork. He could occupy himself quite well without a job if it was not for the money, but he has a job he likes: 'you have to be happy or there's no point working'. He

---

[1] 'Blow my top' = lose my temper.
[2] 'To take things in her stride' = to manage without difficulty.

just hopes things will carry on the way they are now. Together they deliberately live in the present – John because his plans have fallen through or turned sour in the past, Pat because she never plans, 'I used to, and have fallen flat on my face so many times that I've given up. For instance, I used to get very depressed whenever I gave up a job and worried about the next one. And anyway whenever we've got going with saving and so on, something has always cropped up.' They do not try to control their future and consequently cannot visualize it. 'I suppose at some point it will just be the two of us again, like at the beginning when we were courting,' Pat says, 'but it's a strange thought.'

They feel that they have control of their lives on a day-to-day basis. They do not feel oppressed by bosses, the local council, or their families. 'We just plod on, doing our own thing. Not ruled by anyone.' They do not feel thwarted; they do not say, 'If only I'd had a break'. They have no plans to move, to buy a house, to change jobs, to start their own business. John would like to become more skilled by taking evening classes in moulding, but at present he works too much overtime to fit them in. Maybe his guvnor will let him do daytime classes, since he would benefit from having a moulder in the firm. John would enjoy having his own business but 'if it comes, it comes'. Perhaps eventually he will run Pat's parents' do-it-yourself shop, but he is not counting on it.

If the Bateses take life as it comes, the Masons do not. Eileen 'can't just live from day to day. I have to have something to look forward to, even if it is just a few weeks ahead, like holidays. Or next week it's my nephew's birthday party and I'm doing all the cakes for it. It's having something like that that keeps you going.' She copes with the present by setting it against the recent past (which was worse) and against the future (which will be better). 'I often look back' she says, 'because that stops me getting depressed again. Each time I look back I take another step forward. More determined. A couple of years back I'd never have thought I had it in me' (to set up a macramé business). At the moment she feels capable of coping with things; other times they really get her down. We have already seen how she juggles her routine to avoid boredom and strives to achieve something. She cannot understand people with no ambition. This is where she differs from her mum: 'She'll just sit back and do nothing. She does all her housework – and used to look after us – and that was enough for her. She never has expected to have anything else.'

Eileen talks in terms of problems and problem solving. When she visits friends they 'swop problems', both mums 'come round to tell us their problems; and so on. Daily life for her is problem-ridden, but gets easier (or more satisfying?) as she deals with these problems. For instance 'once the little one starts at nursery school, that's another problem out of the way'. If either she or David has a problem they discuss it for hours and try to think of a solution. They talk all night sometimes: 'That's how we cope with all the family problems.'

Eileen has known what it is like to be beyond coping with daily life. She has been afraid to go out of the house, spent day after day alone at home with two tiny children, beseeched David to do the shopping and all outside chores. Analysing her depression into solvable problems, tackling each with David's encouragement, planning, willing herself on, hauled her out of her breakdown and has perhaps become a formula for the future. She expresses great faith in planning. 'I used to believe in luck a lot but I don't now. I think it is what you make it. If things go wrong you haven't planned it right. You have to try a bit harder.' She thinks people could change most things if they wanted to, 'but subconsciously you don't want to change. It's easier to put up with things'. While she believes people largely control their lives, she knows that in her own case this conflicts with the demands of her friends and family. 'The only way I'd be in control is if I moved away because it's people that stop you, put on you,[1] block your plans. But I don't want to move away, so if they stop my plans working out I try a bit harder and hope I'll get a break between times.'

David claims to believe more in luck and less in planning than his wife: 'It's all luck. Or most of it's luck – getting the

---

[1] 'Put on you' = impose on you.

right break[1] at the right time. But it helps if people know you work hard. That's how I got this job.' As for planning, 'Nothing's planned with me. You can't plan – just hope. I can't plan because I'm very impatient, have to do things on the spur of the moment.' Nevertheless he knows where he would like to be in a year's time: 'Within a year, hopefully – but I doubt it – I'll have a business paint-spraying, a decent car, and be thinking seriously about buying a house instead of just dreaming. If I stay in this firm, with it being so big, I'm going to win, and if I start a business I'll make it work. So I win either way. You have to be confident', he says, 'and I'm willing to work all the hours of the day if I'm getting the money.'

[1] 'A break' = an opportunity or piece of good luck.

8 Inner-city livelihood

There is nothing at all sinister about classifying people, households, urban areas, or anything else. Classification is a normal prelude to understanding the relation between one person/place/thing and another. Thinking depends on it: there is no way of making sense of the environment without first dividing it up into items that are like and unlike in one respect or another. But it is only the *process* of sorting things out that is inevitable; the *way* they are sorted varies from one person or situation or setting to another, and even the best of typologies is useful only for some purposes, never for every purpose. In the same way as it is sometimes more useful to classify animals by size than by number of legs or the nature of their coats, for some purposes it is enough to divide the city into inner and outer areas without differentiating one inner area from another, and it may be more useful to know where people were born than where or how they live.

In this perspective, official or bureaucratic typologies are neither wrong nor wrongheaded, they are simply not appropriate to more than a very limited number of classificatory purposes. Their usefulness depends on what the officials want to know. Thus, typologies used in the census allow Her Majesty's Government to know where people are on the night of the count, and to calculate national or regional trends in family size and population movement, but they cannot reflect the fact that household units expand and contract to suit different contexts and different phases of livelihood, nor do they say much about people's reasons for moving from one house, street, or borough to another.

These limitations cause problems only when they are ignored – that is, when people or places that can properly be lumped together by virtue of one characteristic are assumed to be alike in every respect, or when static qualities are read as social processes. We began this study by observing that 'inner-cityness' and minority ethnic status colour both popular and official expectations of any household that can be classified in those terms. The body of the book differentiates them as resource systems. The point has not been to make a new and 'better' typology of households, but to show up aspects of inner-city livelihood that typology can only obscure.

THE 'CAPABILITY' OF THE CITY

The 'capability' of any environment is a product of the options it offers. Here, the number of ways in which eight households manage livelihood in a single neighbourhood demonstrates its scope as well as theirs. They do not all use the inner-London setting in the same say, but their 'conditions of possibility' are both enhanced and limited by the 'capabilities' of the local system. Some features of this local system may be peculiar to it: two of them are striking exactly because they go against received wisdom about inner-city areas. The first is its economic resilience, even in periods of deep recession – probably due to an unusual variety of industries making up the local economy, and the transportation facilities available to residents who are willing to travel long distances away from home to work when the local job options fail. The second has less bearing on the resources available than on their distribution. It shows in Battersea's potential for integrating newcomers noted in Chapter 1, and again as localism in Chapter 3, and is reflected in the kind of neighbourhood that LARA has become. All these eight households could be locally involved if they chose; on the whole if LARA residents do not use local resources, it is because they have other options and other choices to make and not because they are denied access to the local system.

Even those among the eight whose stories make no mention of local support or local identity probably have some sense of local belonging. It would be hard not to. All of them have lived in the area for at least five years, and the regular residents of an urban neighbourhood of this sort inevitably get to know each other by sight. They meet shopping, standing at the bus stop, or walking in the street, and so learn, over time, the public habits and timetables of people they do not know by name and probably never visit at home. Recognizing and being recognized by others creates a sense of belonging in an inner-city area just as it does in a rural village. No doubt this is what is meant by saying that London is not a large impersonal city but a collection of villages; certainly the capabilities of this 'village' ensure against urban anomie.

THE 'VIABILITY' OF HOUSEHOLDS

Do all these eight households 'manage' equally well? If some turn out to be more viable than others, is it because they have access to better resources, because they manage similar resources more successfully, or because the fates have dealt with them more kindly? More important: What is the proper measure of viability? Whose valuation of a successful livelihood are we to use?

Leaving 'what the neighbours say' aside, there are three perspectives on viability that recur more or less explicitly throughout this book: the *official* view, the *actor's* view, and the *observer's* view. Each evaluates the way these households manage very differently. By official and bureaucratic criteria, the most successful livelihood has to be the one that puts least drain or strain on statutory services. The actors' view is of course more variable: 'success' depends on what it is measured against, what was expected, what else is happening, etc. On the specific question of official resources, one household may feel that getting the most out of the government is a good thing while another is humiliated by the 'failure' of dependence. The range of observer's criteria for 'success' is nearly as wide, but is simplified by the privilege of detachment: observers by definition are not required to decide between conflicting priorities or to suffer the fact that gain in one domain too often goes with loss in another. In this observer's view, viability depends on the balanced use of all the resources available – which means knowing about them, having access to them, and managing them appropriately. By this measure all these eight households are 'viable', but they have different resource circumstances and different styles of resource management. The cumulated evidence of these few cases make it clear that no one resource makes the difference between managing and not managing. The 'success' of those who manage best (by any criteria) is not a matter of having a better job, more money, more kin, more education, or a higher general status than the people next door; nor is it, in this sample at least, a matter of a 'better' ethnic origin. Viability depends on combinations of style and circumstance – on the functioning of the household as a 'whole' resource system in a particular environment.

STYLE AND CIRCUMSTANCE

These households are similar but different. They are similar to the extent that they all belong in the same London 'village' (described in Chapter 1) and were selected to have five objective characteristics in common (Chapter 3). Broadly speaking, these features together put them in comparable relation to the material/structural resources of the environment, even though the eight could be subdivided by other typological criteria (as they have been by being paired under the four labels which provide titles for Chapters 4–7). At the same time they differ, both in terms of the kind and quantity of organizing resources they have, and in the way they use/work/convert those resources into livelihood (Chapter 2). The narrative chapters (4–7) suggest a consistency in the differences; each household, like each inner-city setting, maintains the same style of livelihood even when its objective circumstances change. In a follow-up survey made to monitor the effect of three years' recession on the employment situation of the LARA neighbourhood as a whole (p. 7 and Wallman *et al.*

1982: 182), each of these eight remains broadly in character. The circumstances of the Charleses household are most significantly altered. In 1978 Olive was unemployed, totally dependent on 'welfare', and 'not in control' of her life; now she has a part-time job as a cleaner in the neighbourhood. The household still needs state benefits and is financially no better off, but Olive now feels she is 'more in control'. She has a new confidence which shows in her appearance and in her general satisfaction with 'the way things are going'. This contrast apart, the household continues as before: the household system is geared to the well-being and future prospects of the children, and it depends narrowly on neighbourhood contacts for both practical and emotional support.

The locus of identity

Other households are no less consistent in matters of this kind. But just as no one-dimensional typology of households can say much that is useful about household processes (pp. 18–21), so there can be no neat typology of styles of livelihood. There are nevertheless themes or strands of style which combine differently but consistently in each of these eight cases. One is the extent of involvement in the local area: unlike the Charleses, some households are characteristically committed to and dependent on family and ethnic communities, or on their breadwinners' places of work. For example, neither the Kelly nor the Mason households was ever really involved in neighbourhood affairs, both mentioned plans to move in 1978 (Appendix) and both had left the area three years later, apparently with little damage to their sense of belonging. Although the Irving household was and is rooted in the area by home ownership and long residence, its members are not involved in neighbourhood activities and identify themselves by their family and (ethnic) church commitments, and its economy depends on jobs outside the area achieved through non-local, non-ethnic, and largely impersonal contacts.

Boundary styles

Even households that identify in similar ways may have different boundary styles, each tending either to expand or to contract the range and scope of its various 'us' categories. Although definitions of 'us' change from one situation to the next, they seem to be consistently extensive or intensive in each case. For example, Cynthia Abraham and her children address an unrelated neighbour as a kinsman and describe him as a member of the household (p. 81), and include relatively large numbers of people in their 'close friend' category with no fear of being 'used' by 'hangers-on' (p. 85). Bruce Rapier by contrast is not sure that his co-resident father should be counted part of the household, and is 'distant or estranged from most of his kin' (p. 147). His wife Edie enjoys very sociable local contacts, but only exchanges friendship or support with a handful of them and describes herself as 'not all that close' to the daughters of her first marriage who live nearby. Edie's situation is formally parallel to Alice Kelly's: they are both native south Londoners (south London ethnics by the criteria of *Table 6*, p. 15), both are active and extrovert women aged forty-two, and both are raising second families with steady and reclusive second husbands. But the two households define and use 'the family circle' quite differently. Edie Rapier puts the boundary around a small tight group of four – herself and Bruce and their two children – and depends on it for 'the support she needs to go out into the world and play an active role' (p. 150). For Alice Kelly 'the family' is that unit *plus* the parents, uncles, and grandparents of her own childhood, the daughters of her first marriage, their husbands or boy friends, their children – anyone who is related at all is one of 'us'. Given Alice's 'special position in the extended family group' (p.152), this definition makes the small Kelly household the focus of practical and emotional support for many more than four people and gives it an extensive boundary style, making it in this respect more like the Abraham household than like the relatively intensive Rapiers. Incidentally, Alice's reaction to her own intense crisis suggests a limitation on the resource

value of large numbers of 'close' contacts: when she badly
needed emotional support herself, her sense of belonging in
this large family group evaporated and she looked to specifically defined state services for help (p. 160).

Earlier discussions of resource values (Chapter 2) and
affective networks (Chapter 3) indicated that the same
quantities of people (or other) resources may be an asset for
some purposes and a liability for others. Thus the Masons'
huge kin network gives their household all kinds of practical
help but is 'a strain' which absorbs time, money, and
emotional energy (p. 170). It is arguable that their situation is
less a result of boundary style than of the role they are
somehow made to play in the wider family circle. In contrast to
Alice Kelly 'they feel smothered by kin' (p. 171) and are wary of
having neighbours round to the house because 'they tie you
down, like kids; you can't get on with things' (p. 169).
Sometimes, of course, the constraints are circumstantial, not
stylistic. Olive Charles's friends and relatives all had jobs or
domestic commitments that made it impossible for them to
look after her household when she went into hospital, or they
lived so far away that her children could not have boarded with
them without missing school in her absence. Annette Ellison's
many contacts are so like her in age, life stage, and economic
status that they need what she needs: none of them can provide
the childminding services that would allow the others to go out
to work because they all want or need a job, and they are all
'stuck' at home with pre-school children. But all these cases
equally demonstrate that a large number of people known to
or even 'close' to the household does not assure it of the
support it needs in all the circumstances of livelihood.

Changing v. sticking

A third strand of household style shows in the tendency to
move or to stay, to change or to stick. As always, the options
are limited by circumstance, but some households, or more
importantly the resource-keepers of those households, seem to
prefer to continue doing what they are doing, while others
regularly decide in favour of change. Whether they do so

because, like Cliff Ellison, they 'get bored' (p. 113), or because, like Eileen Mason, they 'cannot understand people with no ambition' (p. 208), their households have a livelihood very different from the Rapiers' – built as it is on the fact that Bruce 'accepts things the way they are; the house they live in, the job he does for a living, and the way his family life is structured' (p. 144). There are occasional echoes of these styles in the regularity of timetables and the assignment of household tasks. Bruce Rapier, for example, co-operates with Edith in running the house and raising their children but he does specific things at the same time each day, each week; it is not that household's style to change about or make *ad hoc* arrangements. Cliff Ellison also helps at home, but he tends more often to pitch in when Annette needs help – as when the new baby arrived – than to make commitments that become part of the household routine.

Planning v. not planning

The fourth dimension of style is the matter of planning or not planning. Households that have the habit of planning are likely also to be future oriented (see the section on time perspectives in Chapter 2), and to be reasonably confident that they have the resources necessary to bring their plans about. The Bates and Mason households, as we have noted, have very different time perspectives: the Masons plan the future, the Bateses concentrate on the present, solving small problems, one at a time. Nevertheless the Bateses feel they have control of their lives on a day-to-day basis, 'They don't feel oppressed by bosses, the local council, or their families' (p. 207). Households differ also in terms of how much they plan and what they plan about. There is no household among these eight that plans nothing. Households that do not have the confidence to plan at all are probably 'problem households', not, like these, able to manage a succession of 'ordinary' problems one way or another by pulling their various resources together. But since plans are impossible without a sense of being in control of their outcome, it may be that the scope of a household's planning shrinks when times are hard for it, so that it concentrates its energies on the most immediate and/or soluble problems, such as shopping for today's food but not putting in the application for a better flat; or asking neighbours about jobs but not pursuing any they say are available.

Investment patterns

Each of these households has patches in which livelihood is not the same as normal, and in every case it is impossible to separate the effects of style and circumstance. The final dimension of style affects these eight stories in ways that suggest it is crucial to every circumstance. It shows generally in the way households take up the options offered by the environment and specifically in the way they deploy their resources across the various domains of livelihood. On the evidence of these households, more seems to be better on both counts: it is 'better' not to be narrowly dependent on specific resources, and not to be narrowly involved in only one sphere of activity. By this measure the Charles household is worse off when its economy depends entirely on state welfare and Olive only identifies herself as a mother, than when she has part-time employment and she and her children are involved in neighbourhood affairs; the Irvings can manage Matthew's precarious social and economic status both because his daughters earn small but steady wages at their jobs and because the whole household is 'uplifted' by the work it does for the church.

RESOURCE OPTIONS

These observations are persuasive because they match common sense, but their significance is underlined by two analogies. One stems from psychology and the other from economics. The first is demonstrated by the finding that it is psychologically healthier for the individual to enjoy a range of activities than to be absorbed with any one of them; better, for example, to have identity investments in all kinds of work so that each role gets and gives its due resources, than to be a 'workaholic' obsessed with job satisfaction or career success alone. Very likely the balance is easier to maintain in small-scale settings in which role frames tend to be overlaid and individuals (or a household) bring more than one identity to bear in each context, or interact with other people who know about other aspects of their (or its) livelihood without being told. In such settings the likelihood of *anomie* is remote; so is total identification with a single aspect of livelihood (Wallman 1979b: 17). Although it is popularly assumed that only rural villages can be healthy environments in this respect, the characteristics of the very urban area that is the setting of these eight households give them a similarly broad range of identity options. (It is important however that these characteristics are features of Battersea; other inner-city settings might be less generous.)

The second analogy is with economic notions of 'occupational pluralism' (Wadel 1969) or 'occupational multiplicity' (Lowenthal 1972). Both refer to strategies or styles of resource management, although only in specifically economic domains of livelihood, and again, only in rural areas. The effect of either is that 'the focus of economic activity at any point is not solely determined by what brings in the largest amount of income, but also by its interrelations or linkages to other activities, and by other factors such as tradition, place of residence, or by what a man would prefer to be doing' (Wadel 1969: 45). In that setting too, 'the feasibility of any combination of activities turns out to be a matter of age, household composition, infrastructure and the like – i.e. of the 'total' resource system ... and no one occupation is expected to bear the brunt of economic support for the whole household' (Wadel 1969: 48). The strategy is sensible, not to say 'viable', because it spreads the risk of failure by expanding the household's economic options.

If something like resource domain is substituted for 'occupation', and 'support' is extended to cover the affective as well as the economic needs of the household, then the same logic is illustrated here: given the general limitations of inner-city environments at this time, no one domain of livelihood can be expected to provide sufficiently for all a household's needs; but given the capabilities of *this* inner-city environment, households of all kinds manage 'best' by spreading their resource base across all the options it offers.

Appendix
Survey responses of the eight households

Table A.1 Household profile; employment; institutional support; shopping patterns

name of household	adult birth place	no. of adults in house	age of adults	no. of children in house	years in Battersea[1]	present employment	source of information re: job	use of formal services over 12 months	church attendance	main shopping
Abraham	West Africa	1	44	2	5 +	factory worker	friend	none	monthly	Battersea
Charles	West Indies	1	45	3	15 +	none	—	hospital social services DHSS[2]	weekly	Battersea
Ellison	West Indies	2	21, 28	2	15 +	(f) part-time nursery assistant (m) driver	local contacts advertisement	maternity clinic	once a year	S. London
Irving	West Indies	4	58, 58, 34, 25	2	20 +	(f) none (m) minister (dghts) clerks	— — job centre	DHSS[2]	daily	Battersea Brixton
Rapier	S. London	3	42, 38, 74	2	since birth	(f) part-time childminder (m) clerk	local contacts advertisement	none	twice a year	Battersea
Kelly	S. London Ireland	2	42, 42	2	10	(f) part-time canteen assistant (m) driver/ storeman	job centre local contacts	social services hospital	never	Battersea
Bates	S. London	2	25, 27	2	since birth	(f) part-time cleaner (m) carpenter	friend local contacts	police	never	Battersea
Mason	S. London	2	26, 27	2	5 +	(f) none (m) foreman	— friend	hospital	special events only	Battersea

Notes: [1] Refers to adult with longest residence.
[2] Department of Health and Social Security.

Table A.2 Location of close kin and friends: use of local centre; plans to move

name of household	wife's parents' residence	husband's parents' residence	other relatives' residence	absent children's residence	close friends' residence	use of local centre	plans to move	why?	where?
Abraham	Africa	—	Battersea UK	—	LARA	never	none	—	—
Charles	West Indies	—	Battersea N. and S. London	West Indies	LARA N. and S. London	often	none	—	—
Ellison	S. London	LARA	S. and E. London other UK	—	LARA	often	(f) yes (m) no	wants a garden	S. London
Irving	—	—	S. and other London other UK	S. London	LARA Battersea S. London other UK	never	none	—	—
Rapier	S. London N. London	father 'lives in'	S. and other London	S. and E. London	LARA	often	none	—	—
Kelly	London other UK	Ireland	Battersea S. London	LARA Battersea S. London	Battersea	sometimes	yes	street unfriendly	somewhere better
Bates	Battersea	Battersea	Battersea S. London	—	LARA	often	none	—	—
Mason	S. London	S. London	S. London	—	S. London	often	yes	to own a house	S. London

References

Agar, M. H. (1980) *The Professional Stranger: An Informal Introduction to Ethnography*. New York: Academic Press.

Aijmer, G. (1975) What is a Household? University of Gothenburg. Mimeo.

Apter, D. (1964) Ideology and Discontent. In D. Apter (ed.) *Ideology and Discontent*. Glencoe, Illinois: Free Press.

Arnould, E. J. and Netting, R. McC. (1982) Households: Changing Form and Function. *Current Anthropology* 23 (5).

Barth, F. (1963) Introduction to *The Role of the Entrepreneur in Northern Norway*. Oslo: Scandinavian University Books.

— (1966) *Models of Social Organisation*. Occasional Paper no. 23. London: Royal Anthropological Institute.

Belshaw, C. (1954) *Changing Melanesia: Social Economics of Culture Contact*. Melbourne: Oxford University Press.

— (1967) Theoretical Problems in Economic Anthropology. In M. Freedman (ed.) *Social Organisation: Essays Presented to Raymond Firth*. London: Frank Cass.

Bender, D. (1967) A Refinement of the Concept of Household: Families, Co-residence and Domestic Functions. *American Anthropologist* 69 (5).

Bloch, M. (1977) The Past and the Present in the Present. *Man* 12 (2).

Bohman, K. (1981) Houses, House-work and Kinship: Aspects of the Female Sphere in a Columbian City. *Antropologiska Studier* 30/31 (Stockholm).

Bott, E. (1957) *Family and Social Network*. London: Tavistock Publications.

Bourdieu, P. (1977) *Outline of a Theory of Practice*. Cambridge: Studies in Social Anthropology.

Brenner, Y. S. (1979) *Looking into the Seeds of Time*. Assen: Van Gorcum.

Buchanan, I. H. (1982) Livelihood III: Employment and Work. In Wallman *et al.*

Calley, M. (1965) *God's People: West Indian Pentecostal Sects in Britain*. London: Oxford University Press.

Clark, D. (1982) Production Workers on Shifts: Choice or Constraint? *New Community* 10 (1).

Cohen, A. P. (1982) 'The same – but different': The Allocation of Identity in Whalsay, Shetland. *The Sociological Review* (N.S.) 26 (3).

De Beauvoir, S. (1971) The Age of Discretion. In *A Woman Destroyed*. London: Fontana.

De Tray, D. N. (1977) Household Studies Workshop A/D/C Seminar Report no. 13 May.

Dhooge, Y. (1982) Livelihood II: Local Involvement. In Wallman *et al.*

Ditton, J. (1978) *Part-Time Crime*. London: Macmillan.

Epstein, A. L. (1969) The Network and Urban Social Organisation. In J. Clyde Mitchell (ed.) *Social Networks in Urban Situations*. Manchester: Manchester University Press.

— (1978) *Ethos and Identity*. London: Tavistock Publications.

Fagin, L. (1979) Views from Three Other Disciplines: Psychiatry. In S. Wallman (ed.) *Social Anthropology of Work*. Association of Social Anthropologists Monograph no. 19. London: Academic Press.

Firth, R. (1956) *Elements of Social Organisation*. London: Watts.

Firth, R., Forge, A., and Hubert, J. (1969) *Families and their Relatives*. London: Tavistock Publications.

Flett, H. (1979) Bureaucracy and Ethnicity. In S. Wallman (ed.) *Ethnicity at Work*. London: Macmillan.

Foster, G. M. and Kemper, R. V. (1974) *Anthropologists in Cities*. Boston: Little Brown.

Gans, H. (1962a) *The Urban Villagers*. New York: Free Press.

— (1962b) Urbanism and suburbanism as ways of Life: A Re-evaluation of Definitions. In A. M. Rose (ed.) *Human Behavior and Social Process*. Boston: Houghton Mifflin.

— (1967) *The Levittowners*. New York: Pantheon.

Gellner, E. (1973) Concepts and Society. In I. C. Jarvie and J. Agassi (eds) *Cause and Meaning in the Social Sciences*. London: Routledge & Kegan Paul.

— (1982) *Language, State and Culture*. 6th Radcliffe Brown Memorial Lecture in Social Anthropology. London: The British Academy.

Gershuny, J. I. (1979) *After Industrial Society?* London: Macmillan.

— (1982) Livelihood IV: Household Tasks and the Use of Time. In Wallman *et al.*

Gershuny, J. I. and Thomas, G. S. (1982) *Changing Times: Activity Patterns in the UK 1937–1975*. London: Oxford University Press.

Goffman, E. (1968) *Stigma*. Harmondsworth: Penguin.

— (1978) Gender Display. In L. Tiger and H. Fowler (eds) *Female Hierarchies*. Chicago: Beresford Book Service.

Gonzales, N. (1970) Towards a Definition of matrifocality. In N. Whitten and J. E. Szwed (eds) *Afro-American Anthropology:* Contemporary Perspectives on Theory and Research. New York: The Free Press.

Goody, J. (1958) *The Developmental Cycle in the Domestic Group*. Cambridge Papers in Social Anthropology no. 1. Cambridge University Press.

Hannerz, U. (1969) *Soul Side*. New York: Columbia University Press.

– (1980) *Exploring the City*. New York: Columbia University Press.

Harrison, G. A. (ed.) (1982) *Energy and Effort*. Symposia of the Society for the Study of Human Biology vol. 22. London: Taylor & Francis.

Harrisson, T. (1976) *Living through the Blitz*. London: Collins.

Ingelstam, L. (1980) *Arbetets värde och tidens bruk: en framtidsstudie*. Stockholm: Liber.

Jahoda, M. (1982) *Employment and Unemployment*. Cambridge: Cambridge University press.

Jahoda, M., Lazarsfeld, P., and Zeisel, H. (1972) *Marienthal: The Sociography of an Unemployed Community*. London: Tavistock Publications.

Klein, L. (1976) *New Forms of Work Organisation*. Cambridge: Cambridge University Press.

Kosmin, B. A. (1979) J. R. Archer 1863–1932: A Pan-Africanist in the Battersea Labour Movement. *New Community* 7 (3).

— (1982) Political Identity in Battersea. In Wallman *et al.*

Laslett, P. and Wall, R. (eds) (1972) *Household and Family in Past Time*. Cambridge: Cambridge University Press.

Leach, E. (1961) Two essays concerning the symbolic representation of Time. In E. R. Leach (ed.) *Rethinking Anthropology*. LSE Monographs on Social Anthropology no. 22. London: Athlone.

— (1967) An Anthropologist's Reflections on a Social Survey. In O. Jongmans and P. Gutkind (eds) *Anthropologists in the Field*. Assen: Van Gorcum.

Lessing, D. (1973) *The Summer Before the Dark*. London: Jonathan Cape.

Lewis, O. (1967) *La Vida*. London: Secker & Warburg.

Liebow, E. (1967) *Tally's Corner*. London: Routledge & Kegan Paul.

Liljeström, R. (1979) Time Aspects of Production and Reproduction. University of Gothenburg. Mimeo.

Lowenthal, D. (1972) *West Indian Societies*. Oxford: Oxford University Press/Institute for Race Relations.

McGee, T. G. (1974) *The Persistence of the Protoproletariat: Occupational Structures and Planning of the Future World Cities*. Australian National University, Research School of Pacific Studies, Dept of Human Geography. Mimeo.

Malinowski, B. (1926) *Crime and Custom in Savage Society*. London: Routledge & Kegan Paul.

Mars, G. (1982) *Cheats at Work*. London: Allen & Unwin.

Minge-Klevana, W. (1980) Does labour time decrease with industrialisation? *Current Anthropology* 21 (1).

Mitchell, J.C. (1983) Case and Situation Analysis. *Sociological Review* 31 (2).

Murray, C. (1979) The Work of Men, Women and the Ancestors: Social Reproduction in the Periphery of Southern Africa. In S. Wallman (ed.) *Social Anthropology of Work*. Association of Social Anthropologists Monograph no. 19. London: Academic Press.

New Universities Quarterly (1979) The Culture of Unemployment (special issue).

Oakley, A. (1974) *The Sociology of Housework*. London: Martin Robertson.

Pahl, R. (1980) Employment, Work and the Domestic Division of Labour. *International Journal of Urban and Regional Research* 4 (1).

Pahl, R. E. and Gershuny, J. I. (1979) Work Outside Employment: Some Preliminary Speculations. *New Universities Quarterly* 34 (1).

Paine, R. (1970) Informal Communication and Information Management. *Canadian Review of Sociology and Anthropology* 7 (3).

— (1974) *Second Thoughts about Barth's Models*. Occasional Paper no. 32. London: Royal Anthropological Institute.

— (1976) Two Modes of Exchange and Mediation. In B. Kapferer (ed.) *Transaction and Meaning: Directions in the Anthropology of Exchange and Symbolism*. Association of Social Anthropologists Essays vol. 1. Philadelphia: ISHI.

Radcliffe Brown, A. R. (1952) On Joking Relationships. In *Structure and Function in Primitive Society*. London: Cohen & West.

Sahlins, M. (1974) *Stone Age Economics*. London: Tavistock Publications.

Saifullah Khan, V. (1979) Work and Network: South Asian Women in South London. In S. Wallman (ed.) *Ethnicity at Work*. London: Macmillan.

Santos, M. (1979) Circuits of Work. In S. Wallman (ed.) *Ethnicity at Work*. London: Macmillan.

Scarman, Lord L. G. (1982) *The Scarman Report: the Brixton Disorders 10–12 April 1981*. Harmondsworth: Penguin.

Schapera, I. (1950) Kinship and Marriage among the Tswana. In A. R. Radcliffe-Brown and D. Forde (eds) *African Systems of Kinship and Marriage*. London: Oxford University Press.

Sowell, T. (1975) *Race and Economics*. New York: David McKay.

Speck, R. V. and Attneave, W. (1974) *Family Networks*. New York: Random House.

Suttles, G. D. (1968) *The Social Order of the Slum: Ethnicity and Territory in the Inner City*. Chicago: University of Chicago Press.

Toffler, A. (1970) *Future Shock*. New York: Bantam Books.

Townsend, P. (1979) *Poverty in the United Kingdom*. Harmondsworth: Penguin.

Valentine, C. (1968) *The Culture of Poverty: Critique and Counter Proposals*. Chicago: University of Chicago Press.

Van Velsen, J. (1967) The Extended Case Method and Situational Analysis. In A. L. Epstein (ed.) *The Craft of Social Anthropology*. London: Tavistock Publications.

Wadel, C. (1969) *Marginal Adaptations and Modernization in Newfoundland*. St. John's, Newfoundland: ISER Memorial University.

— (1973) 'Now, whose fault is that?' *The Struggle for Self-esteem in the Face of Chronic Unemployment*. St. John's, Newfoundland: ISER Memorial University.

— (1979) The Hidden Work of Everyday Life. In S. Wallman (ed.) *Social Anthropology of Work*. Association of Social Anthropologists Monograph no. 19. London: Academic Press.

Wallman, S. (1974) Kinship, A-kinship, Anti-kinship: Variation in the Logic of Kinship Situations. In E. Leyton (ed.) *The Compact: Selected Dimensions of Friendship.* St. John's, Newfoundland: ISER Memorial University and in the *Journal of Human Evolution* (1975) 4: 331–41.

— (ed.) (1977) Introduction to *Perceptions of Development.* Cambridge: Cambridge University Press.

— (1978a) The Boundaries of 'Race': Processes of Ethnicity in England. *Man* 13 (2).

— (1978b) Epistemologies of Sex. In L. Tiger and H.T. Fowler (eds) *Female Hierarchies.* Chicago: Beresford Book Service.

— (ed.) (1979a) *Ethnicity at Work.* London: Macmillan.

— (ed.) (1979b) *Social Anthropology of Work.* Association of Social Anthropologists Monograph no. 19. London: Academic Press.

— (1983a) Identity Options. In C. Fried (ed.) *Minorities: Community and Identity.* Dahlem Konferenzen Berlin, Heidelberg, New York: Springer Verlag.

— (1983b) Etnicismo e localismo: La relazione tra struttura e cultura in due aree di Londra. In A. Signorelli (ed.) *Cultura popolare e cultura di massa.* Milan: *La Ricerca Folklorica* 7.

Wallman, S., Dhooge, Y., Goldman, A. and Kosmin, B. A. (1980) Ethnography by Proxy: Strategies for Research in the Inner City. *Ethnos* 45 (1–2).

Wallman, S., Buchanan, I. H., Dhooge, Y., Gershuny, J. I., Kosmin, B. A., and Wann, M. (1982) *Living in South London: Perspectives on Battersea 1871–1981.* London: Gower/London School of Economics.

Wann, M. (1982) Livelihood I: Housing and Housing Action. In Wallman *et al.*

Whyte, W. (1943). *Street Corner Society.* Chicago: University of Chicago Press.

Woodburn, J. (1982) Egalitarian Societies. *Man* 17 (3).

Yanagisako, S. J. (1979) Family and Household: The Analysis of Domestic Groups. *Annual Review of Anthropology 8.*

Young, M. and Willmott, P. (1957) *Family and Kinship in East London.* Harmondsworth: Penguin.

— (1973) *The Symmetrical Family.* Harmondsworth: Penguin.

Zweig, F. (1949). *Labour, Life and Poverty.* London: Gollancz.

Name index

Subject index